MISSION ACCOMPLISHED: KOREAN 2

Author

니콜라 프라스키니 Nicola Fraschini
- 베네치아 카포스카리 대학교 아시아학과(학사), 고려대학교 국어국문학과(석사, 박사) 졸업.
- 전 서강대학교 한국어교육원 전임 강사.
- 전 서호주 대학교(The University of Western Australia) 한국학 조교수(lecturer).
- 현 멜버른 대학교(The University of Melbourne) 한국학 부교수(senior lecturer).
- 호주 한국어교육자 협회(AUATK) 협회장(2021-2022).

김현미 Hyun Mi Kim
- 이화여자대학교 사범대학(학사) 이화여자대학교 한국학과(석사) 졸업.
- 고려대학교 한국어교육센터 한국어교사양성과정 수료.
- 전 캐나다 UBC(University of British Columbia) 한국어 수업 teaching assistant.
- 현 서호주 대학교(The University of Western Australia) 한국학 강사.
- 서호주 주 Department of Education 고등학교 한국어 교육과정 집필 참여.

자문   박현진(전주대학교)
         노정은(한성대학교)

영문 검토 Philippa Freegard
              Gabriel Sparta

MISSION ACCOMPLISHED: KOREAN 2

초판 1쇄 발행 2023년 2월 1일

지은이 니콜라 프라스키니 Nicola Fraschini, 김현미 Hyun Mi Kim
펴낸이 박민우
기획팀 송인성, 김선명, 김선호
편집팀 박우진, 김영주, 김정아, 최미라, 전혜련
관리팀 임선희, 정철호, 김성언, 권주련

펴낸곳 (주)도서출판 하우
주소   서울시 중랑구 망우로68길 48
전화   (02)922-7090
팩스   (02)922-7092
홈페이지 http://www.hawoo.co.kr
e-mail hawoo@hawoo.co.kr
등록번호 제475호

값 42,000원 (MP3 포함)
ISBN 979-11-6748-075-0 14710
ISBN 979-11-6748-073-6 (set)

* 이 책의 저자와 (주)도서출판 하우는 모든 자료의 출처 및 저작권을 확인하고 정상적인 절차를 밟아 사용하였습니다. 일부 누락된 부분이 있을 경우에는 이후 확인 과정을 거쳐 반영하겠습니다.

* 이 책은 저작권법에 따라 보호받는 저작물이므로 무단 전재와 무단 복제를 금지하며, 이 책 내용의 전부 또는 일부를 이용하려면 반드시 저작권자와 (주)도서출판 하우의 서면 동의를 받아야 합니다.

이 저서는 2020년 대한민국 교육부와 한국학중앙연구원(한국학진흥사업단)을 통해 해외한국학중핵대학육성사업의 지원을 받아 수행된 연구임(AKS-2020-OLU-20200039)

MISSION ACCOMPLISHED: KOREAN

목표 달성 한국어!
해외 대학교
초급 학습자를 위한 한국어

Nicola Fraschini
니콜라 프라스키니

Hyun Mi Kim
김현미

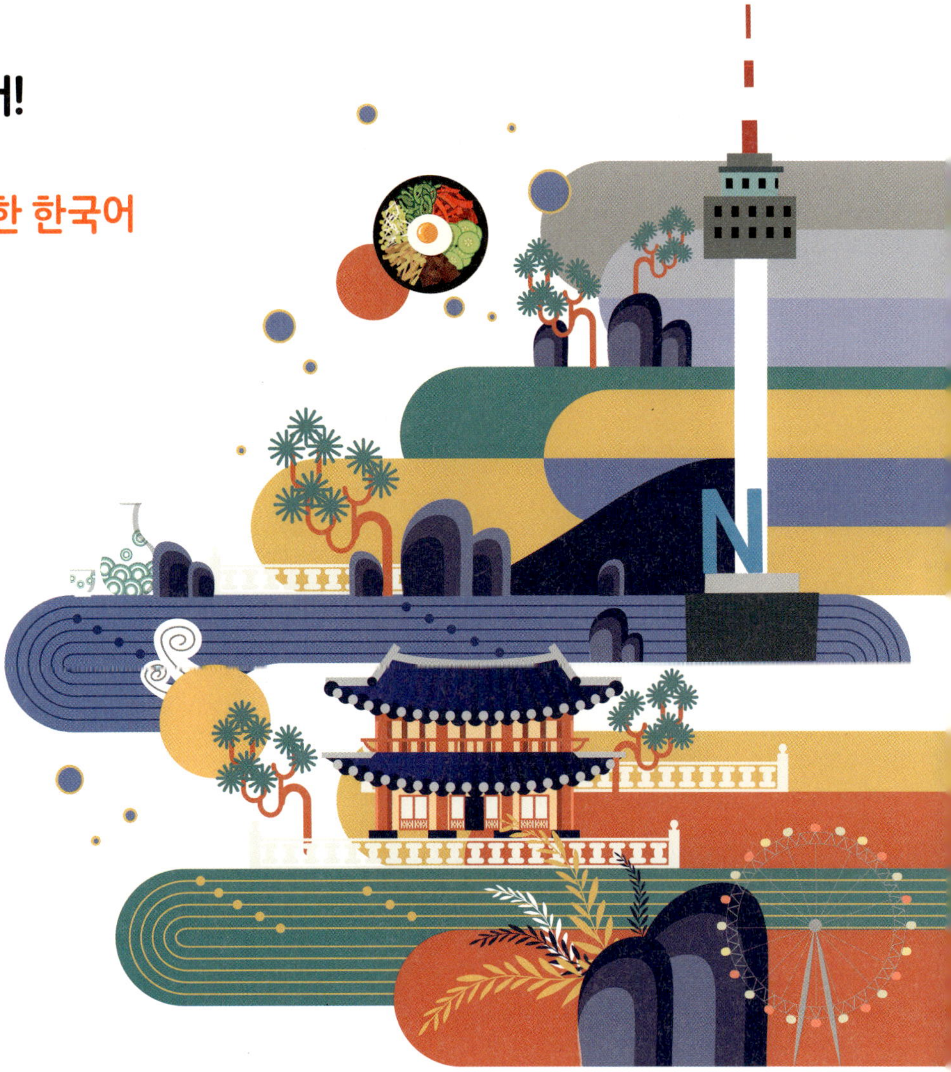

Table of contents

Table of contents ·· 4
About this book ·· 5
Structure ·· 12

Unit 1 ··· 15

Unit 2 ··· 35

Unit 3 ··· 55

Unit 4 ··· 77

Unit 5 ··· 96

Unit 6 ··· 121

Unit 7 ··· 141

Unit 8 ··· 163

Unit 9 ··· 183

Unit 10 ··· 203

Table of conjugations ··· 224
Vocabulary list (Kor-Eng) ·· 228
Vocabulary list (by unit) ·· 236
Vocabulary list (Eng-Kor) ·· 246
Transcripts ·· 252
English translations ··· 258
Answer keys ·· 267

About this book

Aim and goals

This book has been developed to answer the needs of the English-speaking university student who has no or very little previous background knowledge of the Korean language, and with little experience of foreign language learning. The aim of the book is to ease students gently into the journey of learning the Korean language.

The main goals of the book are to allow the student to:

- Apply basic language knowledge to communicate in Korean in most common everyday life situations.
- Demonstrate accuracy when using the basic structures of the language.
- Participate in common conversations that involve an exchange of information.
- Extract relevant information from short written and oral texts about basic topics.
- Produce short written paragraphs about personal matters.
- Be able to use, in real-life situations, a range of functions such as greeting, introducing oneself, talking about past events, making conjectures, asking and giving permission, making requests, expressing ability, and asking or giving instructions and directions.

This volume, together with *Mission Accomplished: Korean 1*, has been developed by adapting the guidelines indicated in the Standard Curriculum for Korean Language.※ Depending on how the instructor intends to use the materials and activities included in the two books, the student will reach level 1~2 of the framework.

What makes this book different?

The past decade has seen a surge in published Korean language textbooks, but *Mission Accomplished: Korean* is different.

The development of this book arose from original research conducted by Nicola Fraschini on Korean language university learner motivation, and the materials and settings of each unit have been designed keeping in mind the results of this research.

The book includes thorough but concise descriptions of the structures and forms of the Korean language. In the authors' experience, and also as indicated by educational research into Korean as a second language, most English-speaking students struggle to produce accurate Korean when taught with an exclusively task-based and communicative approach. The descriptions of language structures support students in approaching a language profoundly different from English. These descriptions are followed by exercises to reinforce accuracy and by communicative activities integrated with engaging and relevant listening and reading materials.

※ National Institute of Korean Language (2020). *Standard Curriculum for Korean Language*. Seoul: Ministry of Culture, Sports and Tourism.

While *Mission Accomplished: Korean 1* provides students with most basic everyday life vocabulary, *Mission Accomplished: Korean 2* introduces new vocabulary along with a generous variety of expressions. All expressions have been selected depending on their frequency in the Korean language, to allow the learner to use them promptly in their communicative exchanges.

The extensive use of photos and pictures not only supports the visual learner, but also helps students to visually contextualize themselves as language users.

The book introduces the learners to relevant aspects of Korean culture and society, and shows how to use the language in a culturally appropriate manner.

The settings of the book follow the university learner's developmental pathway. While many situations in the first book reflect communicative settings located in both Korea and at an English-speaking university, in the second book settings switch mostly to Korea, in order to prepare students with the language skills and real life information needed for their study exchange in Korea.

The book contains numerous appendices that students can use to support self-directed learning. These include: a table that illustrates how the language structures contained in the book conjugate with irregular processive/descriptive verbs; three vocabulary lists (Kor–Eng by unit, Kor–Eng, Eng–Kor); transcripts of all listening activities; translations of dialogues and main listening and reading exercises; and a full set of answer keys.

The book, with the exception of the 문법 (grammar) and 문화 (culture) sections, minimizes the use of English. This is done to help students in their immersion in a Korean language environment. Instructors using this book may wish to provide their students with more English support, depending on the characteristics of their cohort.

How the book is structured

The content of *Mission Accomplished: Korean 2* is organized into ten units. All units follow the same structure:

- 문법 (grammar). This section introduces the students to some of the main forms of the language covered in the unit. Each form is introduced focusing on its meaning and use, and is illustrated by numerous examples. Additional notes expand the explanations with more detailed information for students who wish to learn more. The English terminology of Korean grammar categories follows Yeon, J., and Brown, L. (2011). *Korean: A comprehensive grammar*. Routledge. Therefore, students will be able to easily refer to additional resources for futher in depth study.
- 단어 (words). This section illustrates the vocabulary related to the main topic covered in the unit. All words are presented in Korean with a visual image to help the learner memorize vocabulary. The vocabulary in this section is grouped together by meaning or context of use.
- 연습 (exercises). This section aims to build accuracy in the use of the structures of the language. All exercises related to the use of the same structure are sequenced from a more guided to a more open use of the language. Vocabulary exercises are also included in this section.

- 말하기 (speaking). Each speaking section contains two dialogues. The dialogues illustrate language use in socio-cultural contexts, and the following roleplays permit oral practice of vocabulary and language structures. Although roleplays do not strictly qualify as communicative activities, they have been included in the book as activities that support the student in building confidence in speaking through a guided approach. Further opportunities for communicative speaking activities have been incorporated into the exercises, listening and reading sections.
- 듣기 (listening). All listening activities are divided into three steps. The first step provides students with the context and vocabulary knowledge necessary for the the main listening activity, which follows in the second step. The third step offers the opportunity to expand on the same topic of the main listening task, with either another short follow-up listening or a speaking activity.
- 읽기 (reading). Similarly to the listening activities, all reading activities are divided following the same three-step structure. The first step introduces the students to the core vocabulary used in the main reading, which is presented in step two. Step two is followed by comprehension questions, and by either a follow-up short reading passage or speaking activity.
- 쓰기 (writing). Each writing section is divided into two steps. Students follow the first step to brainstorm their writing, and the second step to engage directly in writing activity.
- 문화 (culture). This section shows a socio-cultural or sociolinguistic aspect of Korea in relation to the main topic covered in the unit.

How to use this book if you are a teacher

The authors are aware that the structure of the curriculum, and the hours available for face-to-face classes vary greatly depending on the teaching context. Similarly, each language program is different in its teaching approach and its consideration of the amount of self-directed learning. The structure of each units has been designed to be flexible in this regard, and the teacher will notice that the different sections, although dealing with the same topic, can be used as independent modules.

Each unit can be used to cover about 6 x 45/50-minute classes of face-to-face teaching, therefore *Mission Accomplished: Korean 1* and *2* can be used in the context of a 100-120 hour course. However, where a program does not allow for such an amount of classroom interaction, the content can be reduced by assigning some of the sections to self-directed learning.

For the novice teacher, we suggest using the book as follows:
1. Introduce language structures in the grammar explanations together with their related exercises. The teacher may decide to introduce one structure and follow with the related exercises before moving on to the next pattern. Illustration of each grammar pattern and associated exercises can be conducted over 2 x 45/50-minute classes.
2. Let the student practice the dialogue roleplays until they are comfortable in using the grammar pattern in oral interaction. Each dialogue can be integrated with more explanation about language use in context. The practice of both dialogues can be done in 1 x 45/50-minute class.

3. Conduct the listening activity, then the reading activity. Step one of the listening/reading activity aims to introduce the student to core vocabulary and the context of the main listening/reading text. The instructor may decide to integrate this section with vocabulary that the students may not know but need in order to conduct the main listening/reading activity. A highlighted question is included in the description of each main listening/reading activity in step two. That question can be used to direct the students to the central point in the listening/reading text. Listening and reading activities can be done in 1 x 45/50 minute—class each.
4. Guide the student through the writing section. Step one of each writing section can also be conducted as an oral activity where students practice using the core vocabulary. After an oral brainstorming students can then engage in the written composition. The writing practice section can be undertaken in one 45—50 minute class.

If the program does not permit the amount of time suggested, the instructor, depending on the teaching approach and the main goal of the course, may decide to reduce the content by a) conducting only one among of the reading/listening sections, and by alternating reading and listening in every other unit; b) assigning the writing section as self—directed learning activity; c) assigning the overview of the grammar explanations as pre—class self—directed learning activity and using the class time to practice.

The more experienced teacher may decide to adopt a different and more communicative approach by starting from the dialogues or the reading/listening sections to illustrate grammar patterns and vocabulary in context, and by proceeding to illustrate the details of the language structure at a later step.

How to use this book if you are a student

The students will find many helpful resources to help them learn Korean. These are some of our suggestions to help you learn better:

- Read carefully through the structure explanations contained in the 문법 (grammar) section. In particular, take careful notes of the examples. All examples have been designed to show how patterns are used in many different contexts, for example with different tenses, or different subjects.
- The vocabulary is always presented in a cluster of words related to the same topic to help you remember better. All vocabulary is illustrated by a picture so that you can understand its meaning without the need of an English gloss. If you need an English explanation, you can refer to the vocabulary list of the relevant unit in the appendix of the book. Building a strong vocabulary base is important: you cannot hear, read, or name what you do not know.
- When doing the practice exercises there may be some vocabulary that you do not know, or some irregular processive verb/descriptive verb that you are not sure how to conjugate. For the vocabulary, you can always refer to the vocabulary list in the appendix. To understand how to

conjugate irregular processive/descriptive verbs you can check the irregular verb conjugation table, always in the appendix.
- When doing the listening and reading activities, read carefully the bold highlighted question in the instructions of the relevant step two. This is the most important question you should try to answer the first time you listen/read the passage. Do not try to understand all the details the first time you approach a text, just try to get the information to answer the main question, and leave the details for later.
- Reviewing is important. At home, we suggest reviewing all listening activities by reading out loud the script while listening to the file. If you are assigned the writing section as a homework task, make sure you review the reading passage first, observing how sentences are constructed and, most importantly, how each sentence is linked to another to form a text.

Settings

Speaking, reading, and listening activities are focused on the interaction of nine main characters. The characters are used to illustrate the use of the Korean language across a range of social interactions in different cultural contexts. Here is an introduction to the characters that appear in the book:

- 보라 (Bora) is a Korean student studying at a Korean university.
- 수진 (Sujin) is a Korean students. She is Bora's friend, and she studies at the same university.
- 토마스 (Thomas) is an Australian student. He is majoring in Korean Studies, and he is on an exchange program at the Korean university where Bora and Sujin are studying.
- 이예린 팀장님 (Ms. Lee) works in the Australian branch of a Korean company.
- 사라 (Sara) is an Australian Korean Studies student, and she is doing an internship in the same company where Ms. Lee works.
- 다니엘 (Daniel) is a student studying Korean Studies at an Australian university.
- 시메이 (Shimei) is an international student, studying together with Daniel at the same Australian university.
- 지호 (Jiho) is a Korean student studying on exchange in Australia, where he meets Daniel and Shimei.
- 김 선생님 (Ms. Kim) is Daniel's and Shimei's Korean language teacher.

Many places are mentioned in *Mission Accomplished: Korean*. Some of them are in Seoul, while others are in other parts of South Korea. Whenever you see a location mentioned you can find it on the maps below.

South Korea

Seoul

Structure

Unit	Topic	Functions	Grammar	Vocabulary
1	Weather	Expressing politeness (1), descriptive verbs, making conjectures	—습니다 형용사 —겠— (추측)	Weather and climate
2	University life	Expressing obligation, ability and possibility	—아야/어야 해요 —(으)ㄹ 수 있어요 —지만	University and academic life
3	House and living	Making a suggestion, asking for and expressing intention, expressing prohibition	—(으)세요 —지 마세요 —(으)ㄹ래요	Housing and furniture
4	Shopping	Making suggestions, talking about personal experiences	—아/어 보세요 —아/어 봤어요 —아/어 주세요	Clothing and accessories, colors
5	Workplace	Expressing politeness (2)	—(으)시— —고; —거나	Work and job searching
6	Family	Making comparison	보다 (더) 제일 —고 있어요	Relatives and family events
7	Transportation	Giving directions	—(으)려고 (1) —(으)ㄹ게요 —(으)ㄴ 다음에	Transportation and directions
8	Health	Expressing feelings	—아서/어서(이유) —(으)러 가요	Body, illness, medicines, and health remedies
9	Cooking	Expressing ability and intention	—(으)ㄹ 줄 알아요/몰라요 —(으)려고 (2)	Cooking, ingredients, and taste
10	Public services	Asking and giving permission	—아도/어도 돼요 —기 전에	Bank, post office, immigration office, service center

Mission Accomplished: Korean 2

Speaking	Listening	Reading	Writing	Culture & Society
Weather and leisure activities	Weather forecast	Information about a hiking excursion	Describe the weather where you live	Hiking culture
University matters	A university course orientation	Email sent by a student to a lecturer	Write an email to your professor asking for information	The Korean education system
Moving house	Making an enquiry to a real estate agent	University dormitory regulations	Describe the house where you would like to move in	Renting in South Korea
Shopping and past experiences	Buying new clothes at the department store	Fashion review blog	Writing an online shopping review	Freebies
Work matters	Workplace meeting	Stories of successful business people.	Writing a short paragraph about a famous entrepreneur.	Hiring process in Korean big companies
Family and relatives	Going to a housewarming party	Drama review	Describe a member of your family	Kinship terms
Taking public transport	Conversation on how to go and see an event	Story about getting around in Seoul	Messaging subway instructions to reach a destination	Taking the bus and subway in Seoul
Symptoms and physical conditions	Visiting a doctor	Korean health remedies	Writing about a past experience of being sick	Korean hospitals
Cooking and food	Shopping for groceries	Reading a recipe	Writing instructions on how to prepare one's favorite food	Fermented food
Using public services	Opening a bank account	Description of a service center for foreigners	Writing an email to enquire about a service	Korean money

Structure

MP3 Streaming

1과
Unit 1

💡 **In this unit you will learn**

- How to use descriptive verbs as noun modifiers.
- How to make conjectures about future events.
- How to express politeness in a formal context.
- How to talk about the weather in Korea and the weather in your country.
- Vocabulary related to weather.

 문법

 Honorific with -습니다/ㅂ니다 (formal polite form, situation honorific).

Meaning

The use of Korean honorifics depends on two main elements. One is the social relationship between the speakers, which affects the level of formality of the situation. The other is the subject of the sentence. These two elements decide which kind of honorific expression must be used. The formal polite ending -습니다/ㅂ니다 belongs to the first category, since it depends on the relationship between the speakers, and on the formality of the situation.

It is attached to both processive and descriptive verbs, in written and spoken contexts. It is used when formal language is required, for example when talking to guests, or when the speaker is addressing somebody older than themselves.

Use

In spoken language, this ending is used during a formal event when talking to somebody that you do not know very well, when talking to somebody whose social position is higher than yours, or to someone who is older. It is generally also used when speaking in front of an audience, and by TV news announcers. In written language, it is used in formal private mail/email, and in writing which needs a formal tone, such as cover letters.

To attach this ending, drop the infinitive ending -다 from the verb base. Then attach -습니다 to consonant-ending bases, or -ㅂ니다 to vowel-ending bases. Most irregular verbs do not change into their irregular form, however verbs ending in ㄹ will drop ㄹ before attaching -ㅂ니다 (see 만들다 below and the irregular verb conjugation table in the appendices).

Verb base ending in a vowel	Verb base ending in a consonant
+ ㅂ니다	+ 습니다

가다 → 가 + ㅂ니다 → 갑니다
하다 → 하 + ㅂ니다 → 합니다
먹다 → 먹 + 습니다 → 먹습니다
좋다 → 좋 + 습니다 → 좋습니다
듣다 → 듣 + 습니다 → 듣습니다
낫다 → 낫 + 습니다 → 낫습니다
*만들다 → 만드 + ㅂ니다 → 만듭니다

Examples

1. 교실에 학생이 **많습니다**. There are many students in the classroom.
2. 김 선생님은 한국어를 **가르칩니다**. Ms. Kim teaches Korean.
3. 시메이 씨는 케이크를 잘 **만듭니다**. Shimei makes good cakes.
4. 싸이는 유명한 가수**입니다**. Psy is a famous singer.
5. 저는 한국 영화를 **봅니다**. I watch a Korean film.
6. 토마스 씨는 지난주에 한국에 **갔습니다**. Thomas went to Korea last week.
7. 방학 때 보라 씨는 호주 여행을 **할 겁니다**. Bora will travel to Australia during the vacation.

Extra notes

- In interrogative sentences, the suffix −습니까/ㅂ니까 is used instead:

  지금 뭐 **합니까**? What are you doing now?
  한국어를 공부합니다. I study Korean.

- −습니다 is attached to the past tense suffix to make the formal polite form in the past tense, therefore becoming −았/었습니다. ㅂ니다 is attached to −(으)ㄹ 거 to make the formal polite form of the future tense.

  아침 식사를 **했습니다**. I had breakfast.
  어제 학교에 **갔습니다**. Yesterday I went to school.
  방학 때 한국에 **갈 겁니다**. I'll go to Korea during the next vacation.

- As in example 4 above, 입니다 is used as the formal polite form of 이다(이에요/예요), attached to both vowel−ending and consonant−ending nouns. However, in the past tense 이었습니다 (e.g., 선생님이었습니다) is used after consonant−ending nouns, and 였습니다 (e.g., 가수였습니다) after vowel−ending nouns.
- In written language, avoid mixing formal (−습니다/ㅂ니다) and informal endings (−아/어요) in the same text. In spoken language, in particular when the speakers already know each other, it can happen that the two endings are both used. In this case, it may happen that the two speakers talk at the beginning using formal endings, and switch later to a less formal tone.
- Since this is a formal ending, when used in the first person remember to use the pronoun 저.

Descriptive verbs used as noun modifiers

Meaning

Korean descriptive verbs can be used as noun modifiers. In other words, they can be used to specify or modify the characteristics of a noun by being placed before it, in a similar fashion to English adjectives. However, placing a descriptive verb in a pre-nominal position requires the use of a specific modifier attached to the base of the descriptive verb.

Use

The modifier to attach to the base of a descriptive verb in order to use it in a pre-nominal position is -ㄴ/은.

-ㄴ is attached to the base of descriptive verbs that end in vowels, while -은 to the base of descriptive verbs that end in consonants. For descriptive verbs constructed with 있다/없다 (such as 맛있다 or 재미있다), the pre-nominal form attaches -는 instead of -ㄴ/은, i.e., 있는/없는 (see examples further below).

Descriptive verb base ending in a vowel	Descriptive verb base ending in a consonant	있다/없다
+ ㄴ	+ 은	+ 는

크다(be big) → 크 + ㄴ → 큰
예쁘다(be pretty) → 예쁘 + ㄴ → 예쁜
낮다(be short) → 낮 + 은 → 낮은
작다(be small) → 작 + 은 → 작은
맛있다(be delicious) → 맛있 + 는 → 맛있는

Some irregular descriptive verbs modify the verb base before adding -은, as they do with other suffixes or connectives that begin with a vowel.

쉽다(be easy) → 쉽 + 은 → 쉬우 + ㄴ → 쉬운
낫다(be better) → 낫 + 은 → 나 + 은 → 나은

Examples

1. 서울은 큰 도시예요. (크다 → 큰) Seoul is a big city.

2. 백화점에서 큰 가방을 샀어요. (크다 → 큰) I bought a big bag at the department store.

3. 북한산은 아름다운 산이에요. (아름답다 → 아름다운) Mt. Bukhan is a beautiful mountain.

Extra notes

- As mentioned above 있다 and 없다 make the pre-nominal form by attaching –는, as in these examples.

  > <오징어 게임>은 재미있는 드라마예요. "Squid Game" is an interesting drama.
  > 어머니는 맛있는 김치를 만들었어요. My mom made a good kimchi.

- When a descriptive verb is used as noun modifier, it cannot be followed by the copula 예요/이에요. Therefore *the bag is big* can only by said as 가방이 커요 and not as 가방이 큰이에요, which is an incorrect expression.

 Expressing conjecture with –겠–

Meaning

–겠– is a future tense marker that can be used to indicate a conjecture regarding a situation, or about something that may have happened or may happen to another person. It can be attached to both processive and descriptive verbs, and usually the conjecture expressed depends on the personal opinion or thoughts of the speaker.

Use

–겠– is attached to both vowel-ending and consonant-ending bases of processive and descriptive verbs. Irregular verbs do not change the base into their irregular form. After –겠–, an appropriate ending indicating the level of formality and politeness, such as –어요 or –습니다 for example, must be added.

> 가다 → 가 + 겠 → 가겠어요
> 하다 → 하 + 겠 → 하겠어요
> 먹다 → 먹 + 겠어요 → 먹겠어요
> 읽다 → 읽 + 겠 → 읽겠어요
> 좋다 → 좋 + 겠 → 좋겠어요
> 듣다 → 듣 + 겠 → 듣겠어요
> 바쁘다 → 바쁘 + 겠 → 바쁘겠어요

Examples

1. [Context: 토마스 씨는 시험을 잘 봤어요.] 토마스 씨는 기분이 좋겠어요. [Context: Thomas did well in the exam.] He must be happy/He will be happy.

2. [Context: 예린 씨는 요즘 회사 일이 많아요.] 예린 씨는 아주 **바쁘겠어요**. [Context: Yerin has a lot of work (to do) at the company recently.] She must be tired/she will be tired.

3. 수진: 보라 씨, 오늘 날씨가 안 좋아요. The weather doesn't look good today.
   보라: 네, 곧 비가 **오겠어요**. Yes, it may be raining soon.

4. 수진: 보라 씨가 남차 친구와 헤어졌어요. Bora split up with her boyfriend.
   토마스: 정말요? 보라 씨가 많이 **힘들겠어요**. Really? It must be hard for her.

5. 토마스: 오늘 4시간 동안 한국어를 공부했어요. I studied Korean for 4 hours today.
   수진: 아 그래요? **피곤하겠어요**! You must be tired!

Extra notes

- Since −겠− is used to express a conjecture, the subject is usually different from the first person. In other words, the speaker cannot use this form to make a conjecture about themselves.
- −겠− can be attached to the past tense suffix to indicate a conjecture about something that happened in the past, such as in 피곤했겠어요 *you must have been tired!*
- −겠− is also used to indicate the future tense. In this case it is often used by the speaker in the first person to indicate the strong volition of doing something. For example, your teacher may say 수업을 시작하겠습니다 *I am about to begin the calss*, when they want to start the lesson, or you may say 앞으로 열심히 하겠습니다 *I will study hard from now on*, if you want to say that you will put effort in your studies.

단어

계절

봄　　　　　여름　　　　　가을　　　　　겨울

날씨

날씨가 어때요?

(하늘이) 맑다　　(하늘이) 흐리다　　비가 내리다
　　　　　　　　　　　　　　　　비가 오다

눈이 내리다　　바람이 불다
눈이 오다

기온

 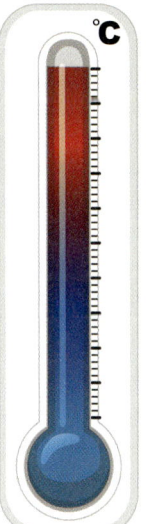

덥다

따뜻하다

시원하다

쌀쌀하다

춥다

1과 21

연습

1 Complete the following sentences by using the verb in brackets. Also, conjugate the verb using the formal polite form (–습니다/ㅂ니다).

| 보기 | 토마스 씨는 오전 10시에 학교에 <u>갑니다</u>. (가다) |

1. 보라 씨는 친구를 집에 .... (초대하다)

2. 예린 씨는 저녁까지 일합니다. 그래서 요즘 친구를 못 .... (만나다)

3. 저는 한국 음식을 자주 .... (먹다)

4. 시메이 씨는 한국어 책을 .... (읽다)

5. 김 선생님은 우리 한국어 선생님 .... (이다)

6. 작년에 대학교에서 한국어 수업을 .... (듣다, *past tense)

7. 3년 동안 태권도를 .... (배우다, *past tense)

2 Fill in the following table with the missing verbs like in the example. Pay attention to the tense!

| 보기 | 가요 ⟷ 갑니다 |

1. .... ⟷ 준비합니다

2. 찾았어요 ⟷ ....

3. 올 거예요 ⟷ ....

4. .... ⟷ 탔습니다

5. 마셔요 ⟷ ....

6. 괜찮아요 ⟷ ....

7. .... ⟷ 많았습니다

8. 들을 거예요 ⟷ ....

3 Using the descriptive verbs suggested, write a sentence about what is represented in the pictures, as in the example.

보기: 시계/비싸다 → 비싼 시계

1.  하늘/맑다

2.  기차/빠르다

3.  선생님/좋다

4.  음식/맛있다

5.  맥주/시원하다

6.  시험/어렵다

7.  산/높다

8.  날씨/춥다

4 Look at the following pictures, then make a conjecture like in the example using the suggestions below.

보기	맛있다		무섭다		무겁다
	기쁘다		비가 오다		춥다

보기: 맛있겠어요.

1.
2.
3.
4.
5.

5 Complete the following mini-dialogues by making a conjecture using a verb (or descriptive verb) + 겠어요.

보기
시메이: 다음 주에 친구들하고 캠핑을 갈 거예요.
사라: 정말 신나겠어요!

1. 보라: 와! _____.

   수진: 보라 씨, 이 쿠키를 제가 만들었어요. 드세요.

2. 보라: 남자 친구한테서 어제 선물을 받았어요.

   수진: 와! _____.

3. 지호: 어제 늦게까지 게임을 했어요. 그래서 늦게 잤어요.

   다니엘: 그래요? 그럼 지금 _____.

4. 다니엘: 사라 씨는 요즘 오전 8시에 출근하고 밤 9시에 퇴근해요.

   시메이: 정말요? 요즘 사라 씨는 많이 _____.

5. 어머니: 지금 2시 50분이에요. 영화 시간은 3시예요.

   보라: _____! 빨리 가요!

6. 다니엘: 날씨가 덥지만 도서관에는 에어컨이 있어요.

   시메이: 그럼 도서관은 _____.

7. 토마스: 아침부터 지금까지 아무것도 못 먹었어요.

   수진: 그럼 토마스 씨는 지금 많이 _____.

6 Fill in the blanks of the following sentences with the most appropriate word.

| 덥습니다 | 내립니다 | 맑습니다 | 겨울 |
| 바람 | 따뜻합니다 | 비 |

한국의 1. _____은 춥습니다. 그리고 겨울에는 눈이 많이

2. _____. 봄은 보통 3월부터 5월까지입니다. 봄은 날씨가

3. _____. 그리고 하늘이 4. _____. 한국의 여름은

5. _____. 그리고 보통 7월에는 한 달 동안 6. _____가

많이 내립니다. 가을 날씨는 좋습니다. 가을에 시원한 7. _____이 붑니다.

말하기

대화 1

Shimei and her teacher Ms. Kim meet together on campus after the vacation. 🎧 1.1

김 선생님: 시메이 씨, 오랜만이에요. 방학을 잘 보냈어요?

시메이: 네, 저는 재미있는 방학을 보냈습니다.

김 선생님: 그래요? 방학을 어떻게 보냈어요?

시메이: 방학 때 한국에 갔다 왔습니다.

💬 Roleplay the dialogue above, changing what Shimei did during her vacation with the suggestions below.

재미있다 + 방학 ➡	한국에서 여행 하다
즐겁다 + 방학 ➡	드라마를 많이 보다
심심하다 + 방학 ➡	공부를 많이 하다
힘들다 + 방학 ➡	아르바이트를 많이 하다

대화 2

Thomas and Bora are talking about the weather for the weekend.

보　라: 토마스 씨, 주말에 뭐 할 거예요?

토마스: 요즘 날씨가 따뜻해요. 그래서 주말에 등산할 거예요.

보　라: 토마스 씨, 일기예보를 못 봤어요? 주말에 비가 올 거예요.

토마스: 아, 정말요?

보　라: 네. 토마스 씨. 속상하겠어요.

Roleplay the dialogue above, changing Thomas' activity and the weather forecast.

듣기

1 Look at the map below, then write the name of the location corresponding to the temperature and its forecast, as in the example.

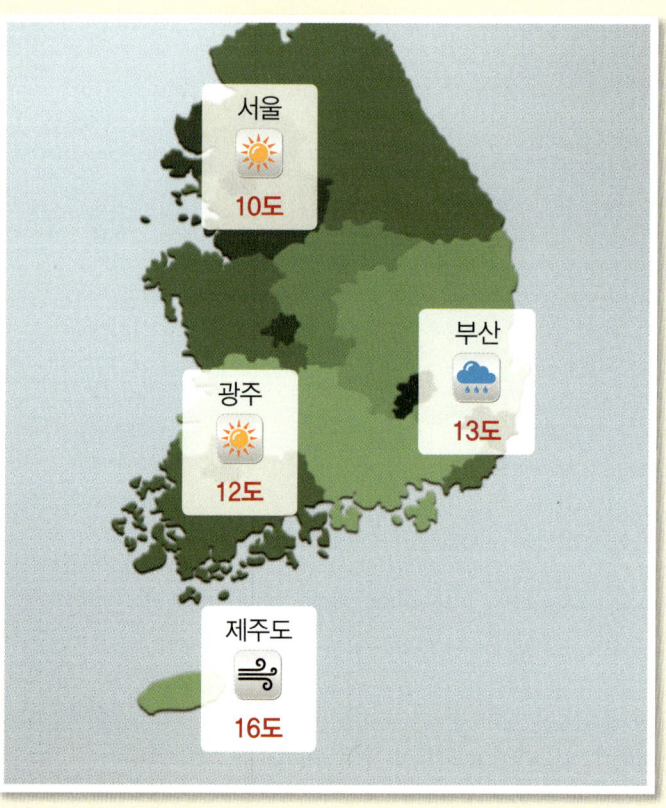

보기	서울은 하늘이 맑습니다. 기온은 10도입니다.

1. ....

   기온은 13도입니다.

2. ....

   기온은 12도입니다.

3. ....

   기온은 16도입니다.

2 Listen to tomorrow's weather forecast for South Korea, then answer the questions below. *What is the forecast for Seoul, Busan, Gwangju, and Jeju island?* 🎧 1.3

Link each location with its forecast for tomorrow.

| 서울 | 부산 | 광주 | 제주도 |

1 2 3 4

3 After listening again to the weather forecast above, listen now to the following statements, then tick whether they are true (O) or false (X). 🎧 1.4

1. O X
2. O X
3. O X
4. O X
5. O X

읽기

1 Write under the photos below one or two expressions that better describe them, choosing from those suggested in the boxes. You can use each expression more than once.

| 보기 흐리다 | 하늘이 맑다 | 쌀쌀하다 | 따뜻하다 |
| 춥다 | 덥다 | 시원하다 | 바람이 불다 |

보기

하늘이 흐립니다
쌀쌀합니다

1.

2.

3.

4.

5.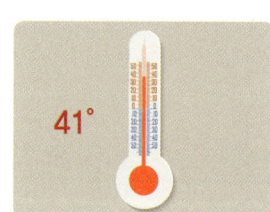

6.

7.

8.

2 This is an announcement for the students of the hiking club. *What are they going to do next Sunday?* Read the announcement, then answer the questions below.

1) 동아리 학생들이 언제, 어디에서 등산합니까?

2) 동아리 학생들이 몇 시부터 등산을 합니까?

3) 다음 주 일요일에 등산합니다. 그러면 무엇을 준비해야 합니까?

4) 토마스 씨는 등산을 하고 싶습니다. 그러면 어떻게 해야 합니까?

5) 다음은 일요일 등산 타임라인입니다. 학생들은 몇 시에 무엇을 합니까?

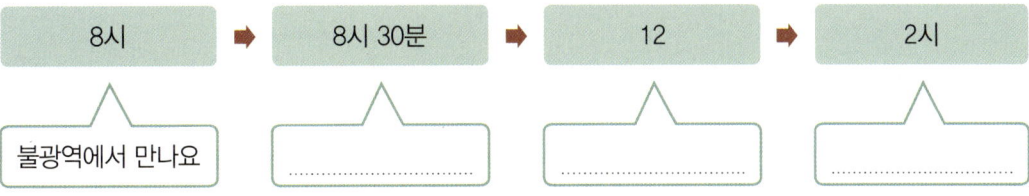

3 여러분, 최근에 야외 활동을 했습니까? 어디에 갔습니까? 날씨가 어땠습니까? 거기에서 무엇을 했습니까? 친구들하고 이야기해 보세요!

 쓰기

1 Look at the following table about the weather in Seoul, then fill in the blanks of the passage below.

계절	기온	날씨	활동
봄 (3월~5월)	22도	따뜻하다 하늘이 맑다	등산하다 자전거를 타다
여름 (6월~8월)	30도	덥다 비가 내리다	수영하다
가을 (9월~11월)	18도	바람이 불다 시원하다	등산하다 자전거를 타다
겨울 (12월~2월)	-3도	눈이 내리다 하늘이 흐리다 아주 춥다	스키를 타다 스케이트를 타다

서울 봄 하늘이 _____. 그리고 날씨가 따뜻합니다. 봄 기온은 보통 _____ 입니다. 봄에 사람들이 등산합니다. 그리고 자전거를 많이 탑니다.

여름에는 _____ 내립니다. 그리고 덥습니다. 사람들은 바다와 수영장에서 _____.

가을은 _____. 가을에는 바람이 _____. 가을에도 사람들이 _____.

겨울은 매우 춥습니다. 기온은 _____ 입니다. 눈도 많이 _____. 그래서 사람들은 겨울에 스키나 스케이트를 _____.

2 What is the weather like in your hometown? Using the example on page 32, fill in the next table with the weather of your hometown. Then, using the information that you used to fill in the table, write a passage about the weather in your hometown, and the leisure activities that people do in each season.

계절	기온	날씨	활동
봄 (월~ 월)			
여름 (월~ 월)			
가을 (월~ 월)			
겨울 (월~ 월)			

문화

Hiking culture

Mountains and forests make up about 64% of the territory of South Korea,[※] and therefore it is not surprising that hiking is one of Koreans' most preferred outdoor activities. A survey conducted by the Korean Forest Service found that about fifteen million people go hiking at least once a month; roughly four out of five Korean adults. Seoul itself is surrounded by mountains, and the capillarity of the public transportation system brings people straight to the base of mountains and the beginning of hiking paths, either by subway or bus.

Near popular hiking sites, in the morning on the weekends, waves of people move from the bus or subway station toward the beginning of hiking paths. Hiking paths cater for different people and vary in lengths and difficulty, and it is possible to go hiking on a 300m 'mountain' for just one hour, or on much higher mountains, on expert-level courses, for many hours. In most cases, people go hiking for a few hours, mainly in the morning.

Due to the proximity of mountains to major cities, the high accessibility of hiking paths, and the fact that it is possible to go hiking in the morning and be back home by early afternoon after lunch, hiking is a popular recreational activity.

A characteristic aspect of Korean hiking culture is what people wear. People usually wear colorful hiking outfits and specialized gear, such as walking poles, to improve safety. It is also not uncommon to see people wearing hiking outfits for other leisure activities. Overall, hiking apparel contributes up to 10% of the total Korean fashion market.[※※]

> ※ Korea Forest Service, https://nifos.forest.go.kr/kfsweb/kfi/kfs/dscss/selectDscss.do?dscssThemaId=441
> ※※ Chung Ang Monthly, https://jmagazine.joins.com/economist/view/330391

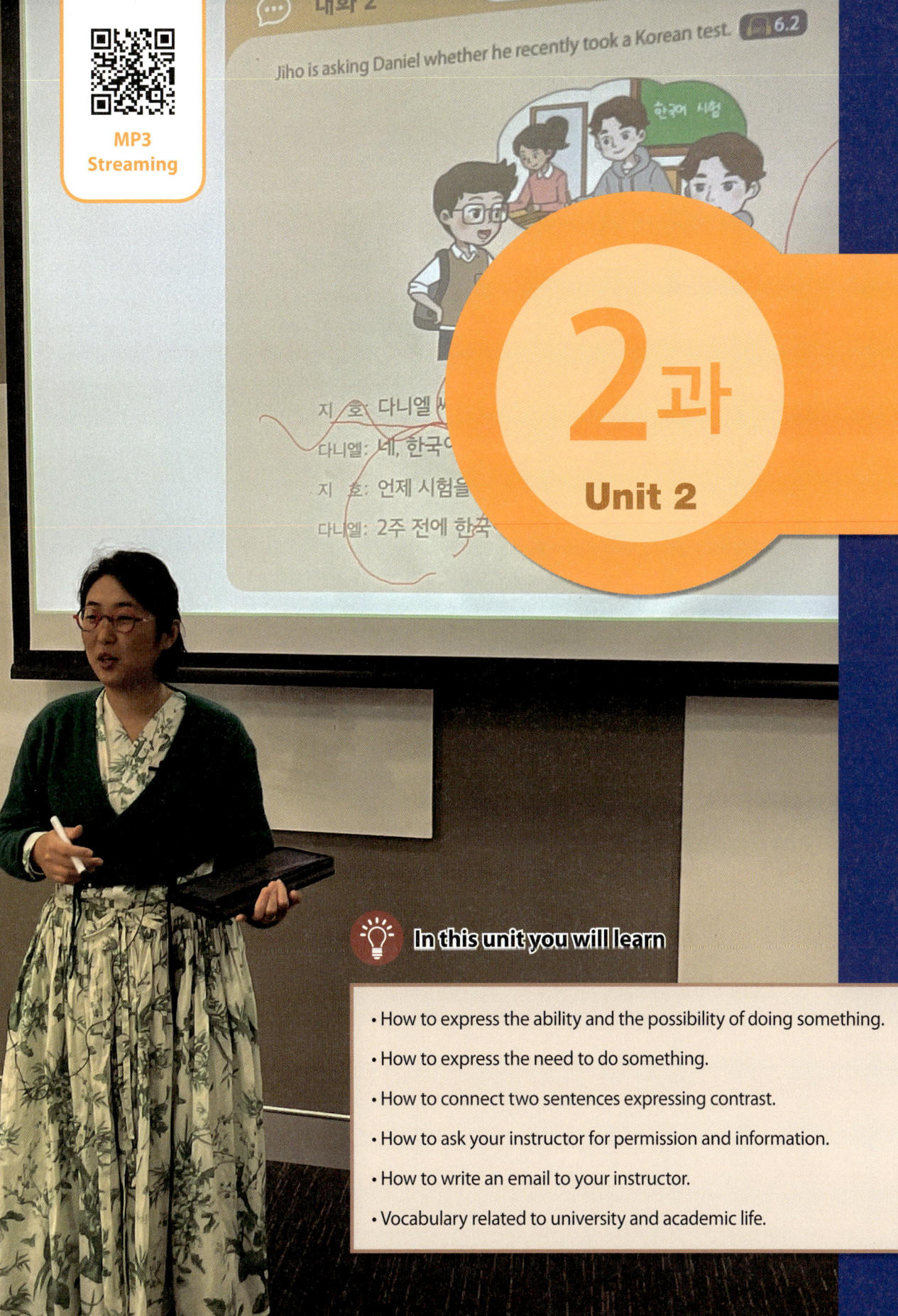

문법

–(으)ㄹ 수 있어요/없어요 (expressing ability or possibility of doing something)

Meaning

The pattern –(으)ㄹ 수 있다/없다 can be used to express the ability or possibility of doing something. For the meaning of ability, it is used to indicate that the speaker, or somebody else, knows how to do something. For the meaning of possibility, it is used to indicate that it is possible to do a certain action within the given circumstances. Its meaning is similar to the English verb can. Whether the meaning implied is that of ability or possibility will depend on the context. This pattern can also be used together with descriptive verbs to indicate the possibility of being in a certain state, and in this way it can also be used to make a conjecture (example 6 below).

Use

The pattern –을 수 있어요 is attached to verb bases ending in consonants, while –ㄹ 수 있어요 to verb bases ending in vowels. Irregular verbs that modify the verb base when attaching a suffix that begins with a vowel will change the base into the irregular form.

Verb base ending in a vowel	Verb base ending in a consonant
+ ㄹ 수 있어요	+ 을 수 있어요

가다 → 가 + ㄹ 수 있어요 → 갈 수 있어요
하다 → 하 + ㄹ 수 있어요 → 할 수 있어요
먹다 → 먹 + 을 수 있어요 → 먹을 수 있어요
듣다 → 듣 + 을 수 있어요 → 들 + 을 수 있어요 → 들을 수 있어요
만들다 → 만들 + 을 수 있어요 → 만들 수 있어요
쉽다 → 쉽 + 을 수 있어요 → 쉬우 + ㄹ 수 있어요 → 쉬울 수 있어요

Examples

1. 수영할 수 있어요. I can swim.

2. 내일까지 숙제를 할 수 있어요? Can you do your homework by tomorrow?

3. 토마스 씨는 노래를 잘 부를 수 있어요. Thomas can sing well.

4. 사진을 잘 찍을 수 있어요. I can (/I know how) to take a photo well.

5. 한국 요리를 할 수 있어요. I can (/I know how) to cook Korean food.

6. 다음주 시험은 어려울 수 있어요. Next week's exam may be difficult.

Extra notes

- This pattern, when used in the negative (−을 수 없다) to indicate not to be able to do something, or that it is not possible to do something, has the same meaning as −지 못하다. The difference is that it is generally not possible to use −지 못하다 with descriptive verbs.

Expressing the need to do something with −아야/어야 해요.

Meaning
−아야/어야 해요 is attached to both verbs and descriptive verbs to indicate that something must be done, or needs to be done.

Use
−아야 해요 is attached to verb bases which contain the vowels ㅏ or ㅗ. −어야 해요 is attached to verb bases which contain any other vowel.

Verb base containing ㅏ or ㅗ	Verb base containing a vowel which is not ㅏ or ㅗ	하다
+ 아야 해요	+ 어야 해요	→ 해야 해요

가다 → 가 + 아야 해요 → 가야 해요
하다 → 하 + 여야 해요 → 해야 해요
배우다 → 배우 + 어야 해요 → 배워야 해요
먹다 → 먹 + 어야 해요 → 먹어야 해요
받다 → 받 + 아야 해요 → 받아야 해요
듣다 → 듣 + 어야 해요 → 들 + 어야 해요 → 들어야 해요
만들다 → 만들 + 어야 해유 → 만들어야 해요

Examples

1. 9시까지 학교에 **가야 해요**. I have to go to school by 9 am.

2. 매일 운동을 **해야 해요**. You need to exercise every day.

3. 다음 주에 시험이 있어요. 그래서 지금 공부**해야 해요**. I have an exam next week. So now I must study.

4. 화요일까지 숙제를 **해야 해요**. I have to do my homework by Tuesday.

5. 한국어 수업에서는 한국어로 **말해야 해요**. You must speak Korean in class.

6. 주말에 집 청소를 **해야 해요**. I have to clean my house on the weekend.

7. 음식이 **맛있어야 해요**. The food must taste good.

Extra notes

- To indicate that something had to be done in the past, the past tense suffix can be attached to both the first and/or the second verb. By using this form in the past tense, the speaker can also show regret for something that should have been done.

  > 한국어를 열심히 공부했어야 해요. I should have studied Korean hard.
  > 한국어를 열심히 공부해야 했어요. I should have studied Korean hard.
  > 한국어를 열심히 공부했어야 했어요. I should have studied Korean hard.

- Instead of –아/어야 + 해요, also –아/어야 + 돼요 can be used without any difference in context of use or meaning, 수업에 늦었어요. 빨리 가야 돼요 *I am late to class, I have to hurry up*.

Expressing contrast using –지만.

Meaning

–지만 is used to connect two sentences indicating that the meaning expressed by the second sentence is in contrast with the meaning expressed by the first sentence. It is can be translated in English as *but*, or *although*.

Use

–지만 is used attached to the base of processive verbs, descriptive verbs, 이다 and 아니다. The same form –지만 is attached to both vowel and consonant ending bases.

> 보다 → 보 + 지만 → 보지만
> 다니다 → 다니 + 지만 → 다니지만
> 하다 → 하 + 지만 → 하지만
> 먹다 → 먹 + 지만 → 먹지만
> 좋다 → 좋 + 지만 → 좋지만
> 쓰다 → 쓰 + 지만 → 쓰지만
> 걷다 → 걷 + 지만 → 걷지만
> 예쁘다 → 예쁘 + 지만 → 예쁘지만
> 멀다 → 멀 + 지만 → 멀지만
> 춥다 → 춥 + 지만 → 춥지만

Examples

1. 수진 씨는 영어를 **잘하지만** 보라 씨는 잘 못해요. Sujin speaks good English, but Bora doesn't.
2. 이 태블릿 PC는 **작지만** 좀 비싸요. This tablet is small but expensive.
3. 퍼스에서 시드니는 **멀지만** 발리는 가까워요. Perth is far from Sydney, but near to Bali.
4. 토요일은 **바쁘지 않았지만** 일요일은 바빴어요. I wasn't busy on Saturday, but I was on Sunday.
5. 사장님은 **안 계시지만** 부장님은 계세요. The boss is not in, but the deputy director is.
6. 저는 한국학 전공이 **아니지만** 한국어를 공부해요. I am not a Korean Studies major (student), but I study Korean.
7. 사라: 학교 식당 음식이 어때요? How is the food of the school restaurant?
   시메이: **싸지만** 맛이 없어요. It's cheap but it's not good.
8. 지호: 한국어 시험이 어땠어요? How was the Korean exam?
   시메이: 공부를 많이 **했지만** 잘못 봤어요. I studied a lot but I didn't do well.

Extra notes

- It is possible to see from the examples above that −지만 can be also attached to a past tense base.
- The subjects of two sentences connected with −지만 can be different.
- −지만 is often used with verbs indicating apologies and when asking a favor:

  미안하지만 문 좀 열어 주세요. I am sorry, can you please open the door (for me)?
  죄송하지만 저는 먼저 집에 가겠습니다. I am sorry but I'll go home early.
  실례지만 김 선생님이 계세요? Excuse me, is Ms. Kim here?
  바쁘겠지만 좀 도와줄 수 있어요? I know you are busy, but could you please help me?

 단어

학교

초등학교   중학교   고등학교   대학교   대학원

대학교

1[일]학년
2[이]학년
3[삼]학년
4[사]학년
졸업(하다)

전공

의학	심리학	경제학
한국학	미디어학	경영학
아시아학	정치학	
언어학	법학	

수업

교실

결석(하다)/출석(하다)

지각(하다)

(한국어를) 공부하다
(한국어/태권도를) 배우다
(단어를) 외우다
복습하다
예습하다

시험을 보다
시험에 합격하다
시험에 떨어지다

# 연습

1 Complete the following sentences using the verb given in brackets and –(으)ㄹ 수 있다/없다.

> 보기   수진 씨는 중국어를 <u>읽을 수 있어요</u>. (읽다)

1. 시메이 씨는 한국어로 잘 _____. (말하다)

2. 어제 커피를 많이 마셨어요. 그래서 밤에 잠을 _____. (자다, *past tense)

3. 토마스 씨는 매운 음식을 잘 _____. (먹다)

4. '여보세요 토마스 씨? 지금 통화 _____?' (하다)

5. 어제 예린 씨는 늦게까지 일했어요. 그래서 일찍 _____. (일어나다 *past tense)

6. 비가 많이 왔어요. 그래서 소풍 _____.(가다, *past tense)

7. '미안해요. 지금 좀 바빠요. 그래서 같이 _____'. (만나다)

8. 수진 씨는 맛있는 김밥을 _____. (만들다).

2 Write your own answers to the following questions. Remember to use –(으)ㄹ 수 있다/없다.

1. 몇 개 국어 할 수 있어요?

   ....

2. 선생님한테 한국어로 이메일을 쓸 수 있어요?

   ....

3. 무슨 운동을 잘할 수 있어요?

   ....

4. 매운 음식을 먹을 수 있어요?

   ....

5. 하루에 몇 시간 공부할 수 있어요?

....

3 Fill in the following sentences with the appropriate processive/descriptive verb conjugated with the form −아야/어야 해요.

| 보기 좋다 | 청소하다 | 사다 | 받다 | 가다 |
| 전화하다 | 연습하다 | 씻다 | 일하다 |

보기 성적이 <u>좋아야 해요</u>. 그럼 교환 학생으로 한국에 갈 수 있어요.

1. 집에 친구를 초대했어요. 그래서 지금 집을 ....

2. 다음 주에 한국어 말하기 시험이 있어요. 그래서 지금 말하기를 ....

3. 중국에 여행을 가고 싶어요. 그럼 비자를 ....

4. 오늘 회사 일이 많아요. 그래서 늦게까지 ....

5. 컴퓨터가 고장 났어요. 그래서 A/S 센터에 ....
   A/S 센터 전화번호 알아요?

6. A: BTS 콘서트에 가고 싶어요.

   B: 그럼 빨리 티켓을 ....

7. 머리가 너무 아파요. 병원에 ....

8. 손이 더러워요. 손을 ....

4 Answer the following questions by using −아야/어야 해요.

1. 한국에 여행을 가고 싶어요. 어떻게 해야 해요?

....

2. 좋은 성적을 받고 싶어요. 어떻게 해야 해요?

....

3. 한국어를 잘하고 싶어요. 어떻게 해야 해요?

   ....

4. 한국 음식을 만들고 싶어요. 어떻게 해야 해요?

   ....

5. 노래를 잘 부르고 싶어요. 어떻게 해야 해요?

   ....

5 Build a sentence using the prompts below and −지만, as in the example.

보기	한국어	어렵다/재미있다
	→ 한국어는 어렵지만 재미있어요.	

1. 하숙집   학교에서 멀다/싸다

   → ....

2. 지하철   사람이 많다/빠르다

   → ....

3. 김치   맵다/맛있다

   → ....

4. 운동   힘들다/신나다

   → ....

5. 학교 식당   맛없다/싸다

   → ....

6 Match the sentences in the left column with those in the right column, and connect them using –지만. Remember that the verb of the first sentence may require the past tense.

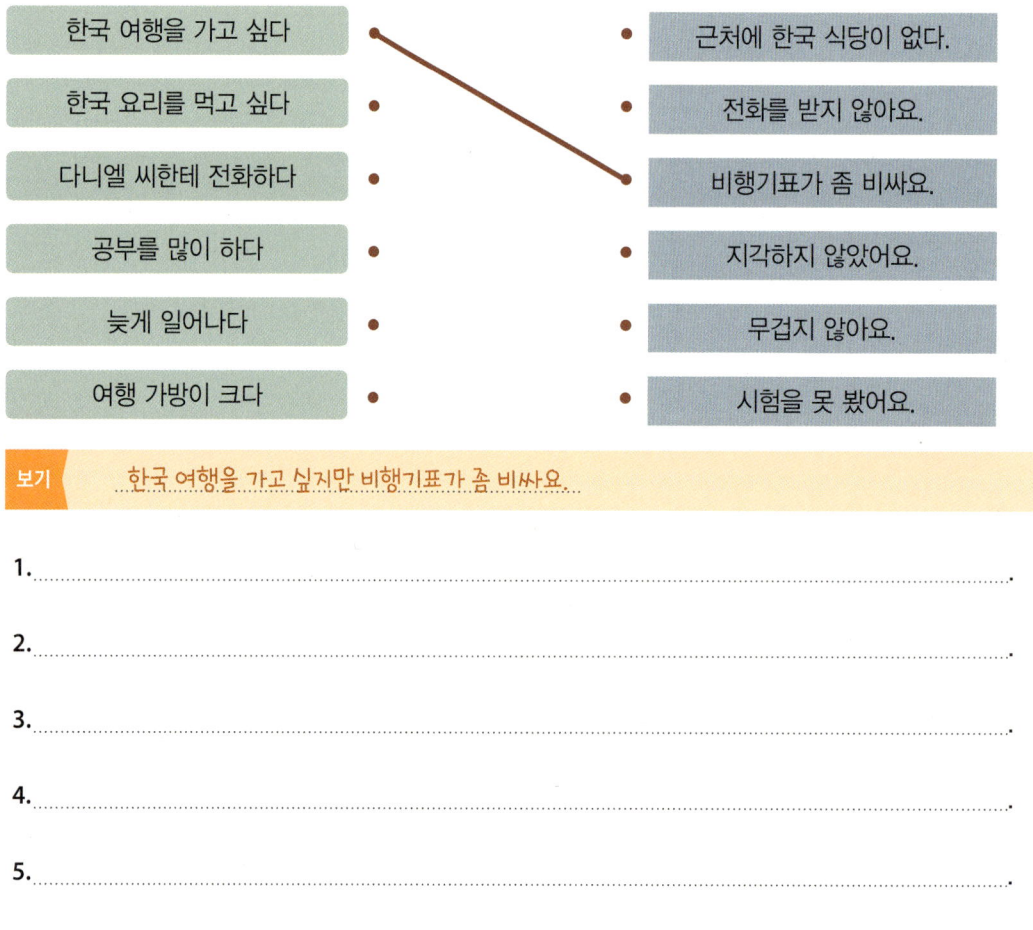

보기 한국 여행을 가고 싶지만 비행기표가 좀 비싸요.

1. _____.
2. _____.
3. _____.
4. _____.
5. _____.

7 Fill in the blanks of the following sentences with the most appropriate word.

| 복습해요 | 졸업해요 | 전공해요 |
| 지각했어요 | 외워요 | 결석해요 |

1. 시메이 씨는 대학교에서 한국어를 공부해요. 그리고 시메이 씨는 한국학을 _____.

2. 토마스 씨는 다음 주에 한국어 시험이 있어요. 그래서 지금 단어를 _____.

3. 지호 씨는 올해 대학교를 _____. 내년에 대학원에 갈 거예요.

4. 다니엘 씨는 오늘도 수업에 오지 않았어요. 다니엘 씨는 요즘 자주
   ....

5. 보라 씨는 매일 영어 수업이 끝나고 집에서 ....

6. 한국어 수업이 9시에 시작해요. 그런데 오늘 수진 씨는 9시 15분에 도착했어요.
   오늘 수진 씨는 ....

말하기

대화 1

Shimei asks a senior student for some tips on learning Korean.

시메이: 선배님, 한국어를 정말 잘해요!

선 배: 아니에요. 아직 잘 못해요.

시메이: 저도 한국어를 잘하고 싶어요. 어떻게 해야 해요?

선 배: 음... 단어를 많이 외워야 해요.

시메이: 아, 그래요? 그리고 또 뭐 해야 해요?

선 배: 그리고 매일 복습해야 해요.

Roleplay the dialogue above, changing the advice on how to improve one's Korean.

💬 대화 2

Daniel and Ms. Kim talk about an upcoming exam. 🎧 2.2

선생님: 여러분, 다음 주 월요일에 중간시험이 있어요.

다니엘: 선생님, 저는 월요일에 다른 수업이 있어요.

선생님: 그럼 화요일에 시험을 볼 수 있어요?

다니엘: 네, 화요일에 볼 수 있어요. 고맙습니다.

💬 Change the upcoming task for the next week with those suggested below.

중간시험이 있다
(시험을 보다)

숙제가 있다
(숙제를 내다)

퀴즈가 있다
(퀴즈를 보다)

한국어 발표가 있다
(발표를 하다)

 듣기

1 Listen to the following sentences, then pair each sentence with the word that describe the sentence the best. 2.3

1. •   • 단어
2. •   • 인터뷰
3. •   • 출석
4. •   • 복습해요
5. •   • 교과서

2 It is the beginning of the semester of your Korean language class, and your teacher Ms. Kim is giving some explanation about the course. *What are the requirements of the course?* 2.4

Listen to the statements below about the course then tick whether they are correct (O) or not (X). 2.5

1. O   X
2. O   X
3. O   X
4. O   X
5. O   X

48 Mission Accomplished: Korean 2

3 Listen again to Ms. Kim's introduction to this semester's course 🎧 2.4. Do you want to ask her any questions? Write down three questions that you may want to ask your teacher, and compare them with your classmates.

질문 1

질문 2

질문 3

 읽기

1 Have you ever written an email to your Korean teacher? What did you ask them? Read the following common situations that students may face, and match the number of that situation with how you would ask your teacher in that situation.

상황 1	다음 주 월요일까지 숙제를 내야 하지만 그때까지 숙제를 할 수 없습니다.
상황 2	한국어 시험이 있지만 그때 다른 수업도 있습니다.
상황 3	교환 학생을 가고 싶습니다.
상황 4	한국어 스터디 그룹에 들어가고 싶습니다. 그런데 친구가 없습니다.

상황 .... 혹시 다른 시간에 시험을 볼 수 있어요?

상황 .... 스터디 그룹에서 같이 공부하고 싶습니다. 어떻게 해야 해요?

상황 .... 이번 학기에 숙제가 많습니다. 다음 주 화요일까지 숙제를 낼 수 있어요?

상황 .... 교환 학생 준비를 어떻게 해야 해요?

2 Shimei writes an email to Ms. Kim because she wants to ask a few questions about the Korean classes. *What does she ask Ms. Kim?*

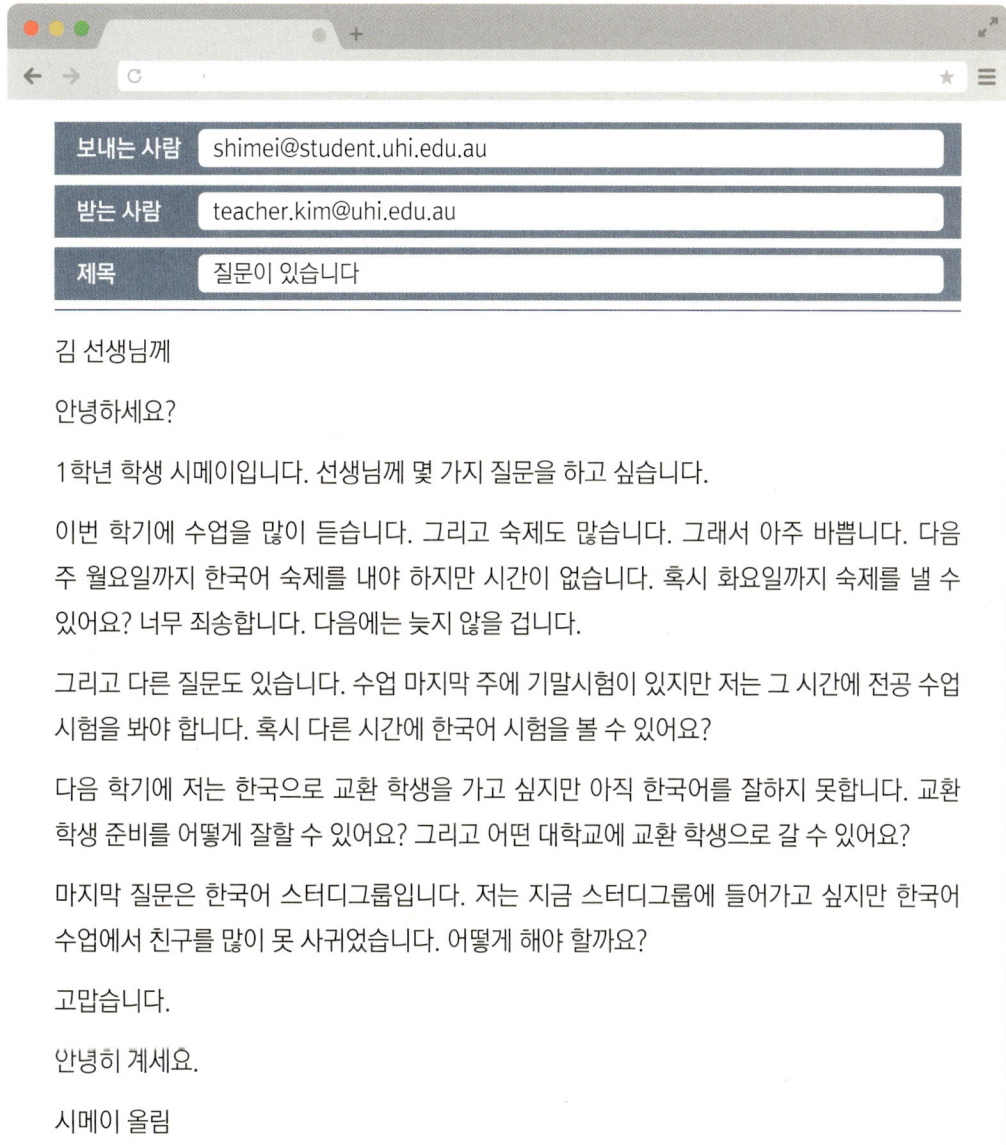

보내는 사람: shimei@student.uhi.edu.au
받는 사람: teacher.kim@uhi.edu.au
제목: 질문이 있습니다

김 선생님께

안녕하세요?

1학년 학생 시메이입니다. 선생님께 몇 가지 질문을 하고 싶습니다.

이번 학기에 수업을 많이 듣습니다. 그리고 숙제도 많습니다. 그래서 아주 바쁩니다. 다음 주 월요일까지 한국어 숙제를 내야 하지만 시간이 없습니다. 혹시 화요일까지 숙제를 낼 수 있어요? 너무 죄송합니다. 다음에는 늦지 않을 겁니다.

그리고 다른 질문도 있습니다. 수업 마지막 주에 기말시험이 있지만 저는 그 시간에 전공 수업 시험을 봐야 합니다. 혹시 다른 시간에 한국어 시험을 볼 수 있어요?

다음 학기에 저는 한국으로 교환 학생을 가고 싶지만 아직 한국어를 잘하지 못합니다. 교환 학생 준비를 어떻게 잘할 수 있어요? 그리고 어떤 대학교에 교환 학생으로 갈 수 있어요?

마지막 질문은 한국어 스터디그룹입니다. 저는 지금 스터디그룹에 들어가고 싶지만 한국어 수업에서 친구를 많이 못 사귀었습니다. 어떻게 해야 할까요?

고맙습니다.

안녕히 계세요.

시메이 올림

Read the statements below and decide whether they are true (O) or false (X).

1. 시메이 씨는 다음 주 월요일에 숙제를 낼 겁니다. O X

2. 시메이 씨는 이번 학기에 수업이 많습니다. O X

3. 시메이 씨는 다음 학기에 교환 학생으로 한국에 가고 싶지 않습니다. O X

4. 시메이 씨는 스터디 그룹 친구가 있습니다. O X

3 If you were Ms. Kim, how would you reply to Shimei? Discuss Ms. Kim's possible reply to Shimei with your classmates, and write it below.

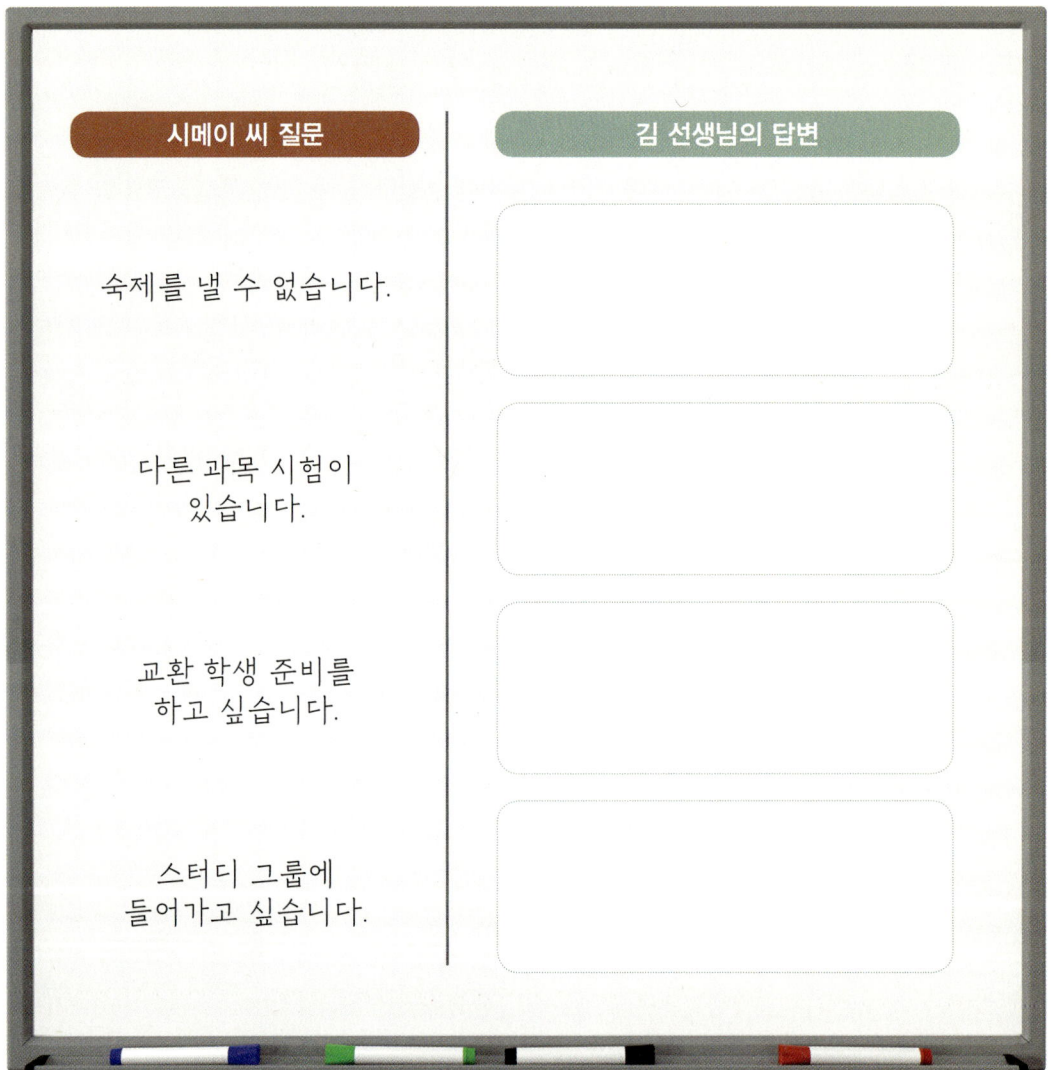

 쓰기

1 Read the following situations, then ask a query to your teacher using the word suggested as in the example.

> 보기
> 교환 학생을 가고 싶습니다. 〈어떤 대학교?〉
> → 교환 학생을 가고 싶습니다. 어떤 대학교에 갈 수 있어요?
>
> 1. 한국어 연습을 많이 하고 싶습니다. 〈좋은 교과서?〉
>   → _____
>
> 2. 한국어 수업 시간에 병원에 가야 합니다. 〈수업에 좀 (늦다)?〉
>   → _____
>
> 3. 시험을 잘못 봤습니다. 〈다음에 어떻게 잘 (보다)?〉
>   → _____

2 Write an email to your Korean language teacher. You want to ask advice 1) for a good Korean language book, 2) whether you can be absent from the next Korean class because you need to go to the hospital, and 3) to check your answers because you are not sure you understood the homework.

문화

Getting into university in Korea

The Korean primary and secondary school system is divided into six years of primary school, three years of middle school, and three years of high school. At the end of high school, students can access university through the university entrance examination (수학능력시험) or through a holistic assessment of their academic results and extracurricular activities over a timeframe of a few years.

The university entrance examination is held in one day, on the same day, for all Korean students. The results give a mark which is scaled against all students taking the exam in that year. The preparation for the exam, which starts at a very young age, takes place not only in schools but mostly in private academies where students usually go after their regular school hours. This has caused the private education sector in South Korea to flourish.

The method which allows university entrance through a holistic assessment of curricular and extracurricular activities includes an evaluation of the student's academic record. This may include marks for each subject, but also activities such as volunteering, internships, awards received by the student and so on.

The two systems have pros and cons. The university entrance examination guarantees more fairness in both the test content and marking, and consequently it does not discriminate against the student's background or socio-economic status. Nevertheless, with this system students play all their cards on one day, and bad luck such as being suddenly unwell may have a negative influence on the exam.

The evaluation of the students' academic record allows for a holistic assessment of the student and their aptitudes. The academic record is compiled over the course of the high school years, and therefore reflects the student's abilities in their entirety. However, this system is often criticized because students from higher socio-economic status have more opportunities to develop extra-curricular activities, and therefore this approach can be misused.

Universities establish a quota of students admitted under one system or the other.

3과
Unit 3

In this unit you will learn

- How to make a polite request, or to politely suggest people do something.
- How to tell people politely not to do something (imperative negative).
- How to ask somebody whether they have the intention of doing something.
- How to make an enquiry to a real estate agent.
- How to describe the place where you live.
- Common regulations of a Korean university dormitory.
- Vocabulary related to housing and furniture.

문법

Imperative polite form, -(으)세요.

Meaning

-(으)세요 is made by combining the honorific marker -시- with the informal polite ending -요. The result is an honorific form used when the subject is a person towards whom the speaker is supposed to show respect, either because of age, context, or social position. Different uses of this honorific marker will be dealt with in Unit 5. In this Unit, the associated function is to express a polite request and a polite imperative.

Use

Although -(으)세요 as an honorific ending that can be used with both processive and descriptive verbs, when it is used for making a request, or as an imperative form, it can only be attached to processive verbs. To attach the suffix -(으)세요 to a verb base, drop the infinitive ending -다 and attach -으세요 to consonant-ending bases, and -세요 to vowel-ending bases.

Verb base ending in a vowel	Verb base ending in a consonant
+ 세요	+ 으세요

가다 → 가 + 세요 → 가세요
주다 → 주 + 세요 → 주세요
하다 → 하 + 세요 → 하세요
받다 → 받 + 으세요 → 받으세요
앉다 → 앉 + 으세요 → 앉으세요
듣다 → 듣 + 으세요 → 들 + 으세요 → 들으세요
만들다 → 만들 + 으세요 → 만드 + 세요 → 만드세요

Examples

1. 여기에 전화번호를 **쓰세요**. Please write your phone number here.

2. A: 학생회관이 어디에 있어요? Where is the student union building?
   B: 저쪽으로 **가세요**. Please go that way.

3. 김 선생님: 다니엘 씨, 큰 소리로 교과서를 **읽으세요**. Daniel, please read the textbook out aloud.
   다니엘: 네 선생님, 알겠습니다. Yes, ok.

4. 여기요! 커피 한 잔 **주세요**. Can I have a cup of coffee please?

5. 선생님, 이 의자에 **앉으세요**. Teacher, please sit on this chair.

6. 내일 오전 9시까지 **오세요**. Please come by 9 am.

7. 밖에 나갈 때 마스크를 꼭 **쓰세요**. Please wear a mask when you go outside.

8. 조용히 **하세요**. Please be quiet.

9. 듣기 파일을 잘 **들으세요**. Please listen to the listening files.

Extra notes

- An ending similar to −으세요 which is used to express a polite request or a polite order is −으십시오. While the meaning is the same, the context of use is different. −(으)세요 is generally used in spoken language in everyday life, while −으십시오 is used in spoken language in more formal situations, or in written announcements.
- Some verbs have their own honorific shape. −(으)세요 is attached to the verb base of the honorific shape. The most frequently used are: 먹다 → 드시다 (드세요), 마시다 → 드시다 (드세요), 말하다 → 말씀하다 (말씀하세요). For a more comprehensive list of verbs that have their own honorific shape, refer to Unit 5.
- When used to make a request or an order, due to the *here and now* meaning that these functions imply, −(으)세요 cannot be attached to past or future tense bases.

 Imperative negative polite form, −지 마세요.

Meaning

−지 마세요 is used in opposition to −(으)세요, and is attached to the verb base to indicate prohibition. It is therefore used as an imperative negative form, to tell somebody not to do something.

Use

It is made by combining −지 and the auxiliary verb 말다 (which indicates a negation) together with the honorific ending −(으)세요. Therefore, −지 마세요 is used to politely indicate a prohibition. Due to its meaning, it can be used only with processive verbs and not with descriptive verbs. The same shape is attached to the base of both consonant−ending and vowel−ending verbs.

Verb base ending in a vowel	Verb base ending in a consonant
+ 지 마세요	

가다 → 가 + 지마세요 → 가지 마세요
타다 → 타 + 지 마세요 → 타지 마세요
하다 → 하 + 지 마세요 → 하지 마세요
찍다 → 찍 + 지 마세요 → 찍지 마세요
받다 → 받 + 지 마세요 → 받지 마세요
듣다 → 듣 + 지마세요 → 듣지 마세요
만들다 → 만들 + 지 마세요 → 만들지 마세요

Examples

1. 미술관에서 사진을 **찍지 마세요**. Don't take photos in the art gallery.

2. 추워요. 창문을 **열지 마세요**. It's cold, don't open the window.

3. 수업에 **늦지 마세요**. Don't be late to class.

4. 술을 **마시지 마세요**. Don't drink alcohol.

5. 수업 중에 전화를 **받지 마세요**. Don't pick up the phone in class.

6. 버스를 **타지 마세요**. 지하철을 **타세요**. Don't take the bus, take the subway.

7. A: 매운 음식을 못 먹어요. I cannot eat spicy food.
   B: 그럼 떡볶이를 **드시지 마세요**. 떡볶이는 매워요. 김밥을 **드세요**. So don't eat Ttokbokki, it's spicy. Eat gimbap.

Extra notes

- −지 말다 can also be used in informal situations as −지 마요, without the honorific ending attached, to express a negative request or to suggest not doing something in a less formal tone.

  토마스: 보라 씨, 우리 약속이 몇 시예요?
  보라: 11시예요. 토마스 씨, 늦지 마요!

- Similarly to −(으)십시오, −지 마십시오 can be used in more formal or written contexts.
- −지 마세요 can be used together with verbs that have their own separate honorific form, such as 먹다(드시다), 마시다(드시다), 말하다(말씀하다). Depending on the status and the relationship between the speaker and the hearer, −지 마세요 can be attached to both the regular and honorific form. Therefore both 먹지 마세요 and 드시지 마세요 are acceptable,

although the latter is more polite than the former.

Asking and expressing the will or intention of doing something, –(으)ㄹ래요.

Meaning

The ending –(으)ㄹ래요 is attached to processive verbs, and expresses two similar meanings depending on whether it is used in declarative or interrogative sentences.

In interrogative sentences it is used to ask about somebody's intention or inclination regarding doing something. It is used when the speaker wants to know about the thoughts or intentions of the hearer.

In declarative sentences, it is used by the speaker to express their inclination, intention, or plan for doing something. By using this ending, the speaker reveals what they are planning to do in the (often near) future.

For both interrogative and declarative sentences, –(으)ㄹ래요 is used in informal spoken language.

Use

–(으)ㄹ래요 can be attached only to processive verbs, due to its meaning. If used in interrogative sentences, the subject is usually the second person but can be used also in the first person plural (we) when the speaker asks about the intention of doing something together (example 4 below). If used in declarative sentences, the subject is the first person, either singular or plural. –ㄹ래요 is attached to vowel-ending verb bases, –을래요 is attached to consonant-ending verb bases.

Verb base ending in a vowel	Verb base ending in a consonant
+ ㄹ래요	+ 을래요

가다 → 가 + ㄹ래요 → 갈래요
하다 → 하 + ㄹ래요 → 할래요
먹다 → 먹 + 을래요 → 먹을래요
듣다 → 든 + 을래요 → 들 + 을래요 → 들을래요
만들다 → 만들 + 래요 → 만들래요

Examples

1. A: 여기서 잠깐 **기다릴래요**? Would you mind waiting here for a moment?
   B: 네, 알겠어요. Yes, ok.

2. A: 지하철역 앞에서 만날래요? What about meeting in front of the subway station?
   B: 네, 거기서 **만나요**. Ok, let's meet there.

3. A: 뭐 먹을래요? What do you want to eat?
   B: 저는 김밥 **먹을래요**. I'll have gimbap.

4. A: 같이 맥주 한 잔 **할래요**? Do you want to drink a glass of beer?
   B: 아니요, 오늘 좀 피곤해요. 좀 **쉴래요**. No, I am tired today. I want to take a rest.

5. A: 토마스 씨, 한국어 숙제가 어려워요? 같이 **공부할래요**? Thomas, is the Korean homework hard? Do you want to study together?
   B: 네, 고마워요. 보라 씨. Yes, thank you, Bora.

6. A: 지호 씨, 어디 아파요? 여기에 잠깐 **앉을래요**? Jiho, are you unwell? Do you want to sit here for a moment?
   B: 네, 오늘 머리가 조금 아파요. Yes, I have a headache today.

Extra notes

- −(으)ㄹ래요, when used in interrogative sentences, may have a meaning similar to −(으)ㄹ까요, but there are important differences. −(으)ㄹ까요 is mostly used when the speaker asks about the intention or will of doing something together and therefore can be used in the first person (plural); on the other hand, by using −(으)ㄹ래요, the speaker just asks about the hearer's intention, and therefore in interrogative sentences it cannot be used in the first person.
- Both −(으)ㄹ래요 and −(으)ㄹ까요 cannot be used in interrogative sentences when the subject is a person older than the speaker; however, they are acceptable if used together with the honorific marker −시− (Unit 5), and if the hearer is a person older than the speaker, but who has known the speaker for a long time.
- −(으)ㄹ래요 and −고 싶어요 also may also share a similar meaning. −(으)ㄹ래요 expresses will and intention about something possible in the present situation. On the other hand, −고 싶어요 simply expresses a desire, without considering whether it is possible or not.
- Even if it used with −요 indicating an informal polite level, −(으)ㄹ래요 belongs to the intimate oral language register, and should not be used when talking to older people or in formal contexts. For example, you should not use this form when talking to your teacher, unless you use it together with the appropriate honorific form (see Unit 5).

 단어

집과 건물

아파트

한옥

하숙집

기숙사

집/방을 구하다

이사를 하다

월세를 내다

집의 구성

거실

부엌

화장실

침실

방의 상태

넓다

좁다

깨끗하다

더럽다

밝다

어둡다

가구와 가전

냉장고

세탁기

침대

옷장

식탁

소파

연습

1 Fill out the following table using －(으)세요 for the left column, and －지 마세요 for the right column.

	－(으)세요	－지 마세요
보기 시작하다 →	시작하세요	시작하지 마세요
1. 타다 →		
2. 쓰다 →		
3. 쉬다 →		
4. 앉다 →		
5. 닫다 →		
6. *듣다 →		
7. *만들다 →		
8. **먹다 →		
9. **말하다 →		

2 Fill in the blanks of the following dialogues by making a suggestion/making a polite request to do something.

> 보기
> 손님: 이 식당은 뭐가 맛있어요?
> 종업원: 비빔밥이 맛있어요. 비빔밥을 드세요.

1. 시메이: 한국어를 잘하고 싶어요. 어떻게 해요?

   다니엘: 그럼 한국 친구하고 ＿＿＿＿＿＿＿＿＿.

2. 사라: 옆 집이 너무 시끄러워요.

   예린: 그럼 이사를 ＿＿＿＿＿＿＿＿＿.

3. 보라: 온라인으로 옷을 샀어요. 그런데 너무 작아요.

   수진: 그럼 사이즈를 ....

4. 예린: 배가 좀 아파요.

   사라: 팀장님, 괜찮으세요? 이 의자에 좀 ....

5. 선생님: 다음 주 시험을 잊지 마세요. 주말에 한국어 공부를 많이 ....

   학생: 네, 알겠습니다.

3 Look at the pictures below, then write what is not permitted. Remember to use −지 마세요 as in the example.

| 보기 | 핸드폰을 쓰지 마세요. |

1. ....

2. ....

3. ....

4 Below is the school board, with a notice about things that are forbidden. Fill in the board by writing what it is not permitted at school.

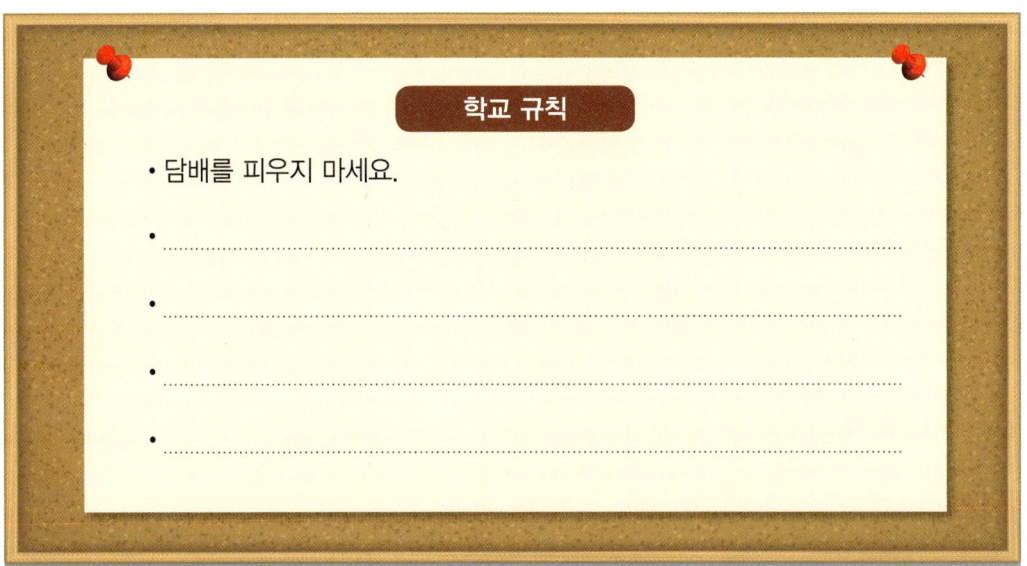

5 Fill in the blanks of following mini-dialogues and sentences by using the verb in brackets conjugated with -(으)ㄹ래요.

| 보기 | 다니엘: 시메이 씨는 뭐 <u>먹을래요?</u> (먹다)
시메이: 저는 라면이요. |

1. 토마스: : 보라 씨, 주말에 같이 _____? (놀다)

   보라: 미안해요. 토마스 씨. 이번 주말에는 시간이 없어요.

2. 수진: 커피를 _____? 차를 _____? (마시다)

   보라: 저는 커피를 _____.

3. 다니엘: 퍼스 시내에 한국 영화 축제가 있어요. 같이 영화를 _____? (보다)

   시메이: 네, 좋아요.

4. 저는 노래방에서 BTS 노래를 _____. (부르다)

5. 버스가 느려요. 그래서 저는 지하철을 _____. (타다)

6. 오늘 몸이 조금 안 좋아요. 그래서 오늘 집에서 _____. (쉬다)

6 Look at the following pictures, then ask your classmate what they prefer to do, like in the example.

보기	A: 한국 영화 볼래요? 미국 영화 볼래요?
	B: 저는 한국 영화를 볼래요.

1. A: ....

   B: ....

2. A: ....

   B: ....

3. A: ....

   B: ....

4. A: ....

   B: ....

5. A: ....

B: ....

7 **Fill in the blanks of the following sentences with the most appropriate word, choosing from those suggested below.**

| 한옥 | 깨끗해요 | 세탁기 |
| 이사 할 거예요 | 거실 | 부엌 |

1. 사라 씨는 자주 집을 청소해요. 그래서 사라 씨 집이 ....

2. 기숙사가 마음에 들지 않아요. 그래서 다음 달에 ....

3. 보라 씨는 .... 에서 요리를 해요.

4. 수진 씨 .... 에는 TV하고 소파가 있어요.

5. 토마스 씨는 .... 에 티셔츠와 바지를 넣었어요.

6. 예린 씨는 .... 에 살아요. 한옥은 한국 옛날 전통 집이에요.

말하기

대화 1

Sujin lives in a boarding house, and she is having a discussion with the landlady because today she broke one of rules. 3.1

아주머니: 수진 학생! 또 늦었어요?

수진: 죄송해요 아주머니!

아주머니: 왜 늦었어요?

수진: 학생모임이 늦게 끝났어요.

아주머니: 하숙집 규칙을 몰라요? 다음에는 늦지 마세요.

수진: 네, 죄송합니다...

Roleplay the dialogue above, changing the rule that Sujin broke and the reason with those suggested below.

늦다	학생모임이 늦게 끝났어요
방에서 요리하다	배고팠어요
방에 친구를 초대하다	같이 시험 준비를 했어요
밤에 세탁기를 돌리다	제 옷이 너무 더러웠어요
방 청소를 하지 않았다	학교 숙제 때문에 너무 바빴어요

💬 대화 2

Thomas is asking Bora for advice about moving houses. 🎧 3.2

토마스: 저는 이사를 하고 싶어요.

보 라: 왜요? 기숙사가 마음에 들지 않아요?

토마스: 네. 기숙사 방이 너무 좁아요. 그래서 새 방을 구하고 싶어요. 어떻게 해야 해요?

보 라: 음…부동산에 문의하세요.

토마스: 부동산이요? 저… 한국어를 잘 못해요… 저 좀 도와줄래요?

💬 Roleplay the dialogue above, then change the reason why Thomas wants to move, and Bora's suggestion.

토마스	보라
방이 너무 좁다	
기숙사가 너무 시끄럽다	부동산에 문의하다
규칙이 너무 많다	
방이 너무 어둡다	
기숙사 밥이 맛이 없다	부동산 앱으로 찾다
방 친구가 마음에 들지 않다	

 듣기

1 Look at the two house descriptions below. Then listen to the statements, and tick off whether they refer to the first house, the second, or both. 🎧 3.3

A
서울 부동산
- 방 2개
- 월세 70만원
- 6층
- 고려대학교에서 5분 거리
- 세탁기, 냉장고 포함
- 침대, TV X

문의전화 02-5437-8953

B
서울 부동산
- 방 1개
- 월세 50만원
- 4층
- 고려대학교에서 30분 거리
- 세탁기, 냉장고, 침대 포함
- 에어컨, TV X

문의전화 02-5437-8953

A	B
1.	
2.	
3.	
4.	
5.	
6.	

2 Thomas and Bora went to the real estate agency to look for a new house for Thomas. *What is the house like that Thomas decides to check out?* Listen to their conversation, then answer the questions below. 🎧 3.4

1. 토마스 씨는 왜 부동산에 갔어요?

2. 토마스 씨는 왜 기차역 근처로 이사를 하지 않을 거예요?

3. 학교 근처 방은 어때요?

4. 학교 근처 방은 월세가 얼마예요?

5. 학교 근처 방에는 무슨 가구와 가전이 있어요?

6. 여러분이 혼자 살 거예요. 그럼 어떤 방을 찾고 싶어요?

3 How is the place you are living now? Answer the following questions, then ask the same questions to your classmates.

	나	친구
집이 어디에 있어요?		
집이 어때요?		
집에 뭐가 있어요?		
그 집이 마음에 들어요? 왜요?		

읽기

1 Have you have lived in a university dormitory or in a college? Did they have specific regulations? Look at the images below, and write what may be forbidden to do in a dormitory, as in the example.

| 보기 | 담배를 피우지 마세요. |

1. _____.

2. _____.

3. _____.

4. _____.

5. _____.

2 This is the list of rules of the student dormitory at Korea University. *What are the students able/not able to do?*

고려대학교 기숙사 규칙

여러분 환영합니다! 저희 기숙사에는 다음 규칙이 있습니다. 규칙을 꼭 지켜야 합니다. 그럼 다 같이 잘 살 수 있습니다. 규칙은 다음과 같습니다.

1) 1주일에 한 번 방을 꼭 청소하세요.

2) 방에서 담배를 피우지 마세요.

3) 기숙사에서 술을 마시지 마세요.

4) 방에 친구를 초대하지 마세요.

5) 방에서 요리하지 마세요.

6) 냉장고에 음식을 넣고 잊어버리지 마세요.

7) 쓰레기를 쓰레기통에 버리세요.

8) 변기에 휴지를 절대 버리지 마세요.

9) 방에서 큰 소리로 말하지 마세요.

10) 밤 10시 이후에는 음악을 이어폰으로 들으세요.

11) 밤 11시 이후에는 기숙사에 들어올 수 없어요.

12) 친구한테 방 열쇠를 주지 마세요.

13) 기숙사 헬스장에서는 오전 7시부터 11시까지, 오후 4시부터 7시까지 운동할 수 있어요.

14) 밤에 세탁기를 돌리지 마세요.

질문이 있어요? 그럼 기숙사 매니저한테 이메일이나 전화로 하세요.

Read the statements below and decide whether they are true (O) or false (X).

1. 기숙사 학생들이 매일 친구를 초대할 수 있어요.   O   X
2. 기숙사 학생들이 다 같이 밤늦게까지 방에서 이야기 할 수 있어요.   O   X
3. 기숙사 학생들이 밤늦게 기숙사에 들어올 수 없어요.   O   X
4. 기숙사 학생들이 항상 헬스장에서 운동할 수 있어요.   O   X
5. 기숙사에 세탁기하고 냉장고가 있어요.   O   X
6. 기숙사 학생들이 방에서 요리할 수 있어요.   O   X

3 What do you think about the dormitory regulations? Do you agree with all of them? Is there any regulation that you don't like? Do you think that there is some regulation missing? Discuss with your classmates, then fill in the table below.

 쓰기

1 Imagine that you are looking for a house to move into. Where would you like to move? What is that house like? Answer the questions below.

1. 여러분 어느 나라에서 살고 싶어요?

2. 어떤 집에서 살고 싶어요?

3. 방이 몇 개 필요해요?

4. 어떤 가구가 필요해요?

5. 어떤 가전이 필요해요?

2 With the answers that you have given to the questions above, write a paragraph where you describe the house you would like to move into.

문화

Renting in South Korea

The most common options for students moving to South Korea and looking for a place to stay are dormitories and boarding houses (하숙집). Dormitories are usually booked through the university, and in most cases students are hosted in twin rooms. 하숙집 are a more traditional option. In this case, a landlady rents rooms in her house to students, and cooks breakfast and dinner for them. The quality of the meals depends on the 하숙집 and the skills of the landlady. Students are usually hosted in single rooms and pay a rent monthly to the landlady; however, in most cases no deposit is required. Many 하숙집 can be found in the proximity of most universities. A cheaper option is the 고시원, but most 고시원 rooms are just a few square meters, and only fit a small bed and a small table. In the case of the 고시원, no meal is provided.

Renting an apartment is much more complex and expensive. In Korea there are two renting options, one where the tenant pays a rent monthly (월세) and another where the tenant pays a lump sum upon signing the contract, which is then returned at the end of the contract (전세). In both cases, contracts are signed for a duration of two years. In the case of a 월세 contract, the tenant is required to provide a deposit, usually equivalent to about a year's rent. The amount of deposit and rent can be agreed between owner and tenant, as the owner may be willing to offer a discount on the rent in exchange for a higher deposit, or vice-versa. On the other hand, 전세 is one of the most popular options for Koreans looking to move into an apartment. Depending on the location, the amount of the lump sum can be considerable. Some lump sums for rental properties in the most expensive districts in Seoul are equivalent to the sum necessary to buy a house in other parts of the country.

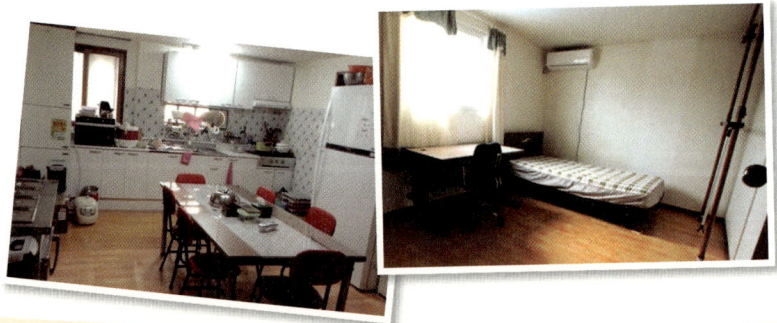

 문법

–아/어 보세요

Meaning

The auxiliary verb 보다 can be attached to the verb base + 아/어 to indicate an attempt to do something. Depending on further endings attached to 보다, it is used either to make suggestions (if used for example in the second person) with the meaning of *try to do...*, or to express the experience of having done something, at least once, in the past (if used in the first person, or in the second person in interrogative clauses), with the meaning of *I tried/have the experience of doing* (first person), or *Have you ever...?* (interrogative).

Since –아/어 보세요 has an honorific meaning (see Unit 5), it is never used in the first person, therefore it expresses the polite suggestion of trying to do something.

Use

Due to its meaning indicating the suggestion of doing something, –아/어 보세요 can only be used with processive verbs.

To use –아/어 보세요, drop the infinitive ending –다 from the verb infinitive form. If the last vowel of the verb base is ㅏ or ㅗ attach –아 보세요. Otherwise, if the last vowel of the verb base is any other vowel, attach –어 보세요. The verb 하다 becomes 해 보세요.

Verb base containing ㅏ or ㅗ	Verb base containing a vowel which is not ㅏ or ㅗ	하다
+ 아 보세요	+ 어 보세요	→ 해 보세요

찾다 → 찾 + 아 보세요 → 찾아 보세요
먹다 → 먹 + 어 보세요 → 먹어 보세요
기다리다 → 기다리 + 어 보세요 → 기다려 보세요
하다 → 하 + 여 보세요 → 해 + 보세요 → 해 보세요
듣다 → 듣 + 어 보세요 → 들 + 어 보세요 → 들어 보세요
눕다 → 눕 + 어 보세요 → 누우 + 어 보세요 → 누워 보세요
부르다 → 부르 + 어 보세요 → 불ㄹ + 어 보세요 → 불러 보세요

Examples

1. 친구: 한국어 수업이 어때요? How are the Korean classes?
   토마스: 재미있어요! 한번 들어 보세요. It's fun! Try them out once.

2. 다니엘: 시험이 언제예요? When is the exam?
   시메이: 잘 모르겠어요. 선생님한테 한번 물어 보세요. I don't know, try asking the teacher.

3. 예린: 이 구두가 마음에 들어요. I like these shoes.
   직원: 그럼 한번 **신어 보세요**. Try them on once.

Extra notes

- As in the examples 1, 2, and 4 above, 한번 is often used together with –아/어 보다 to indicate *one* or *one time*. In this case it is used to suggest doing something which has not been done before.
- Although possible, –아/어 보세요 is usually not attached to the base of the verb 보다 itself. Sentences such as 이 영화를 한번 봐 보세요 *Watch this film once!* sound unnatural and is not very frequently used. It is sufficient simply to use 보세요.

–아/어 봤어요

Meaning

When –아/어 보다 is used in the past tense as in –아/어 봤어요, the speaker expresses (or asks about) some kind of past experience. If the speaker uses –았/었어요 in the first person, they want to say that they had some kind of experience, or that they tried to do something. –아/어 봤어요 can also be used in questions in the second person, when the speaker wants to ask somebody whether they had a certain experience, or tried to do something.

Use

Similarly to –아/어 보세요, –아 봤어요 is attached to verb bases where the vowel is ㅏ or ㅗ. –어 봤어요 is attached to all other verb bases, and 하다 becomes 해 봤어요.

Verb base containing ㅏ or ㅗ	Verb base containing a vowel which is not ㅏ or ㅗ	하다
+ 아 봤어요	+ 어 봤어요	→ 해 봤어요

만나다 → 만나 + 아 봤어요 → 만나 봤어요
읽다 → 읽 + 어 봤어요 → 읽어 봤어요
기다리다 → 기다리 + 어 봤요 → 기다려 봤어요
쓰다 → 쓰 + 어 봤어요 → ㅆ + 어 봤어요 → 써 봤어요
만들다 → 만들 + 어 봤어요 → 만들어 봤어요
걷다 → 걷 + 어 봤어요 → 걸 + 어 봤어요 → 걸어 봤어요
굽다 → 굽 + 어 봤어요 → 구우 + 어 봤어요 → 구워 봤어요
부르다 → 부르 + 어 봤어요 → 불ㄹ + 어 봤어요 → 불러 봤어요

Examples

1. 대학생 때 철학을 공부 **해 봤어요**. *I tried studying philosophy when I was a university student.*

2. 옷 가게에서 새 옷을 **입어 봤어요**. *I tried on my new clothes in the shop.*

3. 유투브 동영상을 **만들어 봤어요**. *I tried to make a Youtube video.*

4. 한국 식당에 한 번 **가 봤어요**. *I tried out the Korean restaurant.*

5. 지호: 시메이 씨, 한국에 **가 봤어요**? *Shimei, have you ever been to Korea?*
   시메이: 네, 한 번 **가 봤어요**. *Yes, I have been there (once).*

Extra notes

- The same pattern can be used by the speaker to say that they have never tried to do something, or have never done something in the past. In this case 한 번도 (not even once) followed by a negative verb is used. For example, 한 번도 한국 음식을 안 먹어 봤어요 *I never tried to eat/I have never eaten Korean food*, or 한 번도 한국에 안 가 봤어요 *I have never been to Korea*.
- When it is used in interrogative sentences, it can be translated with *have you ever...?*, as in example 5 above.
- –아/어 보세요 and –아/어 봤어요 are not the only two patterns in which –아/어 보다 can be used, and many other endings can be attached to –아/어 보다 to add other meanings. For example, –아/어 보고 싶어요 can be used by the speaker to indicate that they want to try to do something (that they have never done before), as in 남극 여행을 한번 해 보고 싶어요 *I want to travel to the South Pole*, 한국 음식을 한번 만들어 보고 싶어요 *I want to try to make Korean food once*.

–아/어 주세요

Meaning

–아/어 attached to the verb base can be followed by the auxiliary verb 주다 to express the request for a favor or help, to offer help or make a promise, or to tell the hearer to do something for somebody else. As for –아/어 보다, many other endings can be attached to –아/어 주다 as well. In this unit we will it used together with the honorific marker as is –아/어 주세요. In this case, it is used in the second person and it indicates the speaker's request for help or a favor.

Use

After dropping the infinitive ending 다 from the verb base, –아 주세요 is attached to the base of verbs containing the vowel ㅏ or ㅗ. –어 주세요 is attached to the base of verbs containing any other vowel. 하다 becomes 해 주세요.

Verb base containing ㅏ or ㅗ	Verb base containing a vowel which is not ㅏ or ㅗ	하다
+ 아 주세요	+ 어 주세요	→ 해 주세요

가다 → 가 + 아 주세요 → 가 주세요
하다 → 하 + 여 주세요 → 해 + 주세요 → 해 주세요
앉다 → 앉 + 아 주세요 → 앉아 주세요
기다리다 → 기다리 + 어 주세요 → 기다려 주세요
읽다 → 읽 + 어 주세요 → 읽어 주세요
만들다 → 만들 + 어 주세요 → 만들어 주세요
쓰다 → 쓰 + 어 주세요 → ㅆ + 어 주세요 → 써 주세요
부르다 → 부르 + 어 주세요 → 불ㄹ + 어 주세요 → 불러 주세요

Examples

1. 여기가 좀 추워요. 창문을 **닫아 주세요**. It's cold here, please close the window.

2. 선생님, 이 단어를 **설명해 주세요**. Teacher, can you please explain this word to me?

3. 고려대학교로 **가 주세요**. Could you please take me to Korea University? (*to a taxi driver*)

4. 집으로 빨리 **와 주세요**. Please, come home quickly.

5. 이 자리에 **앉아 주세요**. Please take a seat here.

6. 제 말 좀 **들어 주세요**. Please listen to me.

7. 너무 시끄러워요. 음악을 좀 **꺼 주세요**. It's too loud. Could you please turn off the music?

Extra notes

- −아/어 주세요 is not attached to the verb 주다, therefore 줘 주세요 is not possible. Instead 주세요 is used alone.
- −아/어 주세요 share with −(으)세요 the meaning of making a request. However, −아/어 주세요 is much more polite when used to make requests, since −(으)세요, although an honorific form itself, is more often used to express a polite order or a command.

쇼핑 장소

가게

시장

백화점

옷

티셔츠

셔츠

치마

바지

한복

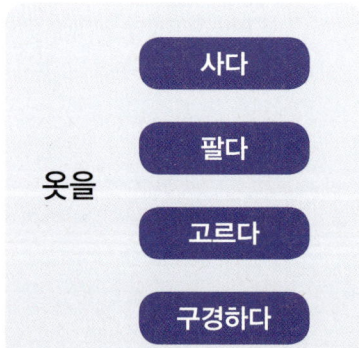

신발

구두 (남자)

구두 (여자)

운동화

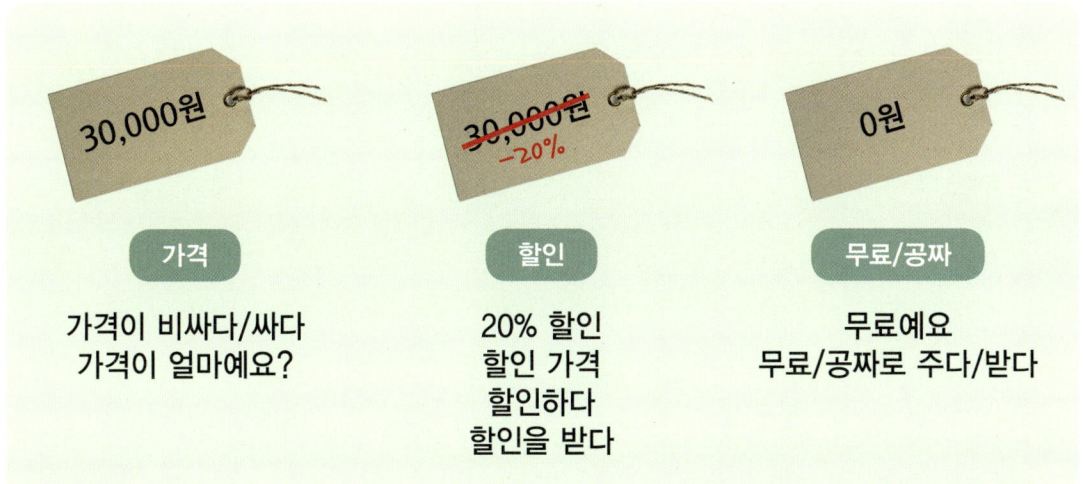

색깔

연습

1 Fill out the following table using —아/어 보세요 for the left column, and —아/어 봤어요 for the right column.

	—아/어 보세요	—아/어 봤어요
보기 먹다 →	먹어 보세요	먹어 봤어요
1. 가다 →		
2. 만들다 →		
3. 보내다 →		
4. 하다 →		
5. 찾다 →		
6. *부르다 →		
7. *듣다 →		
8. *걷다 →		

2 Make a question as in the example, asking your friend if they have ever done what is indicated in the pictures below.

보기

1.
2.
3.
4.
5.
6.
7.

보기	케이크를 만들어 봤어요?

1. ....

2. ....

3. ....

4. ....

5. ....

6. ....

7. ....

3 Make a question as in the example, asking your friend if they have ever done what is indicated in the pictures below.

보기	멋있는 모자예요. 한번 써 보시요.

1. 광화문에 가 봤어요? 한번 ....

2. 이 빵은 정말 맛있어요. 한번 ....

3. 이 치마가 예쁘지 않아요? 한번 ....

4. 편한 운동화예요. 한번 ....

5. 재미있는 책이에요. 한번 ....

6. 막걸리가 맛있어요. 한번 _____.

7. 한국 전통 음악을 안 들어 봤어요? 한번 _____.

4 Complete the following sentences indicating a request, using the verb given in brackets conjugated with –아/어 주세요.

| 보기 | 컴퓨터가 고장 났어요. 좀... | 고치다 ➡ | 고쳐 주세요 |

1. 방이 추워요. 창문을 좀...   닫다 ➡ _____

2. 오늘 핸드폰을 안 가지고 왔어요. 핸드폰을 좀...   빌리다 ➡ _____

3. 여기 경치가 좋아요. 사진을 좀...   찍다 ➡ _____

4. 전화번호가 뭐예요? 좀 ....   가르치다 ➡ _____

5. 선생님, 다시 한 번 ...   말씀하다 ➡ _____

6. 한국 노래를 잘 부르세요? 한번 ...   *부르다 ➡ _____

5 What would you ask in the following situations? Look at the situation, then complete the dialogue by making a request with –아/어 주세요.

| 보기 | 시메이: 핸드폰이 집에 있어요. 미안하지만 핸드폰 좀 _빌려 주세요_ .
다니엘: 네, 여기 있어요. |

1. 다니엘: 한국어 숙제가 어려워요. 좀 _____.

   지호: 네, 알겠어요.

2. 토마스: 아저씨, 병원으로 _____.

   택시 아저씨: 네, 알겠습니다.

3. 시메이: 여보세요? 다니엘 씨 미안해요. 지금 조금 바빠요. 내일 다시 _____.

   다니엘: 네, 알겠어요.

4. 보라: 저는 떡볶이 정말 잘 만들어요!

   토마스: 그래요? 그럼 한번 떡볶이를 ....

5. 수진: 기타를 잘 칠 수 있어요? 한번 ....

   보라: 네, 나중에요.

6 Fill in the sentences below with the most appropriate vocabulary from these suggestions.

| 신었어요 | 썼어요 | 가격 |
| 찼어요 | 벗어야 해요 | 할인 |

1. 이 옷이 예뻐요. 그런데 조금 비싸요. 혹시 .... 을 받을 수 있어요?

2. 한국에서 집 안에 들어가요? 그럼 먼저 신발을 ....

3. 시메이 씨는 파티에 가요. 그래서 예쁜 구두를 ....

4. 사장님은 비싼 시계를 .... 그리고 좋은 안경을 ....

5. 시메이 씨는 온라인에서 원피스를 샀어요. 그 옷 .... 은 50불이었어요.

말하기

대화 1

Daniel is asking Shimei what she did during her trip to Korea.

다니엘: 시메이 씨, 한국 여행 사진을 좀 보여 주세요.

시메이: 네, 여기 있어요.

다니엘: 멋있어요! 여기가 경복궁이지요?

시메이: 네. 다니엘 씨도 경복궁에 가 봤어요?

다니엘: 네, 저도 가 봤어요. 시메이 씨는 경복궁에서 뭐 했어요?

시메이: 경복궁을 구경했어요. 그리고 한복도 입어 봤어요.

Roleplay the dialogue above, changing the place that Shimei visited in Seoul with those below.

경복궁 ➡ 한복을 입다

인사동 ➡ 차를 마시다

광장 시장 ➡ 빈대떡을 먹다

현대 백화점 ➡ 쇼핑하다

한강공원 ➡ 치킨을 먹다

강남 ➡ 공연장에 가다

대화 2

Bora went shopping for new clothes. 🎧 4.2

보라: 저... 이 원피스가 얼마예요?

점원: 12만원이에요. 한번 입어 보세요.

...

보라: 어때요? 잘 어울려요?

점원: 네, 정말 잘 어울리세요.

보라: 저도 이 원피스가 마음에 들어요. 그런데 가격이 좀 비싸네요. 혹시 할인 해 줄 수 있어요?

💬 Roleplay the dialogue above changing the item that Bora wants to buy.

티셔츠 25,000원

치마 60,000원

바지 80,000원

구두 150,000원

모자 40,000원

듣기

1 Listen to the recording, then check if the sentence is spoken by the shopper (고객님), or by the shop clerk (점원). 🎧 4.3

	고객님	점원
1.	☐	☐
2.	☐	☐
3.	☐	☐
4.	☐	☐
5.	☐	☐
6.	☐	☐
7.	☐	☐

2 Sujin went to the department store today. Listen to the recording, then find out *what Sujin bought today*. 🎧 4.4

Listen to the following statements, then tick whether they are true (O) or false (X). 🎧 4.5

1.	O	X
2.	O	X

Mission Accomplished: Korean 2

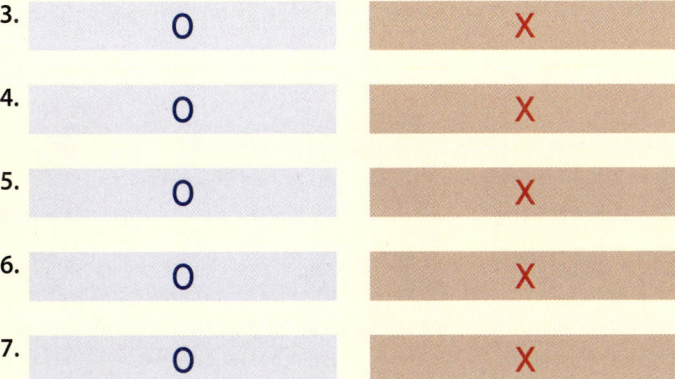

3 Imagine yourself going shopping in a Korean department store. Write below some expressions that you may find useful.

- 바지 있어요? 바지를 보여 주세요.
-
-

-
-
-

Now, together with your classmate, go shopping for some of the following items, and make up a conversation between a shopper and a clerk.

60,000원   45,000원   60,000원   130,000원

35,000원   80,000원   40,000원   20,000원

1 Look at the pictures below, then write their letter next to the corresponding sentence as in the example.

| 보기 | 오늘 시메이 씨는 빨간 스웨터를 입었어요. | 바 |

1. 이 초록색 티셔츠가 마음에 들어요. 그런데 제 사이즈가 없어요. ....

2. 요즘 검은색 반바지가 유행이에요. ....

3. 다니엘 씨는 긴 파란색 바지가 잘 어울려요. ....

4. 흰색 신발이 예쁘지만 조금 비싸요. ....

5. 백화점에서 노란색 치마를 샀어요. ....

2 What would you describe in a fashion blog? Sara writes a fashion blog. Read her post then answer the questions below. *What does Sara suggest?*

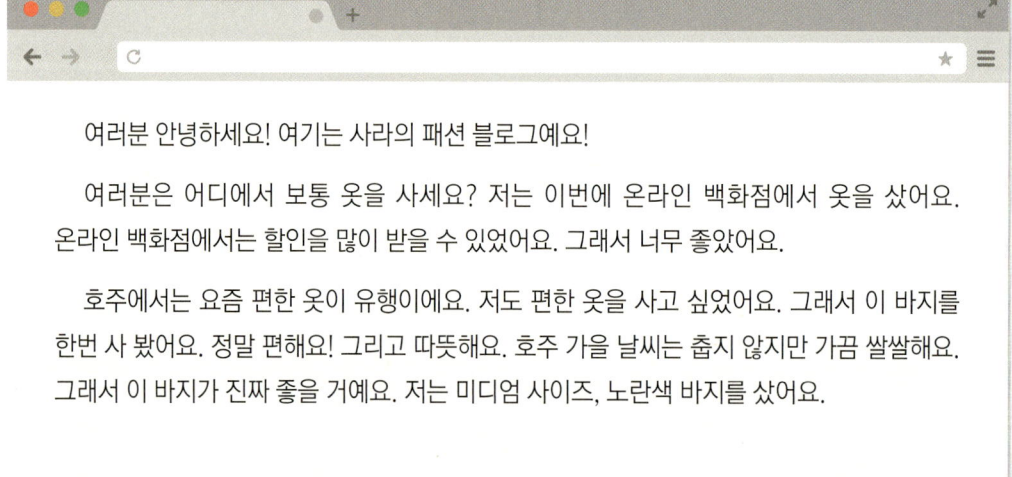

여러분 안녕하세요! 여기는 사라의 패션 블로그예요!

여러분은 어디에서 보통 옷을 사세요? 저는 이번에 온라인 백화점에서 옷을 샀어요. 온라인 백화점에서는 할인을 많이 받을 수 있었어요. 그래서 너무 좋았어요.

호주에서는 요즘 편한 옷이 유행이에요. 저도 편한 옷을 사고 싶었어요. 그래서 이 바지를 한번 사 봤어요. 정말 편해요! 그리고 따뜻해요. 호주 가을 날씨는 춥지 않지만 가끔 쌀쌀해요. 그래서 이 바지가 진짜 좋을 거예요. 저는 미디엄 사이즈, 노란색 바지를 샀어요.

남자친구가 회사에 다녀요. 그래서 남자친구는 정장이 필요해요. 남자친구 생일에 정장을 사 줬어요. 어때요? 멋있죠? 그리고 40% 할인을 받았어요. 남자 친구의 정장은 파란색이에요. 파란색 정장은 요즘 인기가 많아요. 그런데 검은색하고 초록색도 팔아요. 흰 셔츠도 사고 싶었지만 돈이 없었어요. 그래서 흰 셔츠는 남자친구가 샀어요.

여러분도 온라인 백화점에서 한번 옷을 사 보세요. 그리고 아래에 리뷰도 꼭 써 주세요!

What are the best photos that describe what Sara bought? Select which of these pictures best represents what Sara described.

Together with your classmate, reply to the following questions.

1. 사라 씨는 무엇을 샀어요?

....

2. 사라 씨는 어디에서 쇼핑을 했어요?

....

3. 사라 씨는 왜 바지를 샀어요?

4. 사라 씨는 왜 정장을 샀어요?

5. 누가 흰 셔츠를 샀어요?

3 **Read the following comment that a reader posted as a reply to Sara's post, then answer the questions below.**

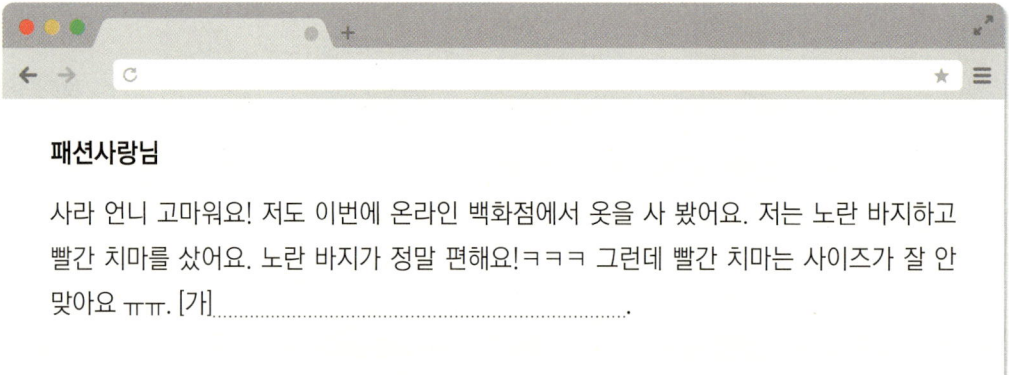

패션사랑님

사라 언니 고마워요! 저도 이번에 온라인 백화점에서 옷을 사 봤어요. 저는 노란 바지하고 빨간 치마를 샀어요. 노란 바지가 정말 편해요! ㅋㅋㅋ 그런데 빨간 치마는 사이즈가 잘 안 맞아요 ㅠㅠ. [가] _____.

Select the best sentence to fill in the blank [가] above.

A) 어떻게 해야 해요? 혹시 저를 도와줄 수 있어요?

B) 혹시 할인해 줄 수 있어요?

C) 그래서 꼭 이메일로 사이즈 문의하세요!

D) 제 남자친구도 정장을 사고 싶어 해요.

 쓰기

1 Look at the questions below, and write your own answer.

1. 언제 쇼핑했어요? 뭐 샀어요?

2. 그것을 어디에서 샀어요?

3. 왜 그것을 샀어요?

4. 무슨 색깔이에요?

5. 입어 봤어요? 어때요?

2 Following your answers, write a review of the item that you purchased.

문화

Freebies

Imagine yourself in Korea. You go to a restaurant and they give you some extra side dish, or maybe some complimentary food. Then you go shopping for groceries. You buy a bit more than usual, and the lady at the mart gives you an extra packet of rice cakes, or a can of coffee. When you go to 노래방 with your friends, you may receive an extra ten minutes.

You may wonder why you receive all these sorts of freebies. These are part of the Korean 덤 culture. 덤 literally means giving "extras" to the customer. Koreans explain this by saying that the 덤 is meant to put the emphasis not on rationality, but on the interpersonal emotional relationship between subjects. In other words, this is an aspect of  Korean culture wherein emotions are highly valued and considered important in establishing a continuing relationship between the vendor and the customer.

While 덤 문화 is more commonly associated with traditional markets, it did not disappear with the growth of large supermarket chains. It simply acquired another form. In fact, it is not uncommon in large supermarkets and in convenience stores to receive a 증정품, literally a "gift", a "freebie". 증정품 are associated with 1+1 or 2+1 offers (buy one or two and get one more), or to special offers where people buy a particular product and receive another one attached to it.

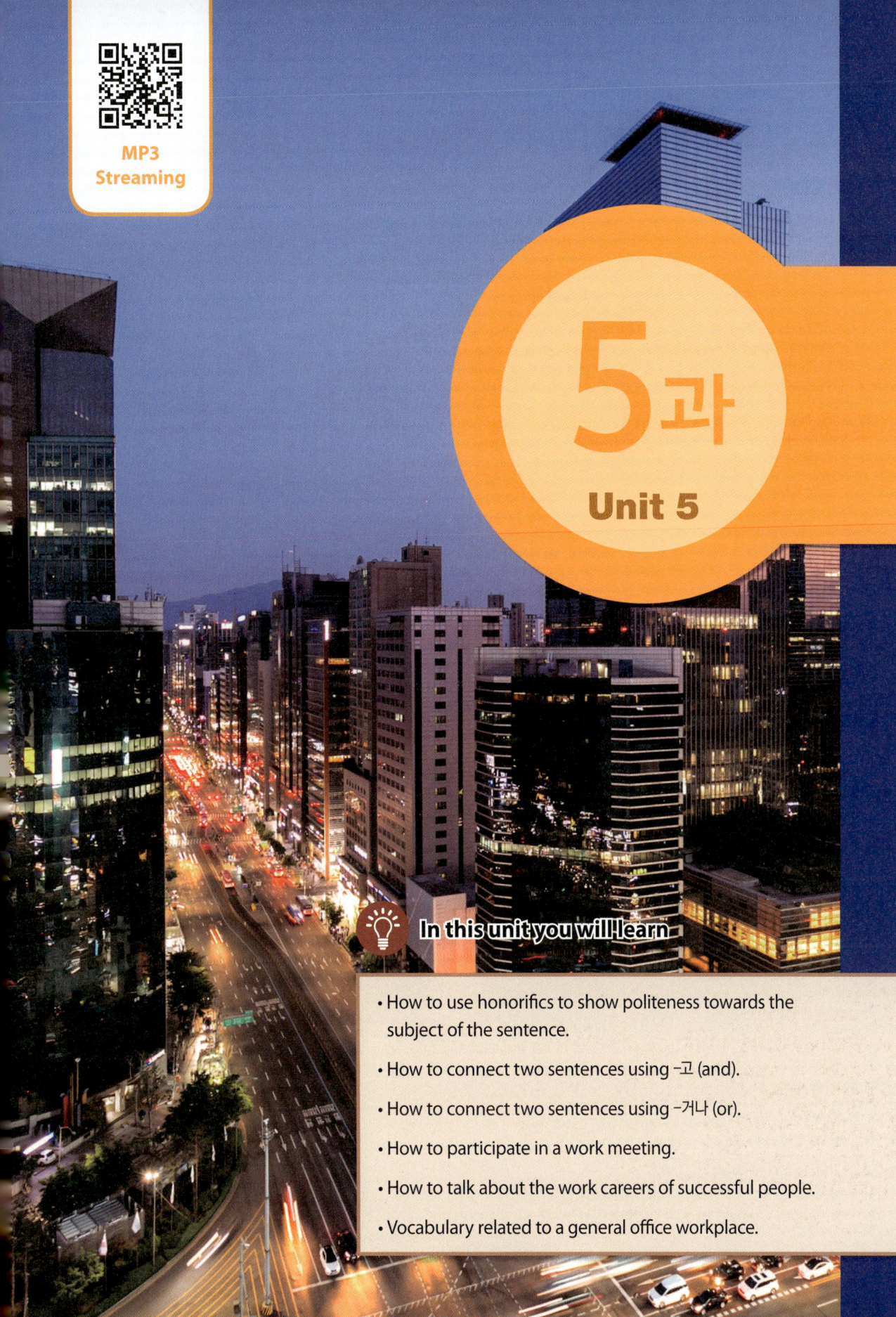

5과
Unit 5

In this unit you will learn

- How to use honorifics to show politeness towards the subject of the sentence.
- How to connect two sentences using -고 (and).
- How to connect two sentences using -거나 (or).
- How to participate in a work meeting.
- How to talk about the work careers of successful people.
- Vocabulary related to a general office workplace.

 문법

 Honorific with −(으)시− (subject and object honorific)

Meaning

In Unit 1 it was mentioned that −습니다 is an honorific ending used to show politeness depending on the formality of the situation, or depending on the relationship between the speaker and the hearer. The Korean language also has a second honorific system, which is used to indicate politeness towards the subject (and sometimes the object) of the sentence. The subject of the sentence can be the hearer (and therefore the second person), but can also be somebody not present at the moment of speaking (and therefore a third person). Since the use of −습니다 depends on the formality of the context, while −(으)시− depends on the subject, they can be used either together or separately.

As mentioned, −(으)시− is attached to the verb base to show politeness towards, in most cases the subject. This can be somebody older than the speaker, somebody that the speaker meets for the first time in a formal situation, or somebody with a social status higher than the speaker.

Use

−(으)시− is a two-shape marker. −으시− is attached to processive and descriptive verb bases ending in consonants. −시− is attached to processive and descriptive verb bases which end in vowels, and to the base of 이다/아니다.

−(으)시− can be followed by the informal polite ending −어요 in the present tense, and by −었어요 at the past tense. In the present tense, there is a further contraction, therefore −시 + 어요 becomes 세요. This contraction does not happen in the past tense. −(으)시− can also be followed by the formal polite ending −습니다, therefore −시 + ㅂ니다 becomes −십니다, while in the past tense −시 + 었 + 습니다 becomes −셨습니다.

Verb base ending in a vowel	Verb base ending in a consonant
+ 세요 (present tense)	+ 으세요 (present tense)
+ 셨어요 (past tense)	+ 으셨어요 (past tense)
+ 실 거예요 (future tense)	+ 으실 거예요 (future tense)

Present tense honorific in an informal polite situation:

```
가다 → 가 + 시 + 어요 → 가세요
하다 → 하 + 시 + 어요 → 하세요
읽다 → 읽 + 으시 + 어요 → 읽으세요
듣다 → 듣 + 으시 + 어요 → 들 + 으시 + 어요 → 들으세요
만들다 → 만들 + 으시 + 어요 → 만드 + 시 + 어요 → 만드세요
```

쓰다 → 쓰 + 시 + 어요 → 쓰세요
덥다 → 덥 + 으시 + 어요 → 더우 + 시 + 어요 → 더우세요

Past tense honorific in an informal polite situation:

가다 → 가 + 시 + 었어요 → 가셨어요
하다 → 하 + 시 + 었어요 → 하셨어요
읽다 → 읽 + 으시 + 었어요 → 읽으셨어요
듣다 → 듣 + 으시 + 었어요 → 들 + 으시 + 었어요 → 들으셨어요
만들다 → 만들 + 으시 + 었어요 → 만드 + 시 + 었어요 → 만드셨어요
쓰다 → 쓰 + 시 + 었어요 → 쓰셨어요
덥다 → 덥 + 으시 + 었어요 → 더우 + 시 + 었어요 → 더우셨어요

For the future tense honorific in an informal polite situation −ㄹ 거예요 is attached after −시−:

가다 → 가실 거예요
하다 → 하실 거예요
읽다 → 읽으실 거예요

In the same sentence where the honorific −(으)시− is used attached to the verb to show politeness towards the subject of the sentence, a few particles may also change into their honorific counterpart. In other words, some particles use a different honorific shape when used in honorific contexts. These are:

이/가 → 께서
은/는 → 께서는
한테 → 께 (example 4 below)
한테서 → 께 (example 5 below)

Examples

1. 선생님**께서** 한국어를 **가르치세요**. The teacher teaches Korean.
2. 사장님**께서** 오늘 일찍 **퇴근하셨습니다**. The boss went home early today.
3. 아버지**께서** 저녁 **식사하세요**. My father is having dinner.
4. 토마스 씨는 선생님**께** 이메일을 보냈어요. Thomas sent an email to the teacher.
5. 토마스 씨는 선생님**께** 이메일을 받았어요. Thomas received an email from the teacher.
6. 지호 선배는 술을 잘 **드세요**. Jiho is a good drinker.

7. 보라: 토마스 씨, 어머니**께서** 어디에 **사세요**? Thomas, where does your mother live?
   토마스: 퍼스에 **사세요**. She lives in Perth.

8. 지호 씨: 선생님, 어디에 **가세요**? Teacher, where are you going?
   김 선생님: 집에 가요. I am going home.

9. 회사원: 사장님, 언제 사무실로 **오세요**? Boss, when do you come back to the office?
   사장님: 오후쯤에 다시 돌아올 거예요. I'll be back in the afternoon.

In examples 1~3 above it is possible to assume that the subject is older or of higher status than the speaker. The speaker therefore uses –(으)시– attached to the verb, and also uses the honorific particle 께서 instead of 이/가.

In example 4 the subject is Thomas, and we can assume that he is not older than the speaker, therefore the verb is not honorific, and neither is the topic particle 는. However, the teacher is probably higher than both Thomas and the speaker, therefore the honorific particle 께 is used in this case instead of 한테.

In example 5 드세요 is used instead of 마셔요, therefore it is possible to see that some verbs change into an honorific counterpart (see extra notes below).

In example 6 Bora uses the honorific form even if the subject of the sentence (Thomas's mother) is not there at the time. This is the case when the honorific is used when the subject is a third person who is not present.

In examples 7~8 it is possible to see that the honorific is not used in the first person.

Extra notes

- Since the use of –습니다 depends on the situation, while –(으)시– depends on the subject, the former can also be used when the subject is the first person (I), but the latter can be used ONLY for the second and third person, and never when the subject is the speaker themselves (examples 8 and 9 above).
- –(으)시– cannot conclude a sentence, therefore it is always followed by another ending to indicate a level of formality.
- Some verbs change into their honorific counterpart when they are used together with the suffix –(으)시–. The most used are:

먹다	eat	드시다	드세요/드십니다	Between the two forms, 드세요/드십니다 is most often used.
마시다	drink	잡수시다	잡수세요/잡수십니다	
있다	be	계시다	계세요/계십니다	Used with the meaning of "to be somewhere".

있다	be	있으시다	있으세요/ 있으십니다	Used with the meaning "to have something".
주다	give	주시다	주세요/ 주십니다	Used when the speaker asks somebody higher to give them something.
주다	give	*드리다	드려요/드립니다	Used when the speaker gives something to somebody higher.
말하다	tell, say	*말씀하다/ 말씀하시다	말씀하세요/ 말씀하십니다	말씀하시다 is used when somebody higher is talking, 말씀하다 is used when somebody lower talks to somebody higher.
만나다	meet	*뵈다	봬요/뵙니다	Used by the speaker to say that they meet somebody higher.
아프다	be sick	편찮으시다	편찮으세요/ 편찮으십니다	Used to indicate that somebody is generally sick or unwell. Mostly used with elderly people with ongoing health issues. Otherwise 아프세요/아프십니다 is used instead.
자다	sleep	주무시다	주무세요/ 주무십니다	Often used in the expression "안녕히 주무세요", to say "goodnight" to higher people.
죽다	die	돌아가시다	돌아가셨어요/ 돌아가셨습니다	Although it is possible to use this in the present tense, due to the nature of its meaning it is mostly used in the past tense.

The verbs marked with (*) in the table above can be considered object honorific, which means they are honorific verbs used by the speaker when the person older or higher is the object (and not the subject). For example.

> 선생님께 한 가지 말씀드리고 싶습니다. Teacher, I'd like to tell you a thing.
> 선생님, 제 우산을 드릴게요. Teacher, I'll give you my umbrella.
> 선생님, 안녕히 가세요. 내일 뵙겠습니다. See you tomorrow teacher (lit. I'll meet you tomorrow).

- The honorific form of descriptive verbs is often overused. It is possible to use the honorific form of descriptive verbs where the subject of the descriptive verb is a person (example A), or a part of the body of that person (example B), but not when the descriptive verb refers to an object belonging to that person (example C).

A) 어머니께서는 친절하세요. My mother is kind.
B) 어머니께서는 키가 크세요. My mother is tall.
C) 어머니께서는 예쁜 가방이 있어요. My mother has a beautiful bag.

Connecting two sentences using −고 (and).

Meaning

The connective −고 is attached to the base of processive and descriptive verbs to connect two actions, events or states by indicating that they happen one after the other, therefore indicating their temporal succession, or by indicating that both happen (also maybe at the same time). It is possible to translate its function in English as *and*.

Use

−고 is attached to the base of both processive and descriptive verbs. The same shape is used attached to both vowel and consonant ending verb bases. Bases of irregular verbs do not change into their irregular form.

가다 → 가 + 고 → 가고
하다 → 하 + 고 → 하고
먹다 → 먹 + 고 → 먹고
듣다 → 듣 + 고 → 듣고
만들다 → 만들 + 고 → 만들고
쓰다 → 쓰 + 고 → 쓰고
춥다 → 춥 + 고 → 춥고

Examples

1. 학생 식당 음식은 싸고 맛있어요. The school canteen is cheap and the food is good.

2. 김치찌개가 맵고 시원해요. Kimchi stew is hot and cool.

3. 오늘 날씨는 춥고 바람이 불어요. Today is cold and windy.

4. 토마스 씨는 지금 열이 나고 머리가 아파요. Thomas has a fever and a headache now.

5. 보라 씨는 공부를 조금 하고 드라마를 봤어요. Bora studied a bit and (then) she watched a drama.

6. 선생님께서 질문을 받고 대답하셨어요. The teacher received a question and replied.

7. 손을 **씻고** 식사하세요. Wash your hands and (then) eat.

8. 저는 **샤워하고** 자요. I have a shower then sleep.

Examples 1~4 above show that −고 is used to connect two events independent of their temporal relation, as they are true at the same time. On the other hand, examples 5~8 show that one event happens before the second.

Extra notes

- When −고 is attached to 이다/아니다, it indicates only that two states are happening, but it cannot be used to indicate temporal succession.
- When −고 is used to indicate temporal succession, the subject of both sentences must be the same. The subject can be different when it is used to indicate that two events simply happened, without specifying any temporal succession.
- −고 can be attached to the past tense base. However, this is possible only when indicating two events without any specific temporal succession (example 1 below). To indicate that two events happened in the past in temporal succession, then the past tense is attached only to the last verb (example 2).

    1) 다니엘 씨는 공부했고 수진 씨는 게임을 했어요. Daniel did his homework and Sujin played computer games (there is no information about which of the two happened first).
    2) 다니엘 씨는 밥을 먹고 게임을 했어요. Daniel did his homework and (then) played computer games.

- A few verbs indicating taking transport (타다), holding (들다), and wearing (입다, 쓰다, 신다) when used together with −고 indicate that the state of the first sentence continues when the event described in the second sentence happens.

    A) 수진 씨는 버스를 타고 학교에 가요. Sujing takes the bus and goes to school.
    B) 김 선생님께서는 가방을 들고 교실에 들어가셨어요. The teacher entered the classroom holding her bag.
    C) 다니엘 씨는 선글라스 쓰고 바닷가에 갔어요. Daniel wears sunglasses and goes to the beach.

Connecting two sentences using –거나 (or).

Meaning

The connective –거나 is attached to the base of processive and descriptive verbs, and 이다/아니다 to indicate a choice between two options. It is therefore translated in English as *or*.

Use

–거나 is attached to the base of verbs and descriptive verbs. The same shape is used attached to both vowel–ending and consonant–ending verb bases. Bases of irregular verbs do not change into their irregular form.

```
가다 → 가 + 거나 → 가거나
하다 → 하 + 거나 → 하거나
앉다 → 앉 + 거나 → 앉거나
읽다 → 읽 + 거나 → 읽거나
좋다 → 좋 + 거나 → 좋거나
쓰다 → 쓰 + 거나 → 쓰거나
듣다 → 듣 + 거나 → 듣거나
살다 → 살 + 거나 → 살거나
```

Examples

1. 숙제를 이메일로 **보내거나** LMS에 올리세요. Send your homework by email or upload it on LMS.

2. 주말에는 보통 음악을 **듣거나** 책을 읽어요. Usually I listen to music or read a book on the weekend.

3. 보라 씨는 저녁에 보통 밥을 **먹거나** 국수를 먹어요. Bora usually has rice or noodles for dinner.

4. 저는 보통 퇴근 후에 **운동하거나** 동료와 함께 식사해요. After work I usually exercise or have dinner with my colleagues.

Extra notes

- –거나 can be used either when the subject of the two sentences is the same, or when it is different.

단어

직장

회사

사무실

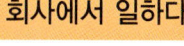
회사에서 일하다
회사에 다니다
직장에 다니다

출근(하다)
출근 시간

퇴근(하다)
퇴근 시간

야근(하다)
늦게까지 야근을 하다

회사원

부장님

동료

문서를 만들다/
작성하다

보고서를 쓰다/
작성하다

회의를 하다
회의에 참석하다
회의를 준비하다

(회사에) 취직하다   직장을 구하다   직장을 그만두다
취직이 어렵다   이력서를 쓰다

연습

1 Put the verbs on the left into their honorific form in the present, past, and future tenses using –(으)세요, –(으)셨어요, –(으)실 거예요.

	현재 (present)	과거 (past)	미래 (future)
보기 읽다 →	읽으세요	읽으셨어요	읽으실 거예요
1. 가다 →			
2. 출근하다 →			
3. *살다 →			
4. *듣다 →			
5. *예쁘다 →			
6. *쓰다 →			
7. **말하다 →			
8. **아프다 →			
9. **자다 →			
10. **먹다 →			

2 Fill in the blanks of the following sentences with the most appropriate verb conjugated with the honorific form with –(으)시–. Be mindful of verbs with a special honorific form.

| 보기 | 보다 | 가르치다 | 자다 | 있다 | 가다 |
| | 오다 | 마시다 | 가다 | 이다 | |

보기 어머니께서 아침에 TV뉴스를 <u>보세요</u>.

1. 부장님께서 오늘 출장 _____. 그래서 회사에 안 나오세요.

2. 우리 아버지께서는 술을 잘 안 _____.

3. 사장님께서는 9시부터 사무실에 _____.

4. 팀장님께서는 오늘 일찍 회사에 _____. 왜냐하면 오늘 일이 많으세요.

5. 김 선생님께서는 한국어를 잘 _____.

6. 사장님께서는 이번 주부터 휴가 _____.

7. 아버지께서는 어제 많이 피곤하셨어요. 그래서 저녁 8시 반에 _____.

8. 어느 나라 사람 _____?

3 Fill in the blanks of the following mini-dialogues by asking a question using the verb in its honorific form, as in the example. Be careful to conjugate the verb in the appropriate tense.

| 보기 | 시메이: *선생님께서 어디에 사세요?* |
| | 선생님: 퍼스 근처에 살아요. |

1. 지호: _____?

   다니엘: 우리 아버지께서는 은행에서 일하세요.

2. 사라: _____?

   사장님: 아니요, 오늘 버스를 타고 회사에 왔어요.

3. 직원: _____?

   손님: 예쁜 치마를 사고 싶어요.

4. 직원: _____?

   고객: 삼성 핸드폰을 찾고 있어요.

5. 지호: _____?

   사장님: 내일은 아침 8시에 출근할 거예요.

6. 사라: _____?

   팀장님: 보통 주말에 영화를 봐요.

7. 의사: _____?

   환자: 머리가 아파요.

4 Connect the following two sentences by using –고.

> 보기 배가 고파요. 그리고 너무 추워요.
> ➡ 배가 고프고 너무 추워요.

1. 토마스 씨는 머리가 아파요. 그리고 열이 나요.

   ➡ _____.

2. 부산 날씨가 맑아요. 그리고 따뜻해요.

   ➡ _____.

3. 다니엘 씨는 오전에는 한국어를 공부해요. 그리고 오후에는 태권도를 배워요.

   ➡ _____.

4. 일요일에 보통 아르바이트를 해요. 그리고 숙제를 해요.

   ➡ _____.

5. 안경을 꼈어요. 그리고 모자를 썼어요. 그리고 집에서 나왔어요.

   ➡ _____.

6. 생강차는 건강에 좋아요. 그리고 맛있어요.

   ➡ _____.

7. 학교에서 수업을 들었어요. 그리고 친구를 만났어요.

   ➡ _____.

8. 보라 씨는 재미있어요. 그리고 친절해요.

   ➡ _____.

5 Look at the pictures, then complete the sentences below, connecting the successive action using —고.

보기: 보라 씨는 아침에 세수하고 운동해요.

1. 시메이 씨는 _____.

2. 수진 씨는 _____.

3. 다니엘 씨는 _____.

6 Connect the following two sentences by using —거나.

보기: 친구한테 연락하고 싶어요. 그럼 문자를 (보내다)/전화해요.
→ 문자를 보내거나 전화를 해요.

1. 몸이 안 좋아요? 그럼 약을 (먹다)/병원에 가요.
→ _____.

2. 한국어 연습을 하고 싶어요? 그럼 한국 신문을 (읽다)/웹툰을 보세요.
→ _____.

3. 기분이 안 좋아요? 그럼 한번 운동을 (하다)/청소를 해 보세요.
→ _____.

4. 시간이 (없다)/피곤하세요? 그럼 택시를 타세요.

   → _____.

5. 호주는 겨울 날씨가 자주 (흐리다)/비가 와요.

   → _____.

6. 저는 운동을 좋아해요. 매일 테니스를 (치다)/달리기 운동을 해요.

   → _____.

7 What do you usually do on the weekend? Look at the following pictures, then tell your friend that you do one activity or the other, as in the example.

| 보기 | 주말에 공부하거나 집을 청소해요. |

1. _____.

2. _____.

3. _____.

4. _____.

5. _____.

8 Fill in the blanks of the following sentences with the most appropriate word, choosing from those suggested below.

보고서   구할 거예요   퇴근해요   동료
출근해요   이력서   참석하셨어요

1. 사장님, 부장님, 팀장님이 모두 회의에 ....

2. 사라 씨는 보통 .... 와/과 함께 점심 식사를 해요.

3. 다니엘 씨는 번역 회사에 취직하고 싶어 해요. 그래서 지금 .... 을/를 써요.

4. 예린 씨는 오전 8시 반에 ....
   그리고 오후 5시에 ....

5. 오늘 사라 씨는 오전에는 .... 를 작성하고 오후에는 회의 준비를 했어요.

6. 지호 씨는 내년에 졸업할 거예요. 지호 씨는 졸업 후에 직장을 ....

말하기

대화 1

Yerin is asking Sara whether she completed a report.

이예린 팀장님: 사라 씨, 보고서를 작성하셨어요?

사라: 아니요. 아직 작성하지 못했어요.

이예린 팀장님: 그럼 보고서를 작성하고 퇴근하세요.

사라: 네, 알겠습니다.

Roleplay the dialogue above, changing Sara's task with those suggested below.

보고서를 작성하다

사장님께 이메일을 보내다

문서를 만들다

회의 준비를 하다

사장님께 전화하다

💬 대화 2

Sara is asking Yerin about the boss. 🎧 5.2

사라: 팀장님, 사장님께서 사무실에 계세요?

이예린 팀장님: 아니요. 오늘 사장님께서 출장 가셨어요.

사라: 아, 그래요? 언제 오세요?

이예린 팀장님: 내일 오실 거예요.

💬 Change what Yerin is saying about the boss with the suggestions below.

출장 가다

몸이 조금 아프다

많이 바쁘다

댁에서 일하다

골프를 치다

 듣기

1 Listen carefully, then fill in the blanks of the sentences below. 5.3

1. 제가 작년부터 이 회사에서 번역 일을 ....

2. 직원들이 다 같이 .... 를 했어요.

3. 요즘 사람들은 온라인으로 .... 을 읽거나 뉴스를 많이 봐요.

4. 좋은 아이디어예요. 여러분은 어떻게 .... ?

5. 버스나 지하철에서 핸드폰을 ....

6. 회사들이 온라인으로 .... 를 많이 해요.

2 Yerin and Sara are in a meeting to decide the marketing strategy of their company. *How are they going to advertise the products of their company?* 5.4

Listen to the following statements, then tick whether they are true (O) or false (X). 5.5

1. O X
2. O X
3. O X

4.   O   X

5.   O   X

3 Imagine you are one of Sara's colleagues. What do you think about her suggestion? Ask your classmate the following questions.

1. 신문에 광고를 해요. 뭐가 안 좋아요?

2. SNS로 광고를 해요. 뭐가 좋아요?

3. 여러분이 사라 씨 동료예요. 어디에 회사 광고를 할 거예요? 왜요?

읽기

1 What's the meaning of the following words? Match the words on the left with their definition on the right.

1) 무역 • • A. 사람입니다. 그리고 이 사람은 회사에서 일합니다.

2) 번역 • • B. 어떤 일을 했습니다. 그런데 앞으로 그 일을 하지 않을 겁니다.

3) 취직합니다 • • C. 어떤 것을 삽니다. 그리고 이것을 다른 나라에 팝니다.

4) 직원 • • D. 한국어를 영어로 바꿉니다.

5) 그만두다 • • E. 직장을 구합니다.

2 A business magazine is introducing the readers to three successful Korean company CEOs. *What kind of companies are they leading?* Read their stories, then answer the questions below.

[가] ....

'오늘의 무역' 신문에서 유명한 사장님 3명을 인터뷰 했습니다. 다음은 김 사장님, 박 사장님과 최 사장님의 이야기입니다.

김 사장님은 '부산무역' 회사의 사장님이십니다. 김 사장님은 대학교 때 큰 무역 회사에서 인턴을 하셨습니다. 그리고 대학교를 졸업하고 같은 회사에 취직하셨습니다. 그때 김 사장님은 매일 아침 일찍 출근하고 늦게 퇴근하셨습니다. 그리고 5년 전에 그 회사를 그만두고 '부산무역'을 만드셨습니다. 지금 '부산무역'은 한국, 싱가포르, 호주, 뉴질랜드에 사무실이 있습니다.

박 사장님은 '번역나라'의 사장님이십니다. 박 사장님은 대학교에서 영어를 전공하셨습니다. 학생 번역 아르바이트를 하셨습니다. 박 사장님은 대학교를 졸업하고 '번역나라' 회사를 만드셨습니다. 처음에는 혼자 일을 하셨습니다. 그리고 나중에 직원을 구했습니다. 지금 박 사장님 회사에서는 인기가 있는 한국 웹툰, 드라마와 영화를 영어로 많이 번역합니다.

최 사장님은 '그린 한국' 회사의 사장님이십니다. 최 사장님은 호주 대학교에서 공부하셨습니다. 최 사장님은 졸업 후에 호주 회사에 취직하셨습니다. 호주에서 10년 동안 일하고 한국으로 돌아오셨습니다. 그리고 7년 전에 '그린 한국' 회사를 만드셨습니다. 이 회사에서는 호주에서 에너지를 삽니다. 그리고 그 에너지를 한국에 팝니다.

Fill in the blank [가] with the most appropriate title for this magazine article.

```
```

Now, together with your classmates, ask and answer the questions below.

1. 김 사장님은 졸업 후에 뭐 하셨습니까?

   ....

2. '부산무역' 사무실은 어느 나라에 있습니까?

   ....

3. 박 사장님은 대학생 때 무엇을 전공하셨습니까?

   ....

4. 박 사장님 회사에서 무엇을 번역합니까?

   ....

5. 최 사장님은 지금 어디에서 일하십니까?

   ....

6. 최 사장님은 무슨 일을 하십니까?

   ....

3 **Read this passage about Daniel, then answer the questions below.**

> 다니엘 씨는 뉴질랜드 사람이에요. 호주 대학교 학생이에요. 호주 대학교에서 한국어를 공부해요. 다니엘 씨는 내년에 교환 학생으로 한국에 가고 싶어 해요. 왜냐하면 거기서 한국어를 잘 배울 수 있어요. 다니엘 씨는 주말에 보통 한국 드라마를 보거나 한국 웹툰을 읽어요. 그리고 한국 영화도 자주 봐요.

1. 다니엘 씨가 대학교를 졸업해요. 그럼 어느 회사에서 일을 할 수 있어요?

2. 여러분이 위 세 개 회사 중에 어느 회사에서 일하고 싶어요? 왜요?

3. 위 회사는 모두 마음에 들지 않아요. 그러면 졸업 후에 어느 회사에 취직하고 싶어요? 무슨 일을 하고 싶어요? 친구하고 이야기 해 보세요.

 쓰기

1 Look at the following information about 이혜진 사장님, then answer the questions below.

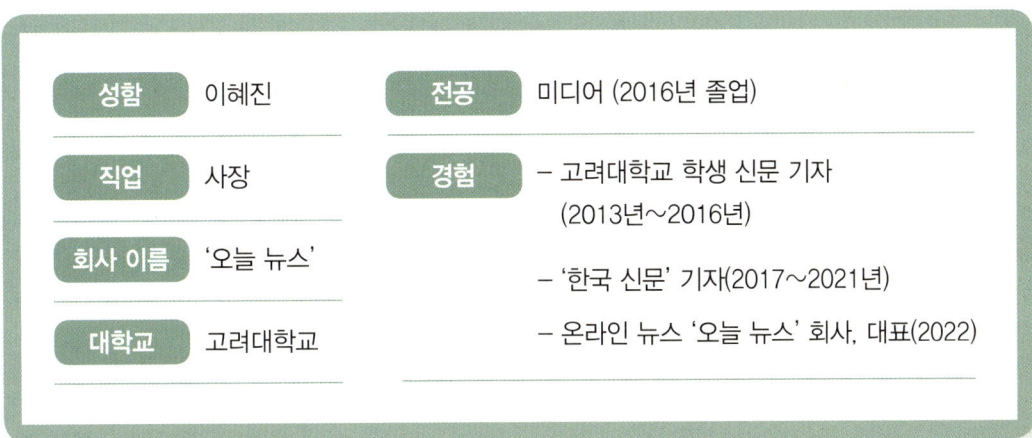

1. 이혜진 사장님은 어디에서, 무엇을 공부하셨어요?

   ....

2. 이혜진 사장님은 졸업 후에 어디에서, 무슨 일을 하셨어요?

   ....

3. 이혜진 사장님은 어떤 회사를 만드셨어요?

   ....

2 Now write a paragraph about 이혜진 사장님 using the information above, and taking as reference the readings of the reading section.

문화

The hiring process in Korean big companies

How do big companies hire people in South Korea? A popular method, although now in decline, is that of an open competitive process (공개채용). Big companies used to run this process regularly twice a year, advertising it well in advance.

This system is used to hire a number of people possessing general skills. Hiring people through this process requires several steps, the first being a written test. The most famous of these written tests is probably Samsung's GSAT (Global Samsung Aptitude Test). The number of candidates sitting these tests can be impressive. In 2015, it was reported that 59,000 students sat the university entrance examination test, 19,000 candidates sat the civil service entry level test, and 10,000 people sat the GSAT.[※] The popularity of the open competitive process is declining: 'only' 4,000 people sat the GSAT in 2017,[※※] but it still attracts a considerable number of candidates. Some of the big companies are moving away from this hiring system, towards processes focused more on hiring people with specialized skills for specific jobs.

Despite the flaws that a generalized hiring system may have, it also has advantages. Companies can hire a large number of people in a short time, and since these people have general skills, they can be moved to different positions if needed. From the perspective of the candidates this system is perceived to be fair, since anybody can have a 'fair go' at securing employment in a big company. This open hiring selection process, characterized by a mass written examination, is similar to the university entrance examination and also to the process used to hire civil servants. It is deeply rooted in Korean history, and comparable to the 과거시험, the examination used to select civil servants during the Choseon period.

※ 장강명(2018). 당선, 합격, 계급. 서울: 민음사.

※※ 장강명, ibid.

 문법

Making comparisons (1), 보다 (더)

Meaning

보다 is a particle attached to nouns to make a comparison, i.e., to say that something is more (than something else). A Korean sentence with a structure such as A는 B보다... corresponds to the English *A is more than B*.

Use

The noun to which 보다 is attached becomes the criteria for the comparison. In the English sentence *Perth is warmer than Seoul*, *Seoul* is the criteria for comparison, therefore in the Korean sentence 서울 will be followed by 보다, as in 퍼스는 서울보다 따뜻해요. In other words, 보다 is attached to the element which, in the English sentence, follows *more than*. 보다 is attached to nouns that end in either vowels or consonants.

Examples

1. 퍼스는 서울**보다** 따뜻해요. Perth is warmer than Seoul.
2. 지하철은 버스**보다** 빨라요. The subway is faster than the bus.
3. 하숙집은 기숙사**보다** 싸요. A boarding house is cheaper than the dormitory.
4. 수진 씨는 보라 씨**보다** 영어를 잘해요. Sujin speaks English better than Bora.
5. 한국어가 수학**보다** 재미있어요. Korean is more fun than mathematics.
6. 호주는 한국**보다** 월세가 비싸요. Rent is more expensive in Australia than in Korea.
7. 한국어가 생각**보다** 쉬워요. Korean is easier than I thought.
8. 지호: 갈비와 삼겹살 **중에서 무엇을 더** 좋아해요? What do you prefer more out of galbi and samgyeopsal?
   시메이: 저는 삼겹살을 **더** 좋아해요. I like samgyeopsal more.

As in sentences 1~3, the most obvious comparison is between two qualities, therefore descriptive verbs are often used in sentences with 보다. Nevertheless, it is also possible to use processive verbs as in example 4, although with processive verbs an adverb is used together (in example 4 the adverb is 잘, lit. *well*). Example 5 shows that the elements of the sentence can be swapped without changing the meaning of the sentence. Example 6 shows how the first term of comparison can be different from the subject of the sentence. In example 6 the subject is 월세. Example 7 illustrates how to use 보다 to say *more than (I) thought*. Lastly, example 8 shows how to ask a question that establishes a preference out of two items, using the adverb 더 (*more*).

Extra notes

- The adverb 더 (*more*) is often used in sentences together with 보다. For example, the same meaning of sentences 1 and 2 above can also be expressed as 퍼스는 서울보다 더 따뜻해요 and 지하철은 버스보다 더 빨라요. By adding 더 the meaning does not change, it adds simply more stress.

- Example 8 shows how to make a question asking for a comparison/preference. Remember that, as in English, depending on the question, the relevant question word may be 무엇, 어디, 누구 etc.

  > 서울과 퍼스 중에서 어디가 더 추워요? Where is colder, Seoul or Perth?
  > 수진 씨와 보라 씨 중에서 누가 영어를 더 잘 해요? Who speaks English better, Sujin or Bora?

- Since 보다 indicates the element which is the criteria for comparison, it can also be used in sentences where the speaker wants to say that A is less than B. In this case, the adverb 덜 is used instead of 더. 퍼스는 서울보다 덜 추워요 means that *Perth is less cold than Seoul*, 수학은 한국어보다 덜 재미있어요 means that *Math is less fun than Korean*.

Making comparison (2), 제일

Meaning

제일 is an adverb used to indicate that something is *the most*, often within a category or a group.

Use

제일 is used in front of processive and descriptive verbs. In interrogative sentences, it can be used as in examples 3~5 below with the pattern "... 중에서 ... 제일...?" to ask what is *the most...* within a category or group.

Examples

1. 한국어 수업이 **제일** 재미있어요. Korean classes are the most fun.

2. 학생들은 학기말에 **제일** 바빠요. The end of the term is when students are the most busy.

3. 지호: 한국 가수 중에서 누구를 **제일** 좋아해요? Who is your most preferred Korean singer?
   시메이: 한국 가수 중에서 아이유를 **제일** 좋아해요. Among Korean singers I prefer IU the most.

4. 수진: 한국 음식 중에서 뭐가 **제일** 맛있어요? What is the most delicious Korean food?
   토마스: 불고기가 **제일** 맛있어요. Bulgogi is the most delicious.

5. 토마스: 한국에서 어디가 제일 아름다워요? Where is the most beautiful place in Korea?
   보라: 제주도가 제일 아름다워요. Jeju island is the most beautiful.

Extra notes

- 제일 can also be used together with other adverbs, often 잘. This happens when the speaker wants to say that somebody or something is the best at doing something, as in 저는 김치찌개를 제일 잘 만들어요 *Kimchi stew is the food I make the best*.

-고 있다 (expressing a continuing action)

Meaning

By attaching the suffix -고 followed by 있다 (-고 있어요) to the base of a processive verb it is possible to express the meaning of a continuing action. It corresponds roughly to the English *be ...~ing*, and therefore can be translated with *to be doing something*. Although the meaning is almost the same of the English *be ...~ing*, Korean and English do not always use the continuous form in the same context, or with the same verbs (see extra notes below). Since the meaning expressed by this form is of a continuing action, it can be used only with (some) processive verbs and not with descriptive verbs.

Use

To make the continous form, attach -고 있다 to the base of the verb. -고 있다 is attached to verb bases that end either with a consonant or with a vowel.

> 가다 → 가 + 고 있어요 → 가고 있어요 (be going)
> 하다 → 하 + 고 있어요 → 하고 있어요 (be doing)
> 먹다 → 먹 + 고 있어요 → 먹고 있어요 (be eating)
> 듣다 → 듣 + 고 있어요 → 듣고 있어요 (be listening)
> 살다 → 살 + 고 있어요 → 살고 있어요 (be living)

To express a continuing action in the past, the past tense suffix is added to the verb 있다

> 먹다 → 먹 + 고 있 + 었어요 → 먹고 있었어요 (was eating)
> 하다 → 하 + 고 있 + 었어요 → 하고 있었어요 (was doing)

Examples

1. 보라 씨는 지금 저녁 식사를 **준비하고 있어요**. Bora is preparing dinner now.

2. 김 선생님은 수업을 **하고 있어요**. Ms. Kim is teaching a class.

3. 토마스 씨는 친구하고 **이야기 하고 있어요**. Thomas is talking to his friend.

4. 수진 씨는 버스를 **기다리고 있었어요**. Sujin was waiting for the bus.

Extra notes

- The future tense can also be added to −고 있다, but instead of a continuing action the meaning expressed is of conjecture about something that may be happening at the time of speaking.

  지호 씨는 자고 있을 거예요. Jiho will be sleeping (now).
  지금 서울에 눈이 오고 있을 거예요. It will be snowing now in Seoul.

- The Korean language often uses the continuous form with verbs that are not usually used in the *be ...~ing* form in English. Some of the most frequent are: 알다 → 알고 있어요 (I know), 모르다 → 모르고 있어요 (I don't know), 기억하다 → 기억하고 있어요 (I remember).
- Similarly, the continuous form can be avoided sometimes with verbs for which it is necessary in English. For example, if somebody calls you while you are eating and asks you what you are doing, you can reply either 밥 먹고 있어요 or 밥 먹어요.
- A number of punctual verbs, i.e., those verbs indicating an action that happens in an instant, can take the continuous form in English but not in Korean. Some examples are the verb *to arrive* and *to die*. In Korean, instead of the expression *the train is arriving*, the expression 기차가 곧 도착할 거예요 (lit. the train will arrive soon) is used instead.
- Verbs indicating *wearing* can have two meanings when used together with −고 있어요. For instance, 다니엘 씨가 티셔츠를 입고 있어요 can be used to indicate either that *Daniel is putting on a shirt*, or that *Daniel is wearing a shirt*.

단어

가족

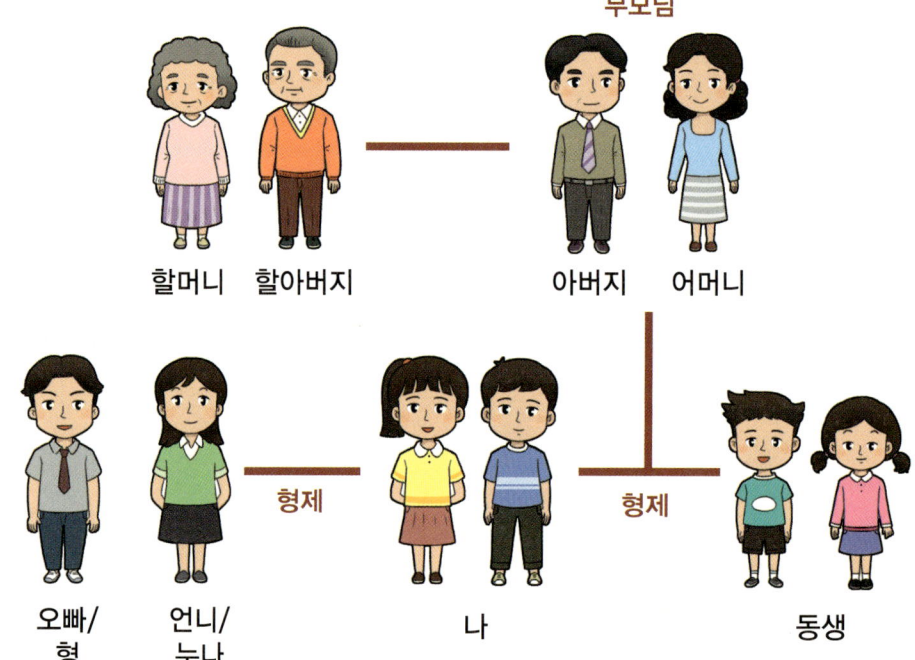

초대

친구를 집에 초대하다

집들이에 초대를 하다/받다

친구 집을 방문하다

손님을 집으로 초대하다

연습

1 Look at the descriptive verbs below, then write a sentence comparing what you see in the pictures, as in the example.

보기	키가 크다
	→ 오빠는 나보다 키가 커요.

1. 키가 작다

   → ....

2. 멀다

   → ....

3. 맛있다

    → ....

4. 싸다

    → ....

5. 비싸다

    → ....

6. 재미있다

    → ....

2 **Form a question comparing what you see in the pictures below, as in the example.**

보기	형/누나(키가 크다)
	→ 형과 누나 중에 누가 키가 더 커요?

1. 한라산/에베레스트산(높다)

    → ....

2. 핫도그/붕어빵(맛있다)

    →

3. 버스/지하철(빠르다)

    →

4. 농구/축구(재미있다)

    →

5. 닭갈비/불고기(좋아하다)

    →

3 Read the following questions, then write your own answer.

1. 한국 영화 중에서 뭐가 제일 재미있어요?

2. 무슨 운동을 제일 좋아해요?

3. 무슨 과목이 제일 재미있어요?

4. 무슨 노래를 제일 좋아해요?

5. 한국 음식 중에서 뭐가 제일 맛있어요?

6. 무슨 음식을 제일 잘 만들어요?

7. 여행을 가요. 뭐가 제일 필요해요?

4 Complete the following sentences using the verb given in brackets and the form —고 있어요.

보기	토마스 씨는 태권도를 <u>배우고 있어요</u>. (배우다)

1. 시메이 씨는 한국어 책을 .... (읽다)

2. 보라 씨는 드라마를 .... (보다)

3. 사라 씨는 2년 전부터 한국어를 .... (공부하다)

4. 지호 씨, 무엇을 .... ? (찾다)

5. 다니엘 씨는 두 달 전부터 열심히 .... (운동하다)

6. 새 핸드폰을 사고 싶어요. 그래서 지금 아르바이트를 .... (하다)

7. 수진 씨는 두꺼운 옷을 .... (입다)

5 What are these people doing?

1.

2.

3.

4.

5.

6.

7.

보기	A: 보라 씨가 뭐 하고 있어요?
	B: 보라 씨는 밥을 먹고 있어요.

1. A: 토마스 씨가 뭐 하고 있어요?

   B: _____

2. A: 예린 씨가 뭐 하고 있어요?

   B: _____

3. A: 선생님이 뭐 하고 있어요?

   B: _____

4. A: 시메이 씨가 뭐 하고 있어요?

   B: _____

5. A: 다니엘 씨가 뭐 하고 있어요?

   B: _____

6. A: 수진 씨는 뭐 하고 있어요?

   B: _____

7. A: 지호 씨는 뭐 하고 있어요?

   B: _____

6 Fill in the blank of the sentences with the most appropriate word among those below.

부인	오빠	할머니
형제	부모님	형

1. 수진 씨 _____은/는 수진 씨보다 4살 많아요. 회사에서 일해요.

2. 지호 씨 _____은/는 3년 전에 결혼했어요. 형은 _____ 하고 서울에서 살아요.

3. 보라 씨는 _____이/가 2명이에요. 언니하고 남동생이 있어요.

4. 우리 가족은 3명이에요. 저하고 _____이에요.

5. _____께서 연세가 많으세요. 그렇지만 항상 운동을 열심히 하세요.

 말하기

대화 1

Bora is asking Thomas about his family. 6.1

보　라: 토마스 씨, 형제가 어떻게 돼요?

토마스: 형이 한 명 있어요.

보　라: 그래요? 형은 어떤 사람이에요?

토마스: 형은 착한 사람이에요. 그리고 저보다 운동을 잘해요. 여기 형 사진이 있어요.

보　라: 형이 토마스 씨하고 많이 닮았어요!

Roleplay the dialogue above, changing the family member Bora and Thomas are talking about.

형	누나	남동생	여동생
착하다	똑똑하다	친절하다	컴퓨터에 관심이 많다
운동을 잘 하다	공부를 잘 하다	춤을 잘 추다	게임을 잘 하다

대화 2

Jiho is calling Sara, but she is busy now. 🎧 6.2

지호: 여보세요? 사라 씨, 지금 잠깐 이야기할 수 있어요?

사라: 미안해요. 지금 좀 바빠요. 일을 하고 있어요.

지호: 어 미안해요.

사라: 아니에요. 괜찮아요. 제가 이따 연락할게요.

지호: 네, 알겠어요. 고마워요.

💬 Roleplay the dialogue above, changing what Sara is doing now.

일하다

집을 청소하다

어머니하고 이야기하다

저녁 식사를 준비하다

한국 드라마를 보다

케이크를 만들다

듣기

1 Listen to the following questions, then match each question with the most appropriate answer. 🎧 6.3

1. •   • A. 회사에 다니세요.
2. •   • B. 휴지는 어때요?
3. •   • C. 우리 오빠는 대학교에서 한국어를 가르치고 있어요.
4. •   • D. 네, 오빠 한 명하고 여동생 한 명이 있어요.
5. •   • E. 착하고 친절하세요.

2 Bora is inviting Thomas to her brother's party. *Why is Bora's brother organising a party? What present is Thomas going to bring to the party?* 🎧 6.4

Listen to the following statements, then tick whether they are true (O) or false (X). 🎧 6.5

1. O X
2. O X
3. O X
4. O X
5. O X

3 Write down your answers to the following questions, then ask the same questions to your classmates.

1. 가족과 같이 살아요? 혼자 살아요?

2. 형제가 어떻게 돼요?

3. 오빠/형/누나/언니/동생은 어떤 사람이에요?

4. 오빠/형/누나/언니/동생은 뭐 해요?

5. 오빠/형/누나/언니는 결혼했어요?

 읽기

1 Look at the following picture of the characters of the drama *My unfamiliar family*, then answer the questions below.

출처: TVN 〈아는 건 별로 없지만 가족입니다〉 공식 홈페이지

1. 가족이 몇 명이에요?

2. 딸이 몇 명이에요?

3. 첫째 딸은 결혼했어요?

4. 드라마의 제목은 왜 '아는 건 별로 없지만 가족입니다'('My unfamiliar family')일까요? 무슨 이야기일까요?

2 Sujin writes drama reviews for a student magazine. This month she wrote a review about the drama *My unfamiliar family*. *Why did she like this drama?*

이번 달 드라마
아는 건 별로 없지만 가족입니다(수진 리뷰)

안녕하세요! 여러분, 제가 그동안 리뷰를 잘 쓰지 못했지만 오늘은 드라마 리뷰를 하나 하겠습니다. 그럼 바로 리뷰를 시작하겠습니다.

지난달에 '아는 건 별로 없지만 가족입니다' 드라마를 봤습니다. 이 드라마는 한 가족의 이야기입니다. 이 가족은 아버지, 어머니, 큰언니, 작은언니, 그리고 남동생이 있습니다. 큰언니는 결혼했습니다. 그래서 남편하고 같이 삽니다. 남동생은 부모님하고 같이 삽니다. 그리고 작은언니는 혼자 삽니다. [가]

보통 사람들이 가족을 제일 잘 압니다. 그런데 이 드라마에서는 사람들이 가족을 사랑하지만 자기 이야기를 가족한테 잘 말하지 않습니다. 그래서 서로를 잘 모릅니다. 아이는 부모님을 잘 모르고, 부인은 남편을 잘 모르고, 형제들도 서로 잘 모릅니다. 그래서 모두 많이 힘듭니다. [나]

드라마 가족이 조금씩 같이 이야기하고 나중에는 모두가 서로 잘 압니다. 이 드라마가 지난달 드라마 중에서 제일 마음에 들었습니다. 왜냐하면 저한테 가족이 중요합니다. 그리고 저는 이 드라마를 보고 한 가지를 배웠습니다. 가족하고 이야기를 많이 해야 합니다. [다]

리뷰는 여기까지입니다. 다음 달에 다른 드라마 리뷰를 하겠습니다. 그러면 또 뵙겠습니다.

출처: TVN 〈아는 건 별로 없지만 가족입니다〉 공식 홈페이지

Read the passage above, the tick whether the following statements are true (O) or false (X).

1. 이 드라마 이야기는 가족 이야기입니다. O X

2. 이 드라마의 가족들은 모두가 같이 삽니다. O X

3. 이 드라마의 가족들은 서로 모두 잘 압니다. O X

4. 이 드라마의 가족들은 서로 잘 모릅니다. 그래서 힘듭니다. O X

5. 수진 씨는 이 드라마를 좋아했습니다.
   왜냐하면 수진 씨한테는 가족이 중요합니다. O X

3 Answer the following questions together with your classmate.

1. 이 드라마는 무슨 이야기를 해요?

2. 이 드라마 사람들은 왜 서로 잘 몰라요?

3. 수진 씨는 왜 이 드라마를 좋아했어요?

4. 다음 문장은 수진 씨 리뷰의 어느 위치에 넣을 수 있어요?

> "그래서 앞으로 저도 동생과 부모님하고 지금보다 더 많이 이야기할 겁니다."

[가]   [나]   [다]

5. 우리 가족들하고 같이 잘 살고 싶어요. 그럼 어떻게 해야 해요? 친구하고 이야기해 보세요.

6. 여러분에게 가족이 어떤 것이에요? 친구하고 이야기해 보세요.

 쓰기

1 Think about a member of your family, and answer the following questions.

1. 누구예요?
   ....

2. 나이/연세가 어떻게 돼요?/되세요?
   ....

3. 어디에서 살아요?
   ....

4. 어떤 사람이에요?
   ....

5. 무슨 일을 해요?
   ....

6. 무엇을 잘 해요?
   ....

2 Now, write a paragraph introducing one of your family members.

문화

Kinship terms

In Australia you use people's name when you wish to address them, and it does not matter whether they are older or younger than you. However, in Korea you rarely address somebody with 'you', and you do not address somebody older directly with their name. Depending on the context, you are more likely to use kinship terms.

If your friend's older sister is 순희, you will never call her just '순희'. You would rather say '순희 언니', or simply '언니'. So the 언니 of your friends becomes your 'older sister', even if she is not your real older sister. How can you specify if somebody is your real older sister or brother? In this case, you can say 친언니 or 친오빠.

In a similar way, the lady or the man working at the small local restaurant becomes your 이모 (aunt) or your 삼촌 (uncle). They are not family members; this is just a way to address people that avoids using their names while at the same time showing respect for their age. This works in an informal environment, but what happens if the environment is more formal? In a formal situation you may address people with kinship terms, but what you are likely to hear is 선생님. Pay attention: in this case not everybody called 선생님 is a teacher! It is just another term used to politely refer to somebody.

문법

 Expressing the purpose of doing something with –(으)려고 (1)

Meaning

The suffix –(으)려고 is used to express the purpose or the goal of doing a certain action in the future. In this unit it is introduced in the form of the pattern –(으)려고 + 해요, and therefore it is used to express the intention of doing something. Other uses of –(으)려고 are covered in Unit 9.

Use

–으려고 is attached to processive verb bases ending in consonant, –려고 is attached to processive verb bases ending in vowels or ㄹ.

Verb base ending in a vowel	Verb base ending in ㄹ	Verb base ending in a consonant
+ 려고 (해요)		+ 으려고 (해요)

가다 → 가 + 려고 → 가려고
하다 → 하 + 려고 → 하려고
쓰다 → 쓰 + 려고 → 쓰려고
읽다 → 읽 + 으려고 → 읽으려고
찾다 → 찾 + 으려고 → 찾으려고
듣다 → 듣 + 으려고 → 들 + 으려고 → 들으려고
돕다 → 돕 + 으려고 → 도우 + 려고 → 도우려고
살다 → 살 + 려고 → 살려고

Examples

1. 다음 학기부터 태권도를 **배우려고 해요**. I plan/have the intention of learning taekwondo from next semester.

2. 시메이 씨는 오전에 도서관에 **가려고 했어요**. Shimei had the intention of going to the library in the morning.

3. 지호 씨는 저녁에 친구를 **만나려고 해요**. Jiho plans/has the intention of meeting up with friends in the evening.

4. 선생님께서 학생한테 이메일을 **보내려고 해요**. The teacher has the intention of sending an email to the student.

5. 밤에 치킨을 **먹으려고 해요**. I plan to eat fried chicken tonight.

6. 지호: 내년에 뭐 할 거예요? What will you do next year?
   다니엘: 직업을 **구하려고 해요**. I have the intention of looking for a job.

7. 보라: 방학 때 무슨 계획이 있어요? What's your plan for the vacation?

   수진: 호주 **여행을 하려고 해요**. I have the intention of travelling to Australia.

Extra notes

- As in example 2 above, the tense is expressed through the verb 하다, at the end of the sentence. –(으)려고 cannot be attached to a past or a future tense base.
- When the subject is a person, –(으)려고 해요 expresses the intention of the subject. However, –(으)려고 해요 is also used with a non-animated subjects to indicate that something is about to start happening, or that seems to be starting soon, as in 비가 오려고 해요 *It's about to rain*.
- –(으)려고 해요 indicates something that may happen in the future, therefore is also used as a future tense. However, the difference is that the future tense expressed with –(으)ㄹ 거예요 indicates something that will probably happen in the future, while –(으)려고 해요 indicates only the intention of the subject, and therefore implies less certainty that the event will take place.

 Making a promise and expressing will with –(으)ㄹ게요.

Meaning

–(으)ㄹ게요 is an ending indicating a future tense, but it is used only by the speaker to express willingness to do something in the (near) future, often something that has some relation with the hearer. It is also used to make promises about something that the speaker will do in the future.

Use

Due to its meaning of expressing willingness and promise, –(으)ㄹ게요 can be used only with processive verbs, and not with descriptive verbs. For the same reason, it can only be used by the speaker in the first person. Also, –(으)ㄹ게요 is almost exclusively used in spoken language.

–ㄹ게요 is attached to processive verb bases ending in vowels, –(으)ㄹ게요 is attached to processive verb bases ending in consonants.

Verb base ending in a vowel	Verb base ending in a consonant
+ ㄹ게요	+ 을게요

7과

> 가다 → 가 + ㄹ게요 → 갈게요
> 하다 → 하 + ㄹ게요 → 할게요
> 마시다 → 마시 + ㄹ게요 → 마실게요
> 앉다 → 앉 + 을게요 → 앉을게요
> 읽다 → 읽 + 을게요 → 읽을게요
> 듣다 → 듣 + 을게요 → 들 + 을게요 → 들을게요
> 쓰다 → 쓰 + ㄹ게요 → 쓸게요
> 만들다 → 만들 + 을게요 → 만드 + ㄹ게요 → 만들게요

Examples

1. 잠깐 기다려 주세요. **빨리 갈게요**. Hold on a moment, please. I'll be there soon.
2. 저는 여기서 **기다릴게요**. I'll be waiting here.
3. 미안해요. 지금 시간이 많이 없어요. 이따 **전화할게요**. Sorry, I don't have much time now. I'll call you later.
4. 더워요? 그럼 에어컨을 **틀게요**. Is it hot? Then I'll turn on the air conditioning.
5. 팀장님: 사라 씨, 수진 씨하고 내일 일찍 올 수 있어요? Sara, can you please come early tomorrow together with Sujin.
   사라: 네, 팀장님. 8시까지 가겠습니다. 제가 수진 씨한테도 **연락할게요**. Yes, I'll be here by 8 am. I'll also call Sujin.

In the sentences above, is it possible to see that examples 1 and 5 express the speaker's willingness to do something. On the other hand, in examples 2~4 and 6 the speaker uses −(으)ㄹ게요 to make a promise.

Extra notes

- Due to its function of making a promise or expressing willingness, and the fact that it is used only in the first person, −(으)ㄹ게요 cannot be used in interrogative sentences.
- Some verbs expressing knowledge such as 알다 (know) and 모르다 (not know), and other verbs expressing a preference such as 좋아하다 (like) and 싫어하다 (dislike), cannot be used together with −(으)ㄹ게요.
- The use of −(으)ㄹ게요 and −(으)ㄹ 거예요 often creates confusion in Korean language learners. −(으)ㄹ게요 must be used instead of −(으)ㄹ 거예요 when the subject is in the first person, and when the speaker makes some sort of promise which is related in some way to the listener.
- Since −(으)ㄹ게요 carries the meaning of making a sort of promise, or doing something which in some way is in relation to the hearer, it is often used together with the verb 주다 as −아/어 줄게요.

> 수진: 조금 더워요.
> 보라: 네, 알겠어요. 창문을 열어 줄게요.
>
> 보라: 이 가방이 좀 무거워요!
> 토마스: 제가 도와줄게요.
>
> 시메이: 한국어가 정말 어려워요!
> 다니엘: 걱정하지 마세요. 제가 설명해 줄게요.

When the speaker is saying that they will do something for somebody older or higher than them, then the honorific form of 주다, which is 드리다, must be used instead. Therefore in this case –아/어 드릴게요 will be used.

> 선생님: 조금 더워요.
> 보라: 제가 창문을 열어 드릴게요.
>
> 선배님: 이 가방이 좀 무거워요!
> 수진: 선배님, 제가 도와 드릴게요.
>
> 팀장님: 커피 한 잔 할까요?
> 지호: 네, 팀장님. 그런데 이번에는 제가 사 드릴게요.

 ## Doing something after having done something else: –(으)ㄴ 다음에

Meaning

The modifier –(으)ㄴ followed by 다음에 is attached to the base of processive verbs to connect two sentences indicating that the action expressed in the second sentence takes place after the action expressed in the first sentence. Therefore, it can be translated as *after doing~*.

Use

–(으)ㄴ 다음에 is attached only to the base of processive verbs. The subject of the first and the second sentence can be different. –ㄴ 다음에 is attached to vowel–ending verb bases, while –은 다음에 to consonant–ending verb bases.

Verb base ending in a vowel	Verb base ending in a consonant
+ ㄴ 다음에	+ 은 다음에

배우다 ➝ 배우 + ㄴ 다음에 ➝ 배운 다음에
하다 ➝ 하 + ㄴ 다음에 ➝ 한 다음에
쓰다 ➝ 쓰 +ㄴ 다음에 ➝ 쓴 다음에
먹다 ➝ 먹 + 은 다음에 ➝ 먹은 다음에
걷다 ➝ 걷 + 은 다음에 ➝ 걸 + 은 다음에 ➝ 걸은 다음에
살다 ➝ 살 + 은 다음에 ➝ 사 + ㄴ 다음에 ➝ 산 다음에
돕다 ➝ 돕 + 은 다음에 ➝ 도우 + ㄴ 다음에 ➝ 도운 다음에
놀다 ➝ 놀 + 은 다음에 ➝ 노 + ㄴ 다음에 ➝ 논 다음에

Examples

1. 토마스 씨는 서울에 **도착한 다음에** 부모님께 전화했어요. Thomas called his parents after arriving in Seoul.

2. 시메이 씨는 손을 **씻은 다음에** 식사해요. Shimei eats after washing her hands.

3. 수진 씨는 저녁 식사를 **한 다음에** 커피를 마시지 않아요. Sujin doesn't drink coffee after dinner.

4. 사라 씨는 이번 학기가 **끝난 다음에** 한국에 여행 갈 거예요. After this semester finishes Sara will travel to Korea.

5. 지호 씨는 학교에서 시험을 **본 다음에** 바로 집에 갔어요. After the exam at school Jiho went straight home.

6. 숙제를 **한 다음에** 한국 드라마를 봤어요. I watch Korean dramas after doing my homework.

7. 토마스: 수진 씨, 광장 시장에 어떻게 가요? Sujin, how do I go to Gwangjang market?
   수진: 먼저 지하철 1호선을 타야 해요. Firstly, you must take the subway line number 1.
   토마스: 그 다음은요? And after that?
   수진: 1호선을 **탄 다음에** 종로 5가역에서 내려요. After taking the subway line number 1, get off at Jeongno 5ga.

Extra notes

- Also −고 (see Unit 5), when used to connect two sentences, can indicate that the two events expressed took place in a temporal sequence. By using −ㄴ 다음에 however, the speaker wants to stress more that one action happens after the other.
- −(으)ㄴ 다음에 cannot be attached to a past tense base, because the modifier −(으)ㄴ attached to the base of processive verb already implies a past meaning. Therefore, it is only possible to say 한 다음에.
- Instead of −(으)ㄴ 다음에, it is also possible to use other expressions indicating "after", such as −(으)ㄴ 후에 and −(으)ㄴ 뒤에.
- The use of −(으)ㄴ 다음에 attached to a processive verb in the negative form, although not completely unacceptable, sounds unnatural.

 단어

교통

교통이 막히다
교통이 복잡하다
교통 카드를 찍다

자동차를 타다
자동차에서 내리다
자동차를 운전하다
자동차를 세우다
자동차로 가다

지하철/버스를 타다
지하철/버스에서 내리다
(고속)버스 정류장에서 내리다
지하철역에서 내리다
272번 버스로 갈아타다
3호선으로 갈아타다
지하철/버스로 가다
지하철/버스를 타고 가다
버스/지하철을 이용하다

연습

1 Fill in the blanks of the following sentences with one of the verbs suggested using –(으)려고 해요.

| 보기 | 준비하다 | 하다 | 가다 | 보내다 |
| | 빌리다 | 사다 | 입다 | 배우다 |

보기 지금부터 저녁 식사를 <u>준비하려고 해요</u>.

1. 보라 씨는 친구 결혼식에 새 옷을 ....

2. 대학교 책이 비싸요. 그래서 도서관에서 책을 ....

3. 다음 주에 수업에 못 갈 거예요. 그래서 지금 선생님한테 이메일을
   ....

4. 보라: 언제 고향에 가요?

   수진: 다음달 쯤에 ....

5. 시메이: 왜 요리를 이렇게 조금 했어요?

   다니엘: 오늘부터 다이어트를 ....

6. 보라: 토마스 씨, 어디에서 수진 씨 생일 선물을 살 거예요?

   토마스: 아, 백화점에서 ....

7. 선생님: 방학 때 뭐 할 거예요?

   시메이: 한국에서 한국어를 ....

2 What are your plans? Answer the following questions, then ask the same questions to your classmates. Remember to express your intention using –(으)려고 해요.

1. 오늘 저녁에 뭐 먹을 거예요?

   ....

2. 주말에 무슨 계획이 있어요?

   ....

3. 내년에 무엇을 공부할 거예요?

   ....

4. 방학 때 어디 여행을 가요?

   ....

5. 졸업해요. 그 다음 계획이 뭐예요?

   ....

6. SNS에 보통 어떤 사진을 올려요?

   ....

3 **Conjugate the following verbs with –(으)ㄹ게요 as in the example.**

보기	읽다 ➡	읽을게요

1. 타다 ➡ ....

2. 전화하다 ➡ ....

3. 주다 ➡ ....

4. 말하다 ➡ ....

5. 가다 ➡ ....

6. 사다 ➡ ....

7. 닫다 ➡ ....

8. 돌아오다 ➡ ....

9. 내리다 ➡ ....

10. 앉다 ➡ ....

11. 있다 →

12. *열다 →

4 Fill in the following mini-dialogues with an appropriate verb conjugated with –(으)ㄹ게요.

보기: 가다, 기다리다, 하다, 일어나다, 나오다, 공부하다, 사다

보기:
A: 내일 몇 시까지 학교에 올 수 있어요?
B: 내일 9시까지 _갈게요_.

1. 수진: 토마스 씨, 같이 커피를 마실까요?

   토마스: 네, 좋아요. 그런데 오늘은 제가 _____.

2. 어머니: 보라야, 시험을 잘 봤어?

   보라: 아니요 어머니. 내일부터 열심히 _____.

3. 지호: 미안해요. 지금 가야 해요. 먼저 _____.

   시메이: 괜찮아요. 다음에 또 만나요!

4. 다니엘: 미안해요. 지금 조금 바빠요.

   지호: 그럼 제가 내일 다시 전화 _____.

5. 어머니: 오늘 집에 빨리 와!

   수진: 네, 어머니. 학교에서 일찍 _____.

6. 보라: 여보세요 토마스 씨? 미안해요. 저는 약속에 조금 늦을 거예요.

   토마스: 걱정하지 마세요. 그럼 제가 커피숍 안에서 _____.

5 Complete the following sentences as in the example, using –(으)ㄴ 다음에.

보기 예습을 하다 + (으)ㄴ 다음에...
   → 예습을 한 다음에 한국어 수업을 들어요.

1. 세수를 하다 + (으)ㄴ 다음에...

   → ....

2. 한국어 시험을 보다 + (으)ㄴ 다음에...

   → ....

3. 점심을 먹다 + (으)ㄴ 다음에...

   → ....

4. 버스에서 내리다 + (으)ㄴ 다음에...

   → ....

5. 도서관에 가다 + (으)ㄴ 다음에...

   → ....

6. 택시를 부르다 + (으)ㄴ 다음에...

   → ....

6 Fill in the following sentences with the most appropriate word among those suggested below.

| 막혀요 | 세워 주세요 | 이용 방법 | 걸려요 |

| 갈아타세요 | 타세요 | 정거장 |

1. A: 신세계 백화점에 어떻게 가요?

   B: 저기에서 1호선을 .... 그리고 서울역에서 4호선으로 ....

2. (On the bus)

   학생: 여기 앉으세요.

   할아버지: 괜찮아요. 다음 .... 에서 내릴 거예요.

3. 출근 시간에 차가 많이 .... 그래서 지하철이 버스보다 더 빨라요.

4. 대학교에서 지하철역까지 시간이 얼마나 ....?

5. 보라 씨, 버스를 타고 싶어요. 버스 .... 을 좀 설명해 주세요.

6. (In a taxi) 기사님, 저기 ....

말하기

대화 1

Thomas is at Korea University, which is near Anam station. He wants to go to the Kyobo bookstore, and asks a lady for information. 🎧 7.1

토마스: 저 죄송한데요… 교보문고에 가려고 해요. 어떻게 가요?

아주머니: 안암역에서 6호선을 타세요. 그리고 청구역에서 5호선으로 갈아타세요.

토마스: 어디에서 내려요?

아주머니: 광화문역에서 내리세요.

토마스: 고맙습니다.

💬 Change Thomas's destination and the instructions using the subway maps below.

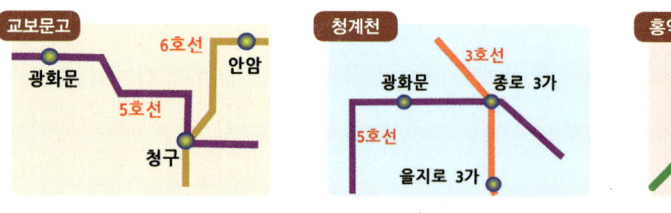

안암역 → 광화문   광화문 → 을지로 3가

서울역 → 홍대입구역

강남역 → 고속터미널

안국역 → 동대문

대화 2

Thomas is asking Sujin how to get to the meeting place.

토마스: 수진 씨, 영화 동아리 모임에 어떻게 가요?

수　진: 먼저 버스를 타야 해요.

토마스: 몇 번 버스를 타야 해요?

수　진: 제가 문자로 보내 줄게요.

토마스: 고마워요.

Change how Sujin will explain to Thomas how to take the bus, using the cues below.

- 문자로 보내다
- 나중에 알리다
- 카카오톡으로 보내다
- 지도를 보내다
- 이메일로 가르치다

듣기

1 Listen to the following description of the Han river park (한강공원), and fill in the blanks in the passage below. 🎧 7.3

> 서울 여름 밤 날씨가 더워요. 그래서 여름에 한강공원은 1)＿＿＿＿＿＿. 사람들이 여기에서 많이 만나요. 친구와 함께 이야기하고 놀아요. 그리고 2)＿＿＿＿＿＿ 맛있는 음식을 먹어요. 공원에서 치킨도 3)＿＿＿＿＿＿.
>
> 여름에 한강공원에서는 4)＿＿＿＿＿＿를 해요. 이때 많은 사람들이 5)＿＿＿＿＿＿를 보려고 해요. 그래서 한강공원 근처는 7)＿＿＿＿＿＿. 한강공원에 한번 가고 싶으세요? 그럼 고려대학교에서 지하철 6호선을 타고 5호선으로 갈아타세요. 그럼 여의도역에 갈 수 있어요.

2 Thomas, Sujin, and Bora are talking about going to the Han river park (한강공원) on Saturday. *What will they do there?* 🎧 7.4

Listen to the following statements, and tick whether they are true (O) or false (X). 🎧 7.5

1. O   X
2. O   X
3. O   X
4. O   X

Mission Accomplished: Korean 2

5.

6.

3 한강공원에서 뭐 해요? Together with your classmates, look at the following activities that you can do at the Han river park. Discuss a trip to the Han river park with them, telling them what you are planning to do there.

밤 사진을 찍다

불꽃놀이를 구경하다

산책을 하다

분수 쇼를 구경하다

63빌딩에 올라가다

오리배를 타다

 읽기

1 Look at the subway timetable of 여의도역, then answer the questions below.

서울 지하철 5호선 열차 시간표 (**평일**)	
여의도역	
신길 방향	여의나루 방향
첫차	
05:30	05:46
막차	
23:39	23:41

서울 지하철 5호선 열차 시간표 (**토요일**)	
여의도역	
신길 방향	여의나루 방향
첫차	
05:30	05:46
막차	
23:39	23:51

서울 지하철 5호선 열차 시간표 (**휴일**)	
여의도역	
신길 방향	여의나루 방향
첫차	
05:30	05:46
막차	
23:39	23:30

1. 평일, 토요일, 휴일의 지하철 시간표가 같아요? 달라요?

2. 여의나루 방향 첫차가 평일에 몇 시에 출발해요?

3. 평일, 토요일, 휴일 중에서 여의나루 방향 막차 시간이 언제가 제일 빨라요?

4. 평일, 토요일, 휴일 중에서 여의나루 방향 막차 시간이 언제가 제일 늦어요?

5. 막차 시간이 지났어요. 그러면 여러분이 어떻게 할 거예요?

2 Thomas, Sujin, and Bora went to watch the fireworks at the Han river Park. *What happened to Thomas?* Read the text below and answer the questions.

토마스 씨는 수진 씨와 보라 씨하고 같이 한강공원에 갔어요.

토마스 씨는 고려대학교에서 지하철 6호선을 탔어요. 그리고 공덕역에서 5호선으로 갈아탔어요. 공덕역에서 토마스 씨는 열차를 잘못 갈아타고 반대 방향으로 갔어요. 다시 여의도 방향 열차를 탄 다음에 5호선 여의도역에서 내렸어요. 여의도역은 한강공원에서 조금 멀어요. 그래서 한강공원까지 20분 정도 걸어서 갔어요. 토마스 씨는 약속 시간에 15분 늦었어요.

한강공원에서 친구들이 토마스 씨를 기다리고 있었어요. 다 같이 63빌딩을 구경한 다음에 산책했어요. 그리고 편의점에서 술을 사고 치킨을 주문했어요. 사람이 많았지만 좋은 자리에 앉았어요. 8시부터 불꽃놀이를 구경했어요.

토마스 씨는 불꽃놀이를 본 다음에 술을 마셨어요. 그리고 친구들과 같이 이야기하고 즐거운 시간을 보냈어요. 시간이 빨리 갔어요. 밤 12시에 토마스 씨는 지하철을 타고 집에 가려고 했지만 막차 시간이 지났어요. 그래서 토마스 씨는 버스를 타려고 했지만 버스 막차 시간도 지났어요. 다음 날 첫차는 오전 5시 46분에 출발해요. 그래서 토마스 씨는 택시를 타려고 했지만 한강공원은 고려대학교 기숙사에서 멀어요. 그리고 택시비가 18,000원이에요.

토마스 씨는 한강공원 근처 찜질방을 찾았어요. 찜질방은 8,000원이에요. 택시비보다 찜질방이 더 [가]_____. 그래서 그날 토마스 씨는 [나]_____.

1. Which title would you give to the text above?

   ....

2. Which word would you write to fill in the blank '가'?

   ....

3. Which sentence would you write to fill in the blank '나'?

   ....

3 Together with your classmates, ask and answer the following questions.

1. 한강공원에 도착한 다음에 토마스 씨는 수진 씨와 보라 씨하고 뭐 했어요?

   ....

2. 토마스 씨는 왜 약속 시간에 늦었어요?

   ....

3. 토마스 씨는 밤 12시에 집에 가려고 했어요. 그런데 왜 집에 가지 못했어요?

   ....

4. 택시비하고 찜질방 가격 중에 뭐가 더 비싸요?

   ....

5. 여러분이 토마스 씨예요. 그러면 어떻게 할 거예요?

   ....

쓰기

1 Thomas is sending a message to Sujin with some instructions to go to Itaewon. Fill in the following sentences with the most appropriate verb.

> 먼저 고려대학교에서 지하철 6호선을 ＿＿＿＿＿＿＿＿＿＿. 그리고 이태원역에서 ＿＿＿＿＿＿＿＿＿＿. 저는 이태원역 3번 출구에서 수진 씨를 기다릴게요.

2 Bora is sending a message to Thomas on how to get to the DDP. Fill in the following sentences with the most appropriate particle.

> 신촌에서 DDP까지 가고 싶어요? 그럼 2호선＿＿＿ 타세요. 그리고 동대문역＿＿＿ 1호선＿＿＿ 갈아타세요. 그 다음에 동대문역사문화공원역＿＿＿ 내리세요.

3 Sujin and Bora decided to go shopping together in 명동. Bora is already there, and Sujin is at City Hall (시청). Bora texts her the instructions to get to 명동. Look at the map, then write her text message.

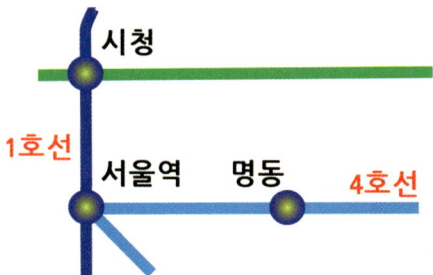

7과 161

문화

Taking the bus and subway in Seoul

It is easy to reach almost any place in Seoul via public transportation, either by subway or by bus. People may prefer the subway during the morning and afternoon rush hour, to avoid being stuck in traffic. Alternatively, they may prefer the bus because of its capillarity, or to avoid walking long distances to transfer from one subway line to another. Whatever means of transportation you decide to take, etiquette is important.

If you take the subway, even during peak times, you will probably notice that despite being crowded there is almost absolute silence. People will talk to each other only in a very low voice, and will be texting instead of making phone calls. Talking aloud, and over the phone, is considered bad behaviour. People making unavoidable phone calls will  cover their mouth with their hand to avoid making too much noise. On the subway you will find seats reserved for the elderly with the script 교통약자석, and pink seats reserved for pregnant women marked with the script 임산부 배려석. During peak times, you may want to give your seat to elderly people. In exchange for the courtesy, they will probably offer to hold your bag for you in

 their lap.

Buses in Seoul are very frequent, with most lines running every five to ten minutes. Since usually different lines stop at the same bus stop, people do not wait in a row before getting on, because it is not possible to know who is waiting for which bus. However, people usually wait in a row when there is just one bus line, and this happens with small local buses, or the red buses connecting central Seoul to the region outside of the capital.

8과
Unit 8

In this unit you will learn

- How to say that you go somewhere to do something.
- How to express the relation of cause/effect between two events.
- How to visit a doctor if you are sick.
- About Korean health remedies.
- How to describe symptoms.
- Vocabulary related to health, health remedies, and the body.

문법

 **Expressing a reason with −아서/어서**

Meaning

−아서/어서 is a connective attached to the base of processive and descriptive verbs, 이다 and 아니다 to express the relation of cause/consequence between two events or facts described in two sentences. It carries the meaning of *so, therefore*, and it is used to explain why a state is the way it is, or the reason why something happened.

The Korean language has several connectives used to express a cause/consequence relation between two sentences. −아서/어서 is mostly used when the consequence expressed in the second sentence is an objective one, or an obvious consequence of the cause expressed in the first sentence.

Use

−아서/어서 is widely used in both written and oral language, and it can also be used when the subject of the first sentence is different from the subject of the second sentence. −아서 is attached to the base of verbs for which the last vowel is ㅏ or ㅗ, −어서 is attached to the base of verbs for which the last vowel is any other vowel, −여서 is attached to 하다 and further contracted in 해서.

Verb base containing ㅏ or ㅗ	Verb base containing a vowel which is not ㅏ or ㅗ	하다
+ 아서	+ 어서	→ 해서

보다 → 보 + 아서 → 봐서
앉다 → 앉 + 아서 → 앉아서
먹다 → 먹 + 어서 → 먹어서
보내다 → 보내 + 어서 → 보내서
하다 → 하 + 여서 → 하여서 → 해서
걷다 → 걷 + 어서 → 걸 + 어서 → 걸어서
쓰다 → 쓰 + 어서 → ㅆ + 어서 → 써서
춥다 → 춥 + 어서 → 추우 + 어서 → 추워서
살다 → 살 + 아서 → 살아서

Examples

1. 토마스 씨는 머리가 **아파서** 오늘 학교에 못 갔어요. Thomas has a headache, so he could not go to school today.

2. 차가 **막혀서** 수진 씨는 약속 시간에 늦었어요. There was a traffic jam so Sujin was late to the appointment.

3. 시메이 씨는 열심히 **공부해서** 좋은 성적을 받을 거예요. Shimei studies hard so she will receive a good mark.

4. 비가 **와서** 소풍을 가지 못했어요. It rained so I could not go on the trip.

5. 다니엘 씨는 요즘 한국 웹툰이 **재미있어서** 웹툰을 많이 봐요. Korean online comics are fun so Daniel reads them often.

6. 요즘 날씨가 **추워서** 보라 씨는 감기에 걸렸어요. It's cold so Bora caught a cold.

7. 지호 씨는 알바도 하고 공부도 **해서** 많이 피곤해요. Jiho works part-time and studies, so he is tired.

8. 사라 씨는 아침을 **먹지 않아서** 힘이 없었어요. Sara didn't have breakfast so she was without energy.

9. BTS는 춤을 잘 추고 노래도 잘 **불러서** 인기가 많아요. BTS dance well and also sing well so they are popular.

10. 시메이: 오늘 헬스장에 왜 안 가요? Why don't you go to the gym today?
    지호: 어제 다리를 다**쳐서요**. Because I hurt my leg yesterday.

11. 지호: 한국어 시험을 잘 봤어요? Did you do well in the Korean exam?
    다니엘: 아니요. 공부를 많이 **못해서** 시험 문제를 다 못 풀었어요. No, the exam was long so I could not answer all questions.

12. 보라: 아직도 열이 나요? Do you still have a fever?
    수진: 아니요. 약을 **먹어서** 지금은 괜찮아요. No, I took medicine so it got better.

Extra notes

- ―아서/어서 cannot be attached to a past tense base or a future tense base. As in examples 1~4, 6, 8, 11, and 12, the tense is expressed by the verb of the second sentence. Nevertheless, in the past decade it has become more common to hear ―어서 sometimes attached to a past tense base. This use is restricted to oral language, and it is not considered totally appropriate.
- ―아서/어서 cannot be used in the first sentence if an imperative or a request are used in the second sentence. Therefore the sentence 시간이 늦어서 빨리 가세요 (*) is grammatically incorrect.
- ―아서/어서 is often used together with verbs expressing gratitude, or being sorry (for something).

> 늦어서 미안해요. Sorry for being late.
> 선생님, 숙제를 하지 못해서 죄송합니다. Sorry for not being able to do the homework.
> 만나서 반갑습니다. I am glad to meet you.
> 오늘 와 주셔서 고맙습니다. Thanks for coming today.

- When –어서 is attached to 이다 and 아니다, it can be used either as 이어서/여서 or (이)라서, and 아니어서/아니라서.

  > 우리 언니는 가수라서/가수여서 노래를 잘 불러요. Since my sister is a singer, she sings well.
  > 점심 시간이라서/점심 시간이어서 식당에 사람이 많아요. It's lunch time so there are many people at the restaurant.

- –아서/어서 can be used as a sentence ending to express a reason, without the need for a further sentence. It is often used to give explanations, and the sentence can be opened by 왜냐하면 (because).

  > 지호: 왜 한국어를 배워요? Why do you study Korean?
  > 시메이: (왜냐하면) 한국 드라마를 좋아해서요. Because I like Korean dramas.

(To go somewhere) to do something, –(으)러 (가요).

Meaning

–(으)러 is a connective attached to a processive verb base which indicates the purpose of a movement. It is used together with verbs indicating movement such as 가다, 오다, 다니다 and it expresses the meaning of *going (somewhere) to do (something)*.

Use

–(으)러 can be used only with processive verbs, and not with descriptive verbs. –(으)러 can be used with all persons, however the subject of the first sentence must be the same as the subject of the second sentence.

–러 is attached to verb bases ending in vowels and to verb bases ending in ㄹ; –(으)러 to verb bases ending in consonants.

Verb base ending in a vowel	Verb base ending in a consonant
+ 러 가요	+ 으러 가요

> 보다 → 보 + 러 → 보러 (가요)
> 하다 → 하 + 러 → 하러 (가요)
> 쓰다 → 쓰 + 러 → 쓰러 (가요)
> 먹다 → 먹 + 으러 → 먹으러 (가요)
> 듣다 → 듣 + 으러 → 들 + 으러 → 들으러 (가요)
> 만들다 → 만들 + 러 → 만들러 (가요)

Examples

1. 보라 씨는 시험 **공부하러** 도서관에 **가요**. Bora goes to the library to study for the exam.

2. 시메이 씨는 오늘 친구를 **만나러** 시내에 **가요**. Shimei goes to the city to meet her friends today.

3. 수진 씨는 요가를 **배우러 다녀요**. Sujin goes to learn yoga.

4. 토마스 씨는 친구와 함께 홍대에 **놀러 갔어요**. Thomas went to Hongdae to hang out together with his friends.

5. 직원: 누구를 **만나러 오셨어요**? Who did you come to meet?
   시메이: 김 선생님을 **만나러 왔어요**. I came to meet with teacher Kim.

Extra notes

- Suffixes indicating tense cannot be used together with –(으)러. To express that somebody went/will go (somewhere) to do something, the tense is attached to the main verb indicating movement, as in 한국어 수업을 들으러 학교에 갔어요 *I went to school to take a Korean class*.
- The negatice form cannot be used together with the verb to which –(으)러 is attached. As with tenses, when saying that somebody does not go (somewhere) to do something, only the verb indicating movement is turned into the negative form, as in 선생님을 만나러 가지 않았어요 *I did not go to meet my teacher*.
- When the destination is indicated, it can be placed both at the beginning of the first sentence, or of the second sentence, therefore 도서관에 공부하러 가요 and 공부하러 도서관에 가요 are both acceptable.
- The same verbs indicating movement cannot be used together with –(으)러 가요. In this case other expressions can be used, but these will be introduced in Unit 9.

몸과 건강

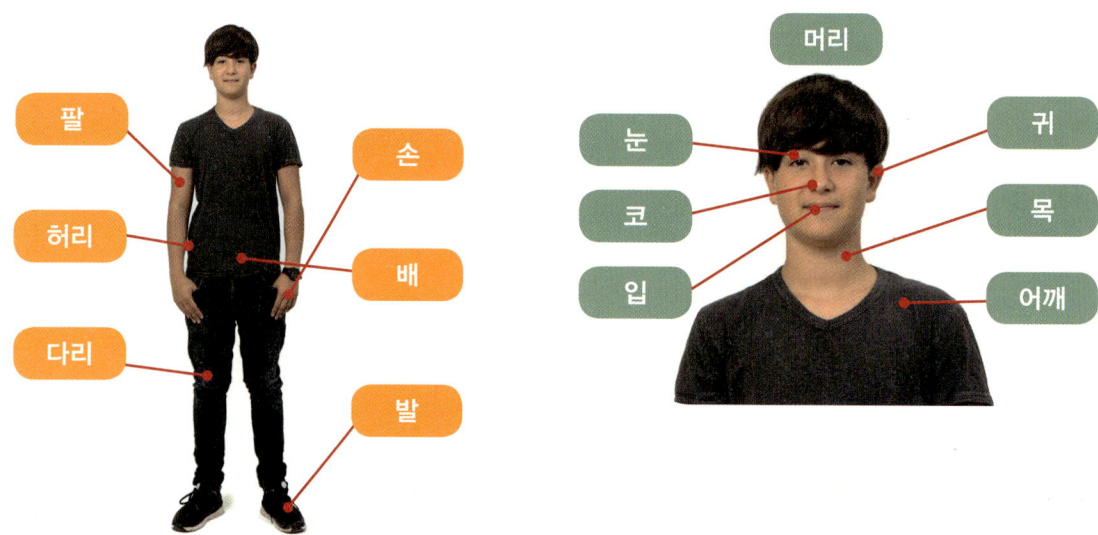

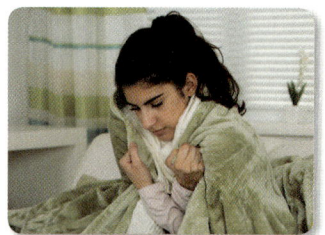

감기에 걸리다

기침이 나다

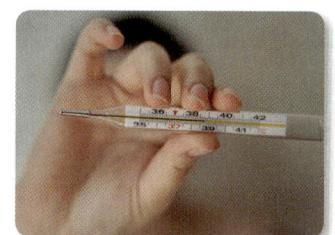

열이 나다

콧물이 나다

눈물이 나다

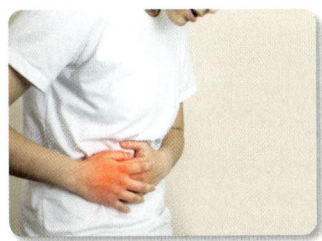
이/머리/배/허리...이/가 아프다

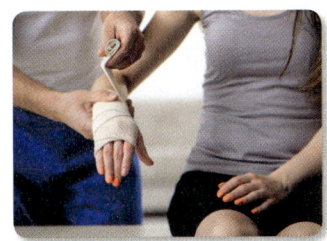
손/다리/머리/허리...을/를 (많이) 다치다

내과

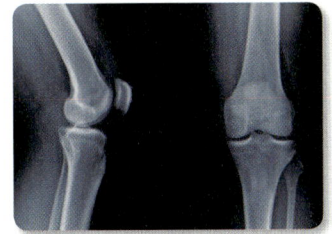
정형외과

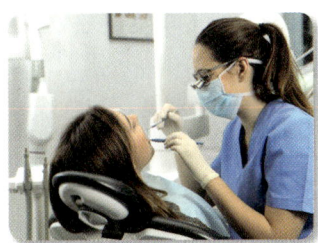
치과

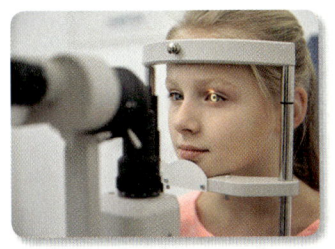
안과

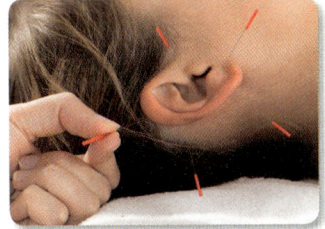
한의원

응급실

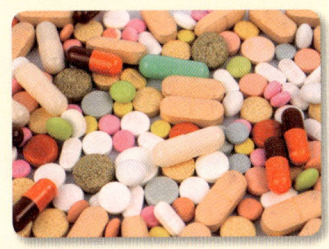

약을 먹다
병원에 입원하다
몸이 좋지 않다
몸이 아프다

건강이 좋지 않다
주사를 맞다
(감기)가 낫다(나아요)

연습

1 Fill in the blanks of the sentences below with the verb indicated in the brackets with -아서/어서.

| 보기 | 사라 씨는 요즘 회사에 일이 _많아서_ 늦게 퇴근해요. (많다) |

1. 토마스 씨는 약속 시간을 _____ 약속 장소에 못 갔어요. (잊다)

2. 예린 씨는 다리를 _____ 일주일 동안 쉬어야 해요. (다치다)

3. 하숙집이 _____ 다른 집으로 이사 가려고 해요. (좁다)

4. 보라: 왜 전화를 안 했어요?

   다니엘: 미안해요. 배터리가 _____ 전화하지 못했어요. (없다)

5. 지호: 요즘 수영장에 자주 가요?

   다니엘: 아니요, 알바를 _____ 수영장에 자주 못 가요. (시작하다)

6. 수진: 닭갈비를 먹어 봤어요?

   토마스: 네. 그런데 너무 _____ 많이 먹지 못했어요. (*맵다)

7. 보라 씨는 이가 _____ 치과에 갔어요 (*아프다)

8. 사라 씨는 하루종일 _____ 많이 피곤해요. (*걷다)

9. 날씨가 _____ 따뜻한 옷을 입었어요. (*춥다)

2 Write down your answer to the following questions, then ask your classmate the same questions. Remember to use -아서/어서.

1. 왜 한국어를 공부해요?

   ....

2. 왜 아르바이트를 해요?

   ....

3. 왜 커피를 안 마셔요?

　　...

4. 왜 인터넷 쇼핑을 해요?

　　...

5. 왜 일찍 학교에 왔어요?

　　...

6. 왜 한국 드라마를 봐요?

　　...

3 Connect the following sentences using −(으)러.

보기	(김 선생님) 공원에 가요. 공원에서 운동해요 ➜ 김 선생님이 운동하러 공원에 가요.

1. (보라 씨) 커피숍에 가요. 커피숍에서 친구를 만나요.

　➜　...

2. (토마스 씨) 백화점에 가요. 백화점에서 쇼핑해요.

　➜　...

3. (수진 씨) 체육관에 가요. 체육관에서 태권도를 배워요.

　➜　...

4. (저는) 학교에 가요. 학교에서 한국어 수업을 들어요.

　➜　...

5. (예린 씨) 고속터미널에 가요. 고속터미널에서 버스를 타요.

　➜　...

6. (지호 씨) 화장실에 가요. 화장실에서 손을 씻어요.

　➜　...

7. (토마스 씨) 피시방에 가요. 피시방에서 게임을 해요.

→ ....

8. (저는) 학원에 다녀요. 학원에서 가야금을 배워요.

→ ....

4 What do you do in these places? Look at the pictures, then ask and answer a question as in the example.

보기 | 1. | 2.

3. | 4. | 5.

6. | 7. | 8.

보기
A: 극장에 뭐 하러 가요?
B: 극장에 알바를 하러 가요.

1. A: ....

B: ....

2. A: ....

B: ....

3. A: ....

   B: ....

4. A: ....

   B: ....

5. A: ....

   B: ....

6. A: ....

   B: ....

7. A: ....

   B: ....

8. A: ....

   B: ....

5 Fill in the blanks of the following text with the words suggested below.

맞고   아프고   내과   걸렸어요

나서   나아서   좋아서

요즘 날씨가 추워서 토마스 씨는 감기에 **1.** .... 머리가

2. .... 열이 **3.** .... 학교에 못 갔어요.

토마스 씨는 몸이 안 **4.** .... 어제 의사 선생님을 만나러

5. .... 에 갔어요. 토마스 씨는 병원에서 주사를

6. .... 집에 온 다음에 감기약도 먹었어요.

이제 토마스 씨는 감기가 다 **7.** .... 내일부터 학교에 가려고 해요.

말하기

대화 1

Ms. Kim is asking Daniel why he did not come to class yesterday. 🎧 8.1

다니엘: 선생님, 지난주에 수업에 못 왔어요. 죄송합니다.

김 선생님: 괜찮아요. 무슨 일이 있었어요?

다니엘: 열이 나서 학교에 못 왔어요.

김 선생님: 지금은 괜찮아요?

다니엘: 네, 지금은 다 나았어요.

💬 Change what happened to Daniel using the cues below.

열이 나다 배탈이 나다 다리를 다치다

이가 아프다 감기에 걸리다

대화 2

Shimei is asking Jiho where he is going. 🎧 8.2

시메이: 지호 씨, 어디에 가요?

지 호: 약국에 약을 사러 가요.

시메이: 왜요?

지 호: 왜냐하면 오늘 몸이 좀 안 좋아서요.

💬 Change the places where Jiho is going, using the cues below.

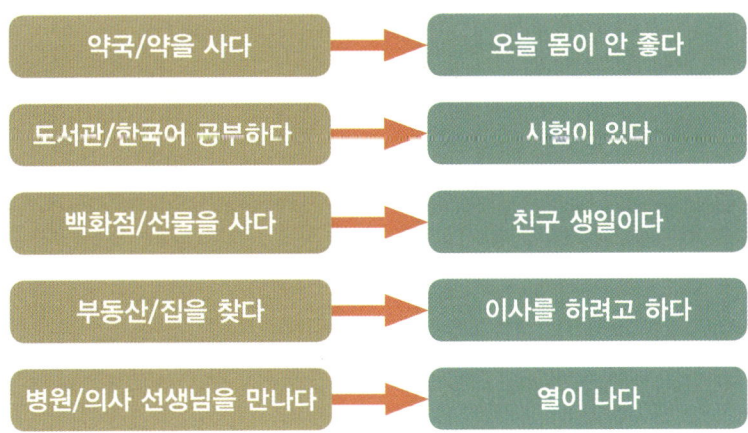

1 Listen to the symptoms that these people are experiencing, then write the relevant number next to the clinic they should visit. 🎧 8.3

안과	치과 ....
정형외과	내과 ....

2 Sujin is sick and she goes to a clinic. *What does the doctor tell her to do?* 🎧 8.4

Listen to the following statements, then check whether they are true (O) or false (X). 🎧 8.5

1. O X
2. O X
3. O X
4. O X
5. O X

3 Listen to this short conversation between Sujin and the pharmacist, then tick the label of the medicine indicated by the pharmacist. 🎧 8.6

Look at the label of the medicines below. Which on did the pharmacist give to Sujin? 가 or 나?

가			
	용법용량	만 15세 이상 및 성인	1일 3회, 1일 2캡슐 식후 30분에 복용
		만 7세 이상 ~ 만 15세 미만	1일 3회, 1일 1캡슐 식후 30분에 복용

나		
	용법용량	성인: 1회 1정 1일 3회 식후에 복용

 읽기

1 When somebody is sick or unwell, what would you suggest they drink or eat? Look at the following symptoms, then discuss with your classmates which remedies may be appropriate.

1. 공부를 많이 해서 피곤해요. 뭐가 좋을까요?

2. 스트레스를 받아서 힘들어요. 뭐가 좋을까요?

3. 머리가 아프고 감기에 걸렸어요. 뭐가 좋을까요?

4. 밥을 먹었지만 힘이 없어요. 뭐가 좋을까요?

5. 운동을 많이 했어요. 뭐가 좋을까요?

6. 목이 아파요. 뭐가 좋을까요?

2 Different cultures have developed different remedies for minor illnesses. They may be truly effective, or they may be just folklore. *When do Koreans eat red ginseng, rice porridge, or drink juice?*

건강 음식과 음료

요즘에 사람들이 건강에 좋은 음식과 음료에 관심이 많아요. 한국인들에게 인기가 있는 건강 음식과 음료는 홍삼, 죽과 즙이에요.

한국 사람들은 홍삼을 잘 먹어요. 홍삼은 건강에 좋아요. 학생들이 공부를 많이 해서 피곤해요. 이때 학생들이 홍삼을 먹고 힘을 내요. 그리고 홍삼을 먹으면 감기에 잘 걸리지 않아요. 홍삼은 먹을 수도 있고 마실 수도 있어요. 왜냐하면 홍삼 사탕도 있고 홍삼차도 있어서요. 한국인들한테 홍삼이 인기가 있어서 좋은 홍삼은 조금 비싸요.

 겨울에 날씨가 추워서 감기에 잘 걸려요? 밥을 먹었지만 힘이 없어요? 그때는 죽을 드셔 보세요. 죽은 쌀로 만들어서 건강에 좋은 음식이에요. 죽은 따뜻하고 맛이 있어서 몸이 아픈 사람들한테 좋아요. 죽은 집에서도 만들 수 있지만 식당에서도 주문할 수 있어요.

즙도 한국인들에게 인기가 있어요. 즙은 여러 종류가 있어요. 어떤 선생님들은 수업이 끝나고 배즙을 마셔요. 왜냐하면 배즙이 목에 좋아서요. 힘든 운동을 한 다음에는 포도즙을 드셔 보세요. 포도즙이 달아서 힘이 생겨요. 보통 즙은 비싸지 않고 약국이나 마트에서 살 수 있어요.

Read the passage above one more time, then select whether the following statements are true (O) or false (X).

1. 배가 많이 아파요. 그러면 홍삼을 먹어요. O X

2. 죽은 쌀로 만들어요. O X

3. 죽은 식당에서만 먹을 수 있어요. O X

4. 운동한 다음에 배즙이 좋아요. O X

5. 선생님들은 말을 많이 해서 목이 아파요. 그래서 배즙을 마셔야 해요. O X

3 Do your habits help you to stay healthy? Look at the checklist below, and tick off the items that you think apply to you.

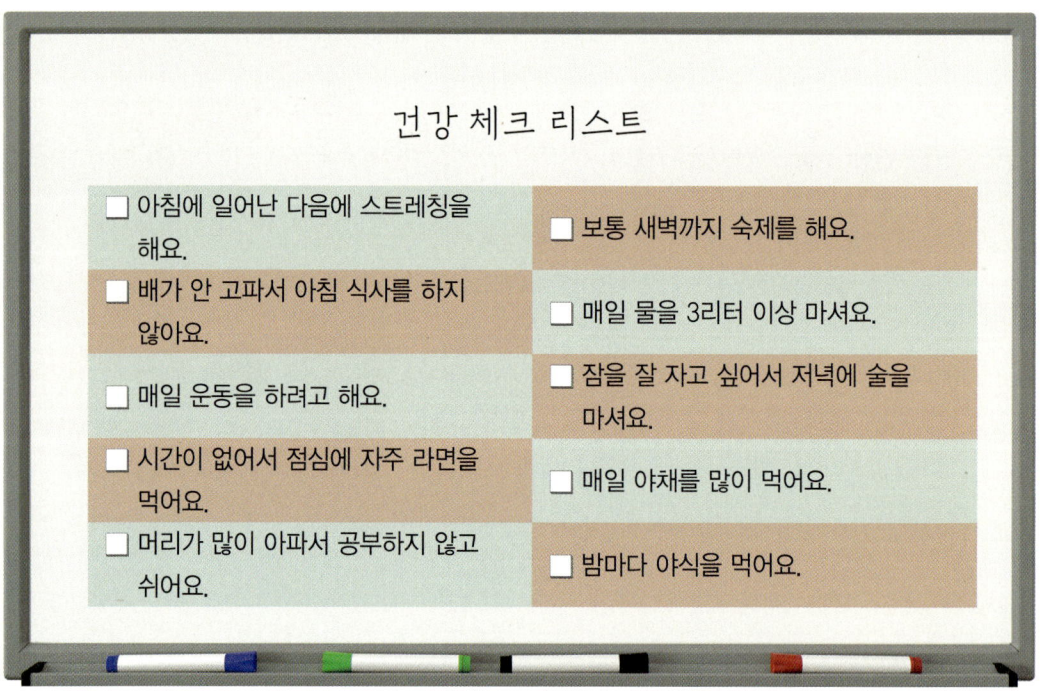

건강에 좋은 것(초록색)을 몇 개 체크 했어요? ....

건강에 안 좋은 것(빨간색)을 몇 개 체크했어요? ....

쓰기

1 Write down what people do in your country when they experience these symptoms.

1. 일을 많이 해서 피곤해요. 어떻게 해요?

   ....

2. 열이 나고 머리가 아파요. 어떻게 해요?

   ....

3. 감기에 걸렸어요. 콧물도 나요. 어떻게 해요?

   ....

4. 목이 아파서 말을 잘 못해요. 어떻게 해요?

   ....

2 Have you ever been unwell? Read Thomas's passage below about when he was sick, then write a similar short passage describing an episode when you have been unwell.

작년 겨울에 날씨가 너무 추워서 감기에 걸렸어요. 머리가 아주 아프고 콧물이 나고 열도 났어요. 그래서 병원에 갔어요. 의사 선생님이 약을 주셨어요. 그리고 3일 동안 약을 먹고 집에서 쉬었어요. 그 다음에 감기가 다 나았어요.

문화

Korean hospitals

What do you do if you are unwell in Korea? In Australia, you would probably go to a GP. However, the Korean health system is different and unfortunately general practitioners do not exist. If you are unwell, you go to the nearest clinic with a doctor specializing in the symptoms that you are experiencing. For example, if you hurt yourself playing sport, you probably want to go to the nearest orthopedic clinic. For this reason, both the small clinic and the big university hospital are called 병원.

If you are unwell, you can visit your local clinic without any appointment. Just drop by, check in at the reception, and wait for your name to be called. You probaly have to wait just for just a few minutes. Koreans rely mainly on private health insurance, but if you do not have any and need to visit a local clinic, you will not end up paying too much, as even without insurance a visit is reasonably priced.

If you have an emergency during the weekend or in the night, when local clinics are closed, then you will probably need to visit the ER. If you call 119, which corresponds to triple-0 in Australia, you will get an ambulance, which is provided free of charge. However, be aware that a visit to the ER of a big hospital, without insurance cover, may result in a hefty bill.

MP3 Streaming

9과
Unit 9

In this unit you will learn

- How to say that you know how to do something or not.
- How to express ability.
- How to express intention.
- How to talk about food and cooking.
- How to shop for groceries.
- How to read a food recipe.
- How to explain how to prepare food.
- Vocabulary for cooking, ingredients, and taste.

 문법

 Expressing the ability of doing something with −(으)ㄹ 줄 알아요/몰라요.

Meaning

The modifier −(으)ㄹ is used together with the bound noun 줄 and followed by a verb of knowledge such as 알아요/몰라요 to create a pattern indicating that the subject knows (or does not know) how to do something. It also has another meaning, to indicate the knowledge of a certain truth; however, this second use is not dealt with in this section.

Use

When −(으)ㄹ 줄 알아요/몰라요 is used with the meaning of knowing (or not knowing) how to do something, it can only be attached to processive verbs.

−을 줄 알아요/몰라요 is attached to consonant-ending verb bases, −ㄹ 줄 알아요/몰라요 to vowel-ending verb bases.

Verb base ending in a vowel	Verb base ending in a consonant
+ ㄹ 줄 알아요/몰라요	+ 을 줄 알아요/몰라요

가다 → 가 + ㄹ 줄 → 갈 줄 알아요/몰라요
하다 → 하 + ㄹ 줄 → 할 줄 알아요/몰라요
쓰다 → 쓰 + ㄹ 줄 → 쓸 줄 알아요/몰라요
읽다 → 읽 + 을 줄 → 읽을 줄 알아요/몰라요
놀다 → 놀 + 을 줄 → 노 + ㄹ 줄 → 놀 줄 알아요/몰라요
살다 → 살 + 을 줄 → 사 + ㄹ 줄 → 살 줄 알아요/몰라요

Examples

1. 다니엘 씨는 한국 음식을 잘 **만들 줄 알아요**. Daniel knows how to cook Korean food well.

2. 시메이 씨는 한국 노래를 잘 **부를 줄 알아요**. Shimei knows how to sing Korean songs well.

3. 토마스 씨는 술을 **마실 줄 몰라요**. Thomas does not know how to drink alcohol (Thomas does not drink alcohol).

4. 지호 씨는 컴퓨터를 잘 **고칠 줄 알아요**. Jiho knows how to fix a computer well.

5. 사장님이 골프를 **칠 줄 아세요**. The boss knows how to play golf.

6. 저는 한글 타자를 **칠 줄 몰라요**. I am not good at typing in Korean.

7. 다니엘 씨는 한자를 **읽을 줄 몰라요**. Daniel does not know how to read Chinese characters.

Extra notes

- When it is used to express how to do something, –(으)ㄹ 줄 알아요/몰라요 denotes the ability (or lack of ability) to perform a certain activity. It therefore has a meaning similar to –(으)ㄹ 수 있어요/없어요, as seen in Unit 2. Despite the shared meaning of expressing the ability to do something, there are also some differences:

1) –(으)ㄹ 수 있어요 can be used to express the meaning of both ability and possibility, while –(으)ㄹ 줄 알아요/몰라요 expresses only the meaning of ability, and does not indicate possibility.

> 다니엘 씨는 수영할 줄 몰라요 means that Daniel does not know how to swim.
>
> 다니엘 씨는 수영할 수 없어요, depending on the context, this can mean either that Daniel does not know how to swim, or that maybe he cannot swim in that situation (but knows how to swim).

Because of this, –(으)ㄹ 줄 알아요/몰라요 is mostly used with verbs indicating something that has been learned.

2) –(으)ㄹ 수 있어요/없어요 can also be used with descriptive verbs when it indicates possibility, but –(으)ㄹ 줄 알아요 only indicates ability, and thus is not used with descriptive verbs.

 Expressing the purpose of doing something with –(으)려고 (2)

Meaning

As described in Unit 7, –(으)려고 is used to express the purpose or the goal of doing a certain action. When used to connect two sentences, the first sentence states the purpose or the goal of the action carried on in the second sentence. It can be translated literally with *doing something in order to....*

Use

When using –(으)려고 to connect two sentences, the subject of the first sentence must be the same as the subject of the second sentence.

–으려고 is attached to verb bases ending in consonants, –려고 is attached to verb bases ending in vowels or ㄹ. For a list of sample verbs conjugated with –(으)려고 *see expressing the purpose of doing something with –(으)려고 (1) in Unit 7.*

Examples

1. 시메이 씨는 단어를 **외우려고** 단어 카드를 만들었어요. Shimei prepares word cards to memorize vocabulary.

2. 다니엘 씨는 극장에서 영화를 **보려고** 티켓을 예매했어요. Daniel booked a ticket to watch a film at the cinema.

3. 아침에 일찍 **일어나려고** 알람 시계를 맞췄어요. I set the alarm to wake up early in the morning.

4. 수진 씨는 주말에 친구하고 **놀려고** 약속을 잡았어요. Sujin makes an appointment with her friends to hang out together on the weekend.

5. 보라 씨는 빨리 학교에 **가려고** 택시를 탔어요. Bora took a taxi to get to school quickly.

6. 지호: 왜 한국 드라마를 봐요? Why do you watch Korean dramas?
   시메이: 듣기 연습을 **하려고** 한국 드라마를 봐요. I watch Korean dramas to do listening exercises.

7. 지호: 왜 한국어를 공부해요? Why do you study Korean?
   다니엘: 한국 여행을 **가려고** 한국어를 공부해요. I study Korean to travel to Korea.

Extra notes

- −(으)려고 cannot be attached to a past tense or a future tense base. As in the examples above, the past tense is attached to the verb of the second sentence.
- Imperative or request suffixes cannot be attached to the verb of the second sentence.
- −(으)려고 and −(으)러 가요 may indicate a similar meaning. However −(으)러 is used only with verbs indicating movement, while −(으)려고 with any other processive verb.

# 단어

요리

볶다

끓이다

삶다

굽다

튀기다

밥을 볶아요
라면을 끓여요
계란/야채/스파게티를 삶아요

고기를 구워요
치킨을 튀겨요

깎다
사과를 깎아요
과일을 깎아요

썰다
양파를 썰어요
당근을 썰어요

섞다
야채하고 간장을 섞어요

넣다
소금을 넣어요

맛

짜다

달다

쓰다

시다

맵다

간장이 짜요
된장찌개가 짜요
과일이 달아요
케이크가 달아요
홍삼이 써요

레몬이 셔요
자몽이 셔요
고추가 매워요
김치가 매워요

재료

주방 용품

연습

1 Fill in the blanks of the following sentences with the most appropriate verb using –(으)ㄹ 줄 알아요.

| 보기 추다 | 하다 | 부르다 | 만들다 |
| 운전하다 | 치다 | 읽다 | 타다 |

보기 저는 춤을 <u>출 줄 알아요</u>

1. 토마스 씨는 한국어를 노래를 _____.
2. 시메이 씨는 자동차를 _____.
3. 수진 씨는 김치볶음밥을 _____.
4. 사라 씨는 스키를 _____.
5. 지호 씨는 테니스를 _____.
6. 시메이 씨는 태권도를 조금 _____.
7. 사라 씨는 한자를 _____.

2 Look at the following photos, then ask and answer questions with your classmate, as in the example.

보기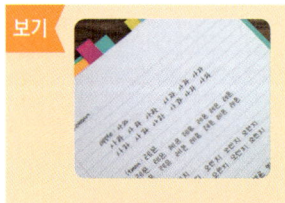
1.
2.
3.
4.
5.
6.
7.

보기
A: 한국어를 읽을 줄 알아요?
B: 네, 한국어를 읽을 줄 알아요.

1. A:
   B:

2. A:
   B:

3. A:
   B:

4. A:
   B:

5. A:
   B:

6. A:
   B:

7. A:
   B:

3 Connect the sentences below using –(으)려고 as in the example.

보기	요리를 배우다 + 요리 학원을 다니다
	→ <u>요리를 배우려고 요리 학원을 다녀요.</u>

1. 한국 여행을 가다 + 아르바이트를 하다

   → _____.

2. 헬스장에서 음악을 듣다 + 이어폰을 사다 (*past tense)

   → _____.

3. 저녁에 친구를 만나다 + 숙제를 빨리 끝내다 (*past tense)

   → _____.

4. 감기에 안 걸리다 + 따뜻한 옷을 입다

    → ....

5. 해외 여행을 가다 + 여권을 만들다 (*past tense)

    → ....

6. 일찍 일어나다 + 일찍 자다

    → ....

7. 불고기를 만들다 + 불고기 재료를 사다 (*past tense)

    → ....

8. 김치찌개를 끓이다 + 레시피를 찾다

    → ....

4 Write down your own answers to the following questions, then ask the same questions to your classmates.

1. 산에 자주 가요? 바다에 자주 가요? 왜요?

    ....

2. 한국 영화를 봐요? 왜요?

    ....

3. 왜 한국어 수업을 들어요?

    ....

4. 클럽에 가요? 왜요?

    ....

5. 왜 대학교에 다녀요?

    ....

6. 인터넷 게임을 해요? 왜요?

　　..

5 Fill in the following blanks with the most appropriate word among those suggested.

| 냄비 | 볶으세요 | 매운 | 삶으세요 | 넣으세요 |

―토마토 소스 스파게티 레시피―

　　먼저 토마토 소스를 만드세요. 양파와 토마토를 썰고 프라이팬에 1. .... 그리고 올리브유하고 잘 볶으세요. 그 다음에 2. .... 에 물을 넣고 끓이세요. 그 물에 스파게티를 넣고 3. .... 스파게티를 삶은 다음에 스파게티를 프라이팬에 넣으세요. 스파게티하고 소스를 잘 섞고 조금 4. .... 한번 맛을 보세요. 여러분이 5. .... 음식을 좋아해요? 그러면 소스에 고추도 조금 넣으세요.

말하기

대화 1

Thomas is asking a favor of Bora. 🎧 9.1

토마스: 보라 씨, 부탁이 있어요.

보 라: 네, 토마스 씨. 뭐예요?

토마스: 한국 요리를 할 줄 알아요?

보 라: 네, 한국 요리를 할 줄 알아요.

토마스: 저는 떡볶이를 한번 만들어 보고 싶어요. 가르쳐 줄 수 있어요?

보 라: 네. 제가 가르쳐 줄게요.

💬 Roleplay the dialogue above, changing the favor that Thomas is asking of Bora.

중국어를 하다
↓
중국어를 배우다

케이크를 만들다
↓
브라우니 케이크를 만들다

동영상을 찍다
↓
SNS에 동영상을 올리다

스케이트를 타다
↓
아이스링크장에 가다

💬 대화 2

Jiho asks Shimei why she studies Korean. 🎧 9.2

지　호: 시메이 씨, 무슨 동영상을 보고 있어요?

시메이: 한국어 수업 동영상을 보고 있어요.

지　호: 그런데 시메이 씨는 왜 한국어를 배워요?

시메이: 나중에 한국 회사에 취직하려고 한국어를 배워요.

💬 **Roleplay the dialogue above, changing the reason why Shimei is studying Korean.**

나중에 한국 회사에 취직하다

나중에 한국에 여행을 가다

나중에 한국 드라마를 보다

나중에 웹툰을 번역하다

나중에 한국어 선생님이 되다

듣기

1 Korean university students usually organize a festival (대학교 축제) every year. Students from different student clubs and departments prepare stalls where they can cook food and offer drinks. Look at the stall menu below and the photos of the food. Which kind of food do you think it is? What kind of ingredients do you think you need to cook it?

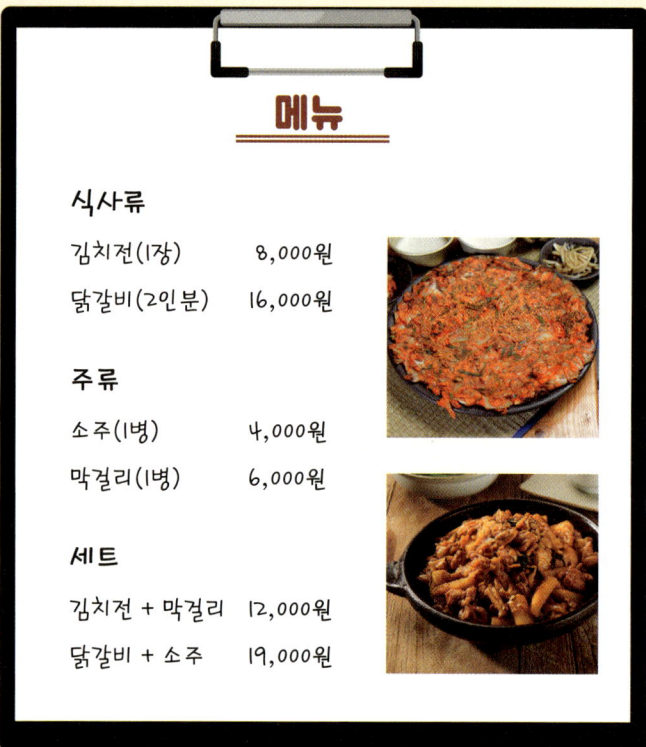

메뉴

식사류
김치전(1장)   8,000원
닭갈비(2인 분)   16,000원

주 류
소주(1병)   4,000원
막걸리(1병)   6,000원

세 트
김치전 + 막걸리 12,000원
닭갈비 + 소주   19,000원

Bora and Thomas want to prepare kimchi pancake and spicy chicken. They are shopping at the supermarket now. Listen to the ingredients, and complete the shopping list. 🎵 9.3

☐ 1. ....
☐ 기름
☐ 파
☐ 3. ....
☐ 고춧가루
☐ 5. ....

☐ 밀가루
☐ 2. ....
☐ 감자
☐ 고추
☐ 4. ....

Mission Accomplished: Korean 2

2 During the university festival week, Bora and Thomas volunteer to cook at the food stall of their student club. They are now at the supermarket to buy the ingredients for their stall. *Which food are they going to sell at their stall?* 🎧 9.4

Listen to the following statements, then tick whether they are true (O) or false (X). 🎧 9.5

1. O   X
2. O   X
3. O   X
4. O   X
5. O   X

3 What do you need to prepare kimchi pancake and spicy chicken? Listen again to the dialogue, then write the ingredients below. 🎧 9.4

김치전 재료	닭갈비 재료

읽기

1 What do you think you need to prepare 떡볶이? Look at the pictures of the ingredients below, then match them with their name.

| 물 | 떡 | 간장 | 설탕 |

| 고추장 | 고춧가루 | 파 |

1.

2.

3.

4. (red pepper powder)

....

5.

6.

7.

....

2 Ms. Kim sometimes posts on her SNS Korean food recipes. *How does she prepare 떡볶이?*

김 선생님 떡볶이 레시피

고등학생 때 떡볶이를 좋아해서 학교 수업이 끝나고 매일 친구와 같이 먹었어요. 학교 앞 식당에서 떡볶이를 먹으려고 항상 학교에서 빨리 나왔어요. 너무 맛이 있어서 지금까지 그 맛을 잊을 수 없어요. 그리고 인터넷에서 아래 떡볶이 레시피를 찾았어요. 오늘 아침에 집에서 떡볶이를 만들려고 장을 보러 갔어요. 이 레시피는 학교 앞 식당 떡볶이 맛과 똑같아서 여러분에게 이 레시피를 알려 드리고 싶어요. 이 레시피는 쉽고 떡볶이를 빨리 만들 수 있어요.

재료
떡볶이 떡: 2컵
물: 2컵
파: 1/2 컵

소스
설탕: 3숟가락
고추장: 1숟가락
고춧가루: 1숟가락
간장: 2숟가락

그럼 지금부터 레시피를 설명해 드릴게요. 먼저 떡을 물에 넣고 30분 동안 기다리세요. 그 다음에 냄비에 이 떡과 새로운 물 2컵과 설탕을 넣고 끓여 주세요. 물이 끓은 다음에 고추장을 넣고 잘 섞어 주세요. 고추장을 잘 섞은 다음에 냄비에 간장을 넣어 주세요. 그리고 고춧가루도 넣고 다시 섞어 주세요. 그 동안 파를 썰고 기다려요. 마지막에 파를 냄비에 넣은 다음에 한 번 더 섞어 주세요. 끝났어요!

참 쉽지요? 여러분도 한번 식당 떡볶이를 집에서 만들어 보세요! 그리고 떡볶이에 다른 재료도 넣을 수 있어요. 저는 항상 계란을 삶은 다음에 떡볶이에 넣어요. 여러분 떡볶이가 너무 매워요? 그러면 치즈를 한번 넣어 보세요. 배가 많이 고파요? 그러면 라면을 넣고 라볶이를 만들어 보세요!

Read the passage above, then tick whether the following statements are true (O) or false (X).

	O	X
1. 이 떡볶이 레시피는 어렵지만 떡볶이는 맛있어요.	O	X
2. 떡볶이 재료는 물, 설탕, 된장, 마늘, 파, 고춧가루예요.	O	X
3. 먼저 떡, 설탕을 물에 넣고 끓여요.	O	X
4. 마지막으로 고춧가루를 넣어요.	O	X
5. 떡볶이에 치즈, 계란, 라면을 넣을 수 있어요.	O	X

3 Look at the following pictures, and put them back in the order indicated by the recipe.

A → .... → .... → .... →
.... → .... → ....

 쓰기

1 What is your favourite food, or a food from your country that you cook particularly well? Think about it, then write a list of the ingredients below.

2 Now write a passage describing why you like this food, how it tastes, and the process to prepare it (its recipe).

문화

Fermented food

Many foods in Korean cuisine are fermented. Fermentation was developed as a method to preserve food for long time, and to make fresh vegetables available during the cold winter months.

Perhaps the most famous Korean fermented food is 김치. There are many types of 김치 made with different vegetables, and there are also countless regional variations. However, the most famous form of 김치 is probably the cabbage kimchi, which is firstly fermented in brine, and then stuffed with other ingredients such as garlic, ginger and crushed red pepper. Many other ingredients, such as preserved seafood, may also be added depending on regional varieties and household recipes.

Fermentation was also used to preserve soy. Fermented soy is the base of two of the most elementary condiments of the Korean cuisine, 된장 and 고추장. 된장 is made by placing fermented soy blocks called 메주 in brine. The result of this process does not only yield 된장, but also soy sauce. 고추장 is made with crushed 메주, then mixed with powdered chilli pepper, cooked glutinous rice, and other ingredients to make a thick and spicy paste.

Small fish, such as anchovies, or seafood, such as small shrimps, are also preserved with salt and used as ingredients for other dishes or as a small side dish. Such preserved seafoods are called 젓갈.

10과
Unit 10

In this unit you will learn

- How to ask and give permission to do something.
- How to say that you do something before doing something else.
- How to make a request for certain services.
- Vocabulary related to public services such as banks, post offices, immigration offices, service centers.
- Vocabulary related to personal pieces of identity.

문법

Asking and expressing permission and approval with −아도/어도 되다.

Meaning

The connective −아도/어도 followed by the verb 되다 is attached to the base of processive and descriptive verbs, 이다 and 아니다 to indicate permission or approval. In English it can be translated as *It is ok to....* It can be used for both asking and giving permission/approval (see examples below).

This expression uses the verb 되다. The basic meaning of this verb is *become, change into, turn into* and therefore it indicates a change of state. However, 되다 is also used in many idiomatic expressions, such as −아/어도 돼요.

Use

−아도 돼요 is attached to the base of processive and descriptive verbs for which the last vowel is ㅏ or ㅗ. −어도 돼요 is attached to the base of the other verbs and descriptive verbs. −여도 돼요 is attached to the base of the verb 하다, and it is further contracted into 해도 돼요.

Verb base containing ㅏ or ㅗ	Verb base containing a vowel which **is not** ㅏ or ㅗ	하다
+ 아도 돼요	+ 어도 돼요	→ 해도 돼요

가다 → 가 +아도 돼요 → 가도 돼요
쓰다 → 쓰 + 어도 돼요 → ㅆ + 어도 돼요 → 써도 돼요
만나다 → 만나 + −아도 돼요 → 만나도 돼요
먹다 → 먹 + 어도 돼요 → 먹어도 돼요
바꾸다 → 바꾸 + 어도 돼요 → 바꿔도 돼요
하다 → 하 +여도 돼요 → 해도 돼요
쓰다 → 쓰 + 어도 돼요 → ㅆ + 어도 돼요 → 써도 돼요
듣다 → 듣 + 어도 돼요 → 들 + 어도 돼요 → 들어도 돼요
모르다 → 모르 + 어도 돼요 → 몰ㄹ + 아도 돼요 → 몰라도 돼요
그렇다 → 그렇 + 어도 돼요 → 그러 + 어도 돼요 → 그래도 돼요

Examples

1. 시메이: 선생님, 저는 오늘 머리가 많이 아파요. Teacher, I feel a bit sick today.
   김 선생님: 그럼 오늘 일찍 집에 **가도 돼요**. You can go home/It's ok to go home.

2. 다니엘: 선생님, 숙제를 내일까지 내야 해요? Teacher, do we have to submit homework by tomorrow?
   김 선생님: 아니요, 다음 주까지 **내도 돼요**. No, it's ok to submit by next week/you can submit by next week.

3. 사라: 팀장님, 오늘 먼저 **퇴근해도 돼요**? Ms. Yerin, can I leave early today?
   이예린 팀장님: 네, 그러세요. Yes, it's ok.

4. 수진: 이거 안 먹어? 내가 **먹어도 돼**? Don't you eat this? Is it ok if I eat it?
   보라: 응, **먹어도 돼**. Yes, it's ok.

5. 지호: 선생님, **질문해도 돼요**? Ms. Kim, is it ok if I ask/can I ask a question?
   김 선생님: 네, 질문하세요. Yes, please ask.

Extra notes

- —어도 돼요 attached to 이다 and 아니다 becomes 이어도 돼요 and 아니어도 돼요. 학생이어도 돼요? *Is it ok even if it's a student?*
- —아/어도 돼요 is not attached to a past tense base.
- With the same meaning, it is also possible to use —아/어도 괜찮아요 as in 집에 가도 괜찮아요? *Is it ok if I go home?*

Doing something before something else, —기 전에

Meaning

The nominal suffix —기 followed by 전에 is attached to the base of processive verbs to connect two sentences indicating that the action expressed in the second sentence happens before the expression indicated in the first sentence. It can be translated into English as *before doing ~*.

Use

—기 전에 is used only together with processive verbs. After dropping the infinitive ending —다, —기 전에 is attached to both vowel-ending and consonant-ending verb bases.

```
가다 → 가 + 기 전에 → 가기 전에
하다 → 하 + 기 전에 → 하기 전에
읽다 → 읽 + 기 전에 → 읽기 전에
먹다 → 먹 + 기 전에 → 먹기 전에
쓰다 → 쓰 + 기 전에 → 쓰기 전에
걷다 → 걷 + 기 전에 → 걷기 전에
살다 → 살 + 기 전에 → 살기 전에
```

Examples

1. 비가 **오기 전에** 빨리 집에 가요. Let's go home before it rains.

2. 시험 **끝나기 전에** 일어나지 마세요. Please don't stand up before the end of the exam.

3. 시메이 씨는 수업에 **가기 전에** 도서관에서 항상 예습을 해요. Shimei always views the material in advance before a class.

4. 지호 씨는 **자기 전에** 샤워를 해요. Jiho has a shower before sleeping.

5. 다니엘 씨는 **운동하기 전에** 스트레칭을 해요. Daniel does some stretching before working out.

6. 보라 씨는 호주에 **가기 전에** 여권을 만들었어요. Bora got her passport before going to Australia.

7. 토마스 씨는 은행이 문을 **닫기 전에** 은행에 가야 해요. Thomas must go to the bank before it closes.

8. 어머니: 약을 먹었어요? Did you take the medicine?
   지호: 아니요. 약을 **먹기 전에** 밥을 먼저 먹으려고 해요. No, I'll eat before taking the medicine.

9. 지호: 시험 기간이라서 도서관에 자리가 없어요. Since it is exam period there are no seats in the library.
   시메이: 보통 저는 도서관에 자리를 잡으려고 도서관이 **문을 열기 전에** 학교에 도착해요. Usually I go to school early before the library opens to get a seat.

Extra notes

- Due to its meaning of *doing something before doing something else*, −기 전에 can only be attached to verbs, and not to descriptive verbs.
- −기 전에 can only be attached to the plain verb base, and not the past or future tense base.
- 전에 can also be used after other nouns, e.g. 시메이 씨는 수업 전에 예습해요 *Shimei views the material in advance before a class*, or 다니엘 씨는 점심 전에 약속이 있었어요 *Daniel had an appointment before lunch*.

 단어

우체국

편지

소포

우표

택배

편지를 쓰다/읽다
편지를 부치다/보내다
편지를 받다
소포를 부치다/보내다
소포를 받다
우표를 붙이다
택배로 보내다/받다
택배를 배달하다

출입국관리사무소

여권

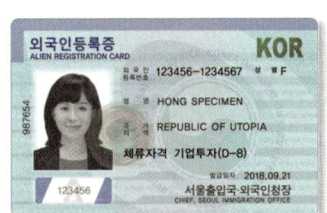
외국인등록증

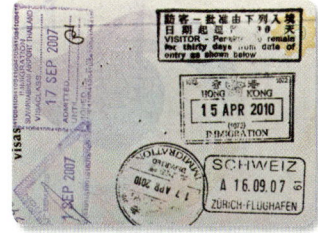
비자

출입국관리사무소

여권을 만들다
외국인등록증을 만들다
비자를 받다
출입국관리사무소를 방문하다

은행

통장

신용/체크카드

현금

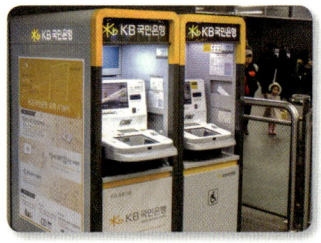
ATM

통장을 만들다
현금을 찾다
은행을 방문하다

지원 센터

지원 센터를 방문하다

지원 센터에 문의하다

지원 센터에서 봉사 활동을 하다

지원 센터를 소개하다

서비스/안내 센터

연습

1 Fill in the following mini-dialogues using the verb suggested in brackets and transforming the verb using -아/어도 돼요 as in the example.

> 보기
> 수진: 이 바지를 <u>입어 봐도 돼요?</u> (입어 보다)
> 직원: 네, 입어 보세요.

1. 토마스: 옷을 좀 _____? (구경하다)

   직원: 네, 천천히 보세요.

2. 시메이: 여기 자리가 있어요? _____? (앉다)

   다니엘: 네. 앉으세요.

3. 다니엘: 여기서 사진을 _____? (찍다)

   박물관 직원: 아니요. 안 돼요.

4. 수진: 일이 있어요. 먼저 _____? (가다)

   보라: 네, 그럼 다음에 봐요.

5. 사라: 팀장님, 저 오늘 몸이 좀 안 좋아서요.

   예린: 그럼 오늘 일찍 _____. (퇴근하다)

6. 토마스: 아저씨, 여기에 차를 _____? (주차하다)

   아저씨: 아니요, 여기는 안 돼요! 저기에 주차 하세요.

10과 209

2 Look at the images, then ask and answer whether you can do the actions represented, as in the example.

보기
1.
2.
3.
4.
5.
6.
7.
8.

| 보기 | 시메이: 여기가 조금 덥네요, 창문을 열어도 돼요? |
| | 지호: 네, 그러세요. |

1. 수진: 여기서 ....?

   보라: 네, 아니요, 안 돼요.

2. 다니엘: 이 물을 ....?

   지호: 네, 그럼요.

3. 사라: 오늘 정말 힘들었어요.

   예린: 그럼 조금 ....

4. 시메이: 자리가 많지 않아요.

   지호: 여기에 ....

5. 시메이: 선생님, 오늘 머리가 아파요.

   선생님: 그럼 집에 _____.

6. 다니엘: 지호 씨, 핸드폰을 좀 _____?

   지호: 네, 여기 있어요.

7. 수진: 이 신발 한번 _____?

   매장 주인: 네, 그러세요.

8. 수진: 맛있겠어요! 조금 _____?

   보라: 네, 여기 젓가락이 있어요.

3 Connect the sentences on the left with the most appropriate sentence on the right, using –기 전에.

1. _____.

2. _____.

3. _____.

4. _____.

5. _____.

6. _____.

4 Write your answers to the following questions, then ask the same questions to your classmates.

1. 졸업하기 전에 뭐 할 거예요?

   _____.

2. 취직하기 전에 뭐 할 거예요?

   _____.

3. 한국에 가기 전에 뭐 할 거예요?

   _____.

4. 유학 가기 전에 뭐 해요?

   _____.

5. 보통 수업 듣기 전에 뭐 해요?

   _____.

6. 약을 먹기 전에 뭐 해야 해요?

   _____.

5 Fill in the blanks of the following sentences with the most appropriate word.

| 부치러 | 현금 | 통장 | 택배 | 외국인등록증 |

1. 토마스 씨는 한국에 도착한 다음에 은행에서 _____를 만들었어요.
   그리고 출입국관리사무소에서 _____도 만들었어요.

2. 수진 씨는 온라인 쇼핑을 했어요. 그래서 지금 _____를
   기다리고 있어요.

3. 다니엘 씨는 소포를 _____ 우체국에 가고 있어요.

4. 보라 씨는 돈이 없어서 ATM에 _____을 찾으러 가요.

말하기

대화 1

Thomas is at the university library and would like to use one of the computers.

🎧 10.1

직 원: 뭐 도와드릴까요?

토마스: 도서관 컴퓨터를 써도 돼요?

직 원: 네, 됩니다. 그런데 컴퓨터를 쓰기 전에 여기에 학생증을 찍으셔야 합니다.

토마스: 아 네, 알겠습니다. 고맙습니다.

💬 Roleplay the dialogue above changing what Thomas is asking the librarian.

- 도서관 컴퓨터를 쓰다
- 책을 빌리다
- 도서관 프린터기를 쓰다
- 여기에 책을 반납하다
- 스터디룸을 예약하다

💬 대화 2

Jiho is asking Sara about the preparation for her upcoming trip to Korea.

지호: 사라 씨, 다음 달에 한국에 가세요?

사라: 네.

지호: 비행기표를 샀어요?

사라: 아니요, 비행기표를 사기 전에 먼저 여권을 만들려고 해요.

지호: 좋은 생각이에요. 그럼 한국에 잘 다녀와요.

사라: 네!

💬 Roleplay the dialogue above changing what Jiho asks Sara.

> 비행기표를 샀어요?

> 따뜻한 옷을 준비했어요?

> 호텔을 예약했어요?

> 하숙집을 구했어요?

> 한국어 학원에 등록했어요?

 듣기

1 Listen to the following sentences, then write the relevant number under the item they are indicating. 🎧 10.3

A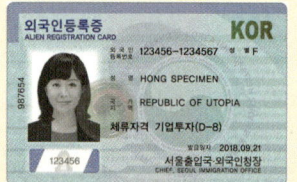

B

C

....

D

E

F

....

2 Thomas is at the bank. *What is he doing there?* 🎧 10.4

Listen again to the dialogue, then tick whether the statements below are correct (O) or wrong (X). 🎧 10.5

1. O   X
2. O   X
3. O   X
4. O   X
5. O   X

3 Listen to the following expressions and decide whether it is more likely to hear them at the bank or at the university library. Then write them down below. 🎧 10.6

은행	대학교 도서관
•	•
•	•
•	•

읽기

1 Read the examples below, and guess the meaning of the words in green.

토마스 한국 생활
- 처음에는 한국 생활이 심심했어요. 왜냐하면 친구가 없었어요.
- 외국인 센터에서 한국 생활 정보를 많이 받았어요.

지원 센터
- 외국인을 위해 한국어 교육 지원 센터가 있어요. 거기서 한국어를 배울 수 있어요.
- 학교 도서관에 디지털 지원 센터가 있어요. 거기서 컴퓨터를 빌릴 수 있어요.

정보
- 토마스 씨는 관광 정보를 받고 싶어서 관광 안내 센터에 문의했어요.
- 요즘 사람들이 인터넷으로 관광 정보를 많이 찾아요.

문화
- 한국 문화에 관심이 있어서 한국어를 배워요.
- 시메이 씨는 한국 전통 문화 중에서 전통 음악에 제일 관심이 많아요.

봉사 활동
- 수진 씨는 주말에 봉사 활동을 해요. 수진 씨는 어린이 병원에서 어린이들과 놀아 줘요.
- 토마스 씨는 봉사 활동으로 한국 할머니와 할아버지들한테 영어를 가르쳐요.

2 Where do you go if you need assistance in Korea? What kind of services does the center below offer? Read the webpage of this center, and answer the questions below.

서울 외국인 지원 센터

서울 외국인 지원 센터가 여러분을 환영합니다. 한국에 오신 다음에 생활이 많이 힘드세요? 그럼 우리 센터를 한번 방문해 보세요. 우리 센터에서는 외국인들에게 한국 생활에 필요한 정보를 알려 드립니다. 우리 센터에서는 한국어와 영어로 안내를 받으실 수 있습니다. 그리고 우리 센터에는 지원 프로그램, 교육 프로그램, 문화 프로그램, 봉사활동 프로그램이 있습니다.

지원 프로그램
- 휴대폰이 필요하세요?
- 은행 통장을 아직 만들지 못하셨어요?
- 아파서 병원에 가셔야 해요?
- 출입국관리사무소에서 외국인등록증을 만드셔야 해요?
- 지하철과 버스 노선이 어려우세요?
- 한국어를 아직 잘 말할 수 없으세요?
- 집을 구하고 계세요?

휴대폰, 은행, 병원 등의 문제가 있어요? 우리 센터에서 도와 드릴 수 있습니다.

교육 프로그램
한국어가 어려우세요? 우리 센터에서는 외국인들이 한국어와 한국 문화를 무료로 배울 수 있습니다.
- 한국어 수업
  - 기간: 10주
  - 레벨: 초급, 중급
  - 장소: 서울 외국인 지원 센터 교실
  - 문의: info@seouljiwon.go.kr

문화 프로그램
- 서울 구경(경복궁, DDP, 북한산)
- 한국 요리 수업(매월 2주차, 4주차 토요일 오전 10시)
- 도서관(영어 책과 잡지, 신문; 한국어 교과서)

봉사 활동

여러분 혹시 봉사 활동을 하고 싶으세요? 우리 센터에서 한국인과 외국인 봉사자를 항상 찾고 있습니다.

- 한국인 봉사자: 한국어 선생님, 문화 프로그램 가이드, 영한 통역/번역.
- 외국인 봉사자: 지원센터 안내, 한영 통역/번역.

문의: volunteering@seouljiwon.go.kr

Together with your classmates, answer the questions below.

1. 서울 외국인 지원 센터는 어떤 곳이에요?

2. 서울 외국인 지원 센터에서 외국인들이 뭐 할 수 있어요?

3. 서울 외국인 지원 센터에서는 어떤 한국어 수업이 있어요?

4. 서울 외국인 지원 센터에 어떤 문화 프로그램이 있어요?

5. 서울 외국인 지원 센터에서 무슨 봉사 활동을 할 수 있어요?

3 **Together with one of your classmates, role play a situation where one of you goes to the centre to ask for information about a program, and the other replies. Then, write down your dialogue.**

지원 센터 직원: 어떻게 오셨어요?

센터 방문자: 프로그램 문의하러 왔어요.

...

...

 쓰기

1 How would you make the following inquiries to the service center introduced above?

1. 한국어 수업 ➡ 언제? 레벨?

2. 도서관 ➡ 무슨 책?

3. 봉사 활동 ➡ 무슨 활동?

2 Write an email to the service center introduced in the reading section, asking for info about Korean classes, cooking classes, and volunteering.

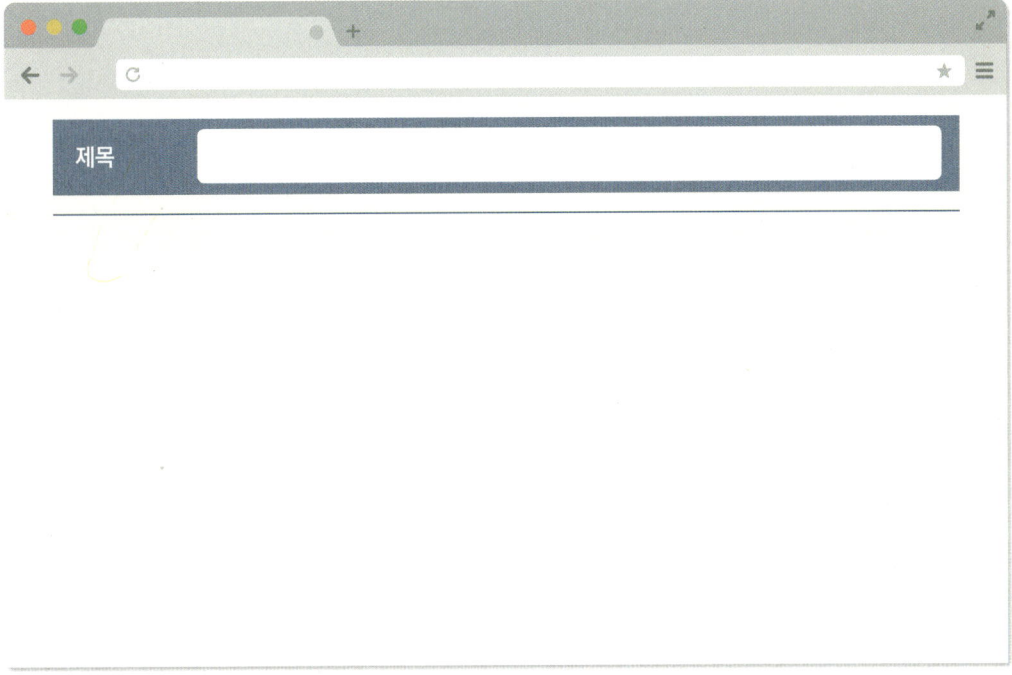

제목

문화

Korean money

The Korean won is available in 1,000 won, 5,000 won, 10,000 won and 50,000 won notes.

이황 (Lee Hwang) a Confucian scholar who lived in the 16th century, is represented on the 1,000 won note. The same note, also shows a plum tree, something 이황 used to love.

이이 (Lee I) is represented on the 5,000 won note. Like Lee Hwang, Lee I too was a Confucian scholar who lived in the 16th century. The black bamboo is also visible on the note, symbolizing the location where Lee I was born.

세종대왕 (King Sejong) is represented on the 10,000 won note. King Sejong, who lived in the 15th century, is remembered not only for the creation of 한글, but also for many other innovations. For example, he introduced several administrative reforms, developed astronomical instruments, directed the compilation of historical accounts, and invented a system to transcribe music which is still used today in classical Korean music. The 10,000 note also shows one of the astronomical instruments invented by the king, alongside a picture of the five peaks and the moon, which was used as a background to the throne by the kings of the Choseon dynasty.

신사임당 is represented on the 50,000 won note. 신사임당, a painter, is the mother of Lee I, making Korea unique in having both a mother and son represented on national banknotes. The 50,000 won is the most recent banknote, being introduced in 2009.

There are voices criticizing who is represented on the national notes. While nobody argues against the importance of King Sejong, many people point out that thousands of years of Korean history should not be represented by figures who lived across only a few centuries. Some critics argue that confucianism is over-represented. Others, were against the choice of 신사임당 for the 50,000 won note, arguing that other female characters would have been more representative. Finally, there are complaints that figures symbolizing the Independence movement are not included.

Table of conjugations

Category	Dictionary form	–습니다/ㅂ니다	–겠–	–아/어야 해요	–(으)ㄹ 수 있어요
regular	받다	받습니다	받겠어요	받아야 해요	받을 수 있어요
regular	보다	봅니다	보겠어요	봐야 해요	볼 수 있어요
regular	가다	갑니다	가겠어요	가야 해요	갈 수 있어요
regular	읽다	읽습니다	읽겠어요	읽어야 해요	읽을 수 있어요
regular	배우다	배웁니다	배우겠어요	배워야 해요	배울 수 있어요
regular	가르치다	가르칩니다	가르치겠어요	가르쳐야 해요	가르칠 수 있어요
ㄷ불규칙	듣다	듣습니다	듣겠어요	들어야 해요	들을 수 있어요
ㅡ불규칙	크다	큽니다	크겠어요	커야 해요	클 수 있어요
ㅡ불규칙	끄다	끕니다	끄겠어요	꺼야 해요	끌 수 있어요
ㄹ불규칙	만들다	만듭니다	만들겠어요	만들어야 해요	만들 수 있어요
ㄹ불규칙	멀다	멉니다	멀겠어요	멀어야 해요	멀 수 있어요
르 불규칙	고르다	고릅니다	고르겠어요	골라야 해요	고를 수 있어요
르 불규칙	빠르다	빠릅니다	빠르겠어요	빨라야 해요	빠를 수 있어요
ㅂ 불규칙	맵다	맵습니다	맵겠어요	매워야 해요	매울 수 있어요
ㅂ 불규칙	돕다	돕습니다	돕겠어요	도와야 해요	도울 수 있어요
ㅅ 불규칙	낫다	낫습니다	낫겠어요	나아야 해요	나을 수 있어요

ㄷ 불규칙 → The last consonant ㄷ of the base changes into ㄹ when a suffix beginning with a vowel is attached, e.g., 듣다.

ㅡ 불규칙 → ㅡ of the verb base is dropped when a suffix beginning with -어 (such as -어요, -었어요) is attached, e.g., 바쁘다.

ㄹ 불규칙 → ㄹ of the verb base is dropped when a suffix beginning with ㄴ, ㅂ, ㅅ, ㅇ is attached, e.g., 만들다.

-(으)세요	-지 마세요	-(으)ㄹ래요	-아/어 주다/보다	-고 있다	-거나
받으세요	받지 마세요	받을래요	받아 보다	받고 있어요	받거나
보세요	보지 마세요	볼래요	/	보고 있어요	보거나
가세요	가지 마세요	갈래요	가 보다	가고 있어요	가거나
읽으세요	읽지 마세요	읽을래요	읽어 보다	읽고 있어요	읽거나
배우세요	배우지 마세요	배울래요	배워 보다	배우고 있어요	배우거나
가르치세요	가르치지 마세요	가르칠래요	가르쳐 보다	가르치고 있어요	가르치거나
들으세요	듣지 마세요	들을래요	들어 보다	듣고 있어요	듣거나
크세요	/	/	/	/	크거나
끄세요	끄지 마세요	끌래요	꺼 보다	끄고 있어요	끄거나
만드세요	만들지 마세요	만들래요	만들어 보다	만들고 있어요	만들거나
머세요	/	/	/	/	멀가나
고르세요	고르지 마세요	고를래요	골라 보다	고르고 있어요	고르거나
빠르세요	/	/	/	/	빠르거나
매우세요	/	/	/	/	맵거나
도우세요	돕지 마세요	도울래요	도와 보다	돕고 있어요	돕거나
나으세요	/	/	/	/	낫거나

르 불규칙 → The verb base drops ㅡ and doubles ㄹ when an ending beginning with a vowel is attached, e.g., 모르다.

ㅂ 불규칙 → ㅂ changes into 우 when suffix beginning with a vowel is attached, e.g., 맵다.

ㅅ 불규칙 → The last consonant ㅅ of the base is dropped when a suffix beginning with a vowel is attached, e.g., 낫다.

Table of conjugations

Category	Dictionary form	-(으)려고	-(으)ㄹ게요	-(으)ㄴ 다음에
regular	받다	받으려고	받을게요	받은 다음에
regular	보다	보려고	볼게요	본 다음에
regular	가다	가려고	갈게요	간 다음에
regular	읽다	읽으려고	읽을게요	읽은 다음에
regular	배우다	배우려고	배울게요	배운 다음에
regular	가르치다	가르치려고	가르칠게요	가르친 다음에
ㄷ불규칙	듣다	들으려고	들을게요	들은 다음에
ㅡ불규칙	크다	/	/	/
ㅡ불규칙	끄다	끄려고	끌게요	끈 다음에
ㄹ불규칙	만들다	만들려고	만들게요	만든 다음에
ㄹ불규칙	멀다	/	/	/
르 불규칙	고르다	고르려고	고를게요	고른 다음에
르 불규칙	빠르다	/	/	/
ㅂ 불규칙	맵다	/	/	/
ㅂ 불규칙	돕다	도우려고	도울게요	도운 다음에
ㅅ 불규칙	낫다	/	/	/

−아/어서	−(으)러	−(으)ㄹ 줄 알아요	−기 전에	−아/어도 돼요
받아서	받으러	받을 줄 알아요	받기 전에	받아도 돼요
봐서	보러	볼 줄 알아요	보기 전에	봐도 돼요
가서	/	갈 줄 알아요	가기 전에	가도 돼요
읽어서	읽으러	읽을 줄 알아요	읽기 전에	읽어도 돼요
배워서	배우러	배울 줄 알아요	배우기 전에	배워도 돼요
가르쳐서	가르치러	가르칠 줄 알아요	가르치기 전에	가르쳐도 돼요
들어서	들으러	들을 줄 알아요	듣기 전에	들어도 돼요
커서	/	/	/	커도 돼요
꺼서	끄러	끌 줄 알아요	끄기 전에	꺼도 돼요
만들어서	만들러	만들 줄 알아요	만들기 전에	만들어도 돼요
멀어서	/	/	/	/
골라서	고르러	고를 줄 알아요	고르기 전에	골라도 돼요
빨라서	/	/	/	/
매워서	/	/	/	/
도와서	도우러	도울 줄 알아요	돕기 전에	도와도 돼요
나아서	/	/	/	/

Korean–English vocabulary list

Korean	English	Unit
A/S 센터	service center	2
가게	shop (noun, place)	4
가격	price	4
가구	furniture	3
가깝다	be near	2
가끔	sometimes	4
가다	go	1
가방	bag	1
가수	singer	1
가을	autumn	1
가전	electric appliances	3
가져가다	bring	7
간식	snack	1
간장	soy sauce	9
갈비	rib (pork or beef, Korean dish)	6
갈아타다	transfer (verb)	7
감기	cold, flu	8
같다	be the same	1
거리	distance	3
거실	living room	3
걱정하다	be worried	7
건강	health	5
걷다	walk (verb)	4
걸리다	take (time)	1
걸리다	catch (a cold, flu)	8
검은색	black	4
겨울	winter	1
결석하다	absent (verb)	2
결혼하다	marry (verb)	6
경치	view, panorama	1
계란	egg	9
계산하다	calculate/prepare the bill	4
계시다	be (somewhere, honorific)	2
계절	season	1
계획	plan	7
고기	meat	9
고등학교	high school	2
고르다	choice (verb), pick up, select	4
고장 나다	be broken	2
고추	chilli pepper	9
고추장	chilli paste	9
고춧가루	chilli powder	9
고치다	fix, repair	4
공부하다	study (verb)	1
공짜	free of charge	4
과목	subject (university course)	6
과일	fruit	9
관광	tourism	10
관심	interest	6
광고	advertisement	5
괜찮다	be fine, be ok	1
교과서	textbook	2
교실	classroom	2
교통	traffic	7
교통 카드	traffic card	7
교환 학생	exchange student	2
구경하다	browse	3
구두	shoes (formal)	4
구하다	find, look for, search for	3
구하다(직원을)	recruit (people)	5
구하다(직장을)	find (a job), get an employment	5
구하다(집을)	find (a house, a place to stay)	3
국수	noodles	5
굽다	roast	9
귀	ear	8
규칙	rule, regulation	3
그냥	just, simply, as it is	7
그릇	bowl	9
그만두다	quit (verb)	5
근처	near, nearby	1
금방	soon	8
기다리다	wait	3
기대하다	expect	10
기분	mood	1
기쁘다	be happy, glad	1
기숙사	dormitory	3
기억하다	remember	6
기온	temperature	1
기차	train	1
김밥	gimpap	2
김치	kimchi	1
김치찌개	kimchi stew	3
깎다	peel (verb)	9

Korean	English	Unit
깨끗하다	be clean	3
꼭	surely, certainly	2
끓다	boil (ramyon, soup etc.)	9
끝나다	finish (intransitive verb)	7
나가다	exit, go out	3
날씨	weather	1
남편	husband	6
낫다	be better	8
낮	day (as opposed to night)	1
내과	internal medicine clinic	8
내다	pay	3
내리다	come down, fall (rain, snow)	1
내리다	get off	7
내일	tomorrow	2
냄비	pot	9
냉장고	fridge	3
넓다	be wide, be spacious	3
넣다	put, put in	9
노란색	yellow	4
노래	song	2
놀다	hang out	2
농구	basketball	6
높다	be high	1
누나	older sister (of a male person)	6
누르다	press	10
눈	snow	1
눈	eye	8
눈물	tear	8
늦다	be late	2
다니다	go, attend	2
다리	leg	8
다이어트	diet	7
다치다	get hurt	8
단어	word, vocab	2
닫다	close	7
달다	be sweet	9
닭갈비	spicy stir-fried chicken	6
닮다	be similar, look like (person)	6
담배	cigarette	3
당근	carrot	9
대리(님)	deputy head of section (usually a young worker)	5

Korean	English	Unit
대학교	university	1
대학원	graduate school	2
댁	house (honorific)	5
더럽다	be dirty	3
덥다	be hot	1
도서관	library	1
도착하다	arrive	7
돌리다(세탁기를)	run the laundry	3
돌아가다	go back	1
돕다	help (verb)	2
동료	colleague	5
동생	younger brother/sister	6
동영상	video	4
돼지고기	pork	9
된장	fermented bean paste	9
된장찌개	soup made with fermented bean paste	9
두껍다	be thick	6
드라마	drama	1
드리다	give (honorific)	5
듣다	listen	1
들어가다	enter, go in, get in	3
등산하다	go hiking	1
디자인	design	4
따뜻하다	be warm	1
딱딱하다	be hard	8
딸	daughter	6
떡볶이	rice cake with spicy sauce	2
떨어지다	fail (an exam)/fall down	2
똑똑하다	be smart	6
라면	ramyon	3
마늘	garlic	9
마스크	mask	3
마시다	drink	1
마음에 들다	like, catch one's fancy	3
막걸리	alcoholic beverage made with fermented rice	4
막차 시간	time of the last train/subway	7
막히다	be jammed	7
만나다	meet	3
만들다	make	1
많다	be many	1

Korean–English vocabulary list

Korean	English	Unit
말씀하다	speak (honorific)	5
말하기 시험	speaking exam	2
말하다	speak, say	2
맑다	be clean (sky)	1
맛	taste	9
맛있다	be delicious	1
맞다(주사를)	get a jab	8
매일	every day	2
맥주	beer	1
맵다	be spicy	2, 9
머리	head	2
먼저	firstly, first of all	4
멀다	be far	2
멋있다	be cool, nice	4
모르다	not know	3
모임	gathering	3
모자	cap, hat	1
목	neck/throat	8
몸	body	8
무겁다	be heavy	1
무료	free of charge	4
무섭다	be scary	1
무슨	which	2
무역	commerce	5
문	door	10
문서	document	5
문의하다	enquire	3
문자	text message	7
문제	problem	8
문화	culture	10
묻다	ask	4
뭐	what	1
미디어학	Media studies	2
미술관	art gallery	3
미안하다	be sorry	2
바꾸다	change	5
바닷가	seaside	5
바람	wind	1
바로	now, straight away	3
바쁘다	be busy	1
바이올린	violin	7
바지	pants	4

Korean	English	Unit
받다	receive	1
발	foot	8
발표	presentation	2
밝다	be bright	3
밥	rice (cooked)	9
방문하다	visit (verb)	6, 10
방학	vacation	1, 3
방향	direction	7
배	stomach, belly, abdomen	8
배	pear	8
배고프다	be hungry	3
배달하다	deliver (verb)	10
배터리	battery	8
백화점	department store	4
버리다	throw away	3
버스	bus	3
번역	translation	5
벗다	take off (clothes)	4
변기	toilet	3
병	bottle	2
병원	hospital	2
보고서	report	5
보내다	send/spend	1
보다	see/watch/look	1
보라색	purple	4
복습하다	review (verb)	2
복잡하다	be complicated/be jammed (traffic)	7
볶다	stir-fry	9
봄	spring	1
봉사활동	volunteering activity	10
부동산	real estate	3
부르다	sing (a song)	2
부모님	parents	6
부부	married couple	6
부엌	kitchen (house kitchen)	3
부인	wife (somebody else's)	6
부장(님)	head of section (on the workplace)	5
부지런하다	be diligent, hard working	6
부치다	send	10
부탁(이 있다)	favour	9

Korean	English	Unit
불	light/fire	10
불꽃놀이	fireworks	7
불다	blow (verb)	1
붕어빵	pancake filled in with sweet bean paste	6
붙이다	attach	10
비	rain	1
비밀번호	PIN number	10
비싸다	be expensive	1
비자	visa	2
비행기	airplane	2
빈대떡	mung-bean pancake	4
빌리다	borrow	2
빙수	shaved ice	3
빠르다	be quick, be fast	1
빨간색	red	4
빵	bread	4
사과	apple	9
사다	buy	1
사무실	office	5
사용하다	use (verb)	10
사이즈	size	4
사이트	website	5
사인하다	sign (verb)	10
사장(님)	boss	5
사진	photo	2
사탕	candy	8
산	mountain	1
살다	live	3
삶다	boil (egg, spaghetti etc.)	9
삼겹살	pork belly	6
새	new	3
새롭다	be new	4
색깔	color	4
생각	thought	5
생각하다	think	5
생강차	ginger tea	5
생일	birthday	3
샤워하다	have a shower	5
섞다	mix (verb)	9
선글라스	sunglasses	4
선물	present	1, 6

Korean	English	Unit
선생님	teacher	1
설명하다	explain	4
설탕	sugar	9
세우다	stop (verb, a mean of transportation)	7
세탁기	laundry machine	3
셔츠	shirt	4
소개하다	introduce, present (verb)	10
소고기	beef	9
소금	salt	9
소주	soju (spirit)	3
소파	sofa	3
소포	parcel	10
소화제	digestive medicine	8
손	hand	8
손님	guest	6
수고가 많다	thank you for your efforts (idiomatic)	5
수업	class	1
수영하다	swim (verb)	1
숙제	homework	2
숟가락	spoon	9
쉬다	rest (verb)	3
스케이트	skate	1
스키	ski	1
스트레칭	stretching	8
시계	watch, clock	1
시끄럽다	be noisy	3
시다	be sour	9
시원하다	be cool	1
시작하다	start (verb)	1
시장	market	4
시험	exam	1
식사	meal	1
식탁	dining table	3
신나다	be excited	1
신다	wear (shoes or socks)	4
신문	newspaper	5
신발	shoes	1
신용카드	credit card	10
신호등	traffic light	7
심리학	Psychology	2

Korean–English vocabulary list

Korean	English	Unit
심심하다	be bored	1
쌀	rice (uncooked)	9
쌀쌀하다	be chilly	1
썰다	slice (verb)	9
쓰다	wear (hat, cap)	4
쓰다	be bitter	9
쓰다	use (verb)	10
쓰레기	trash	3
쓰레기통	trash bin	3
씻다	wash	5
아내	wife (one's own)	6
아들	son	6
아름답다	be beautiful, pretty	1
아마도	perhaps, maybe	1
아버지	father	6
아시아학	Asian Studies	2
아이	child	6
아침	morning	1
아파트	apartment	3
아프다	be sick, be unwell	2
안과	ophtalmology clinic	8
안내	guide	1
앉다	sit (verb)	3
알	pill, capsule	8
알다	know	3
알람시계	alarm clock	9
야근하다	work until late	5
야식	night snack	8
야채	vegetable	9
약	medicine	8
약속	appointment, promise	1
양말	socks	4
양파	onion	9
어깨	shoulders	8
어둡다	be dark	3
어렵다	be difficult	1
어린이	children, kid	10
어머니	mother	1, 6
어울리다	match, fit nice/get along well	4
어제	yesterday	1
언니	older sister (of a female person)	6

Korean	English	Unit
언어	language	1
언어학	Linguistics	2
에어컨	air conditioning	1
여권	passport	10
여름	summer	1
여행	travel	1
연락하다	contact (verb)	7
연세	age (honorific)	6
열	fever	8
열다	open	7
열쇠	key	3
열심히	diligently, hard	6
영화	film	1
예매하다	book (a ticket), make a reservation (verb)	9
예습하다	prepare (view in advance)	2
예약하다	book, make a reservation (verb)	10
오늘	today	1
오다	come	1
오랜만	after a long time	1
오빠	older brother (of a female person)	6
오후	afternoon	5
온라인	online	5
올리다	upload/rise	5
옷	clothes	1
옷장	wardrobe	3
와인	wine	6
외국인등록증	alien registration card	10
외우다	memorize	2
요리	cuisine	1
요즘	recently	1
우리	we, our	1
우산	umbrella	3
우체국	post office	10
우표	stamp	10
운동하다	exercise (sport, verb)	2
운동화	training shoes	4
운전하다	drive	7
원피스	dress	4
월세	rent (monthly)	3
웹툰	webtoon	5

Korean	English	Unit	Korean	English	Unit
유럽	Europe	10	정류장	bus stop	7
유명하다	be famous	1	정말	really	1
유행	trend, vogue, popular	4	정보	information	10
은행	bank	10	정장	suit	4
음식	food	2	정치학	Political Sciences	2
음악	music	1	정형외과	orthopedic clinic	8
응급실	ER	8	조심하다	be careful	3
의사	doctor	8	조용하다	be quite	3
의학	medicine (specialization)	2	졸업하다	graduate (verb)	2
이력서	CV	5	좁다	be narrow	3
이사하다	move (verb, moving house)	3	좋다	be good	1
이야기	story	5	죄송하다	be sorry	2
이어폰	earphone	3	주문하다	order (verb)	7
이틀	two days	8	주사	jab, injection	8
인기(가 있다)	be popular	4	죽	congee	8
일	work	1	준비물	things, material to prepare	1
일기예보	weather forecast	1	준비하다	prepare	1
일어나다	wake up, stand up	2	중간시험	mid-term exam	2
일찍	early	5	중국	China	2
읽다	read	2	중학교	middle school	2
입	mouth	8	지각하다	be late	2
입다	wear	4	지금	now	1
입원하다	get admitted to hospital	8	지난주	last week	1
잊다	forget	3	지원	support	10
자다	sleep (verb)	2	지하철	subway	1
자리	seat	4	직원	employee	5
자몽	grapefruit	9	직장	workplace	5
작다	be small	2	질문	question	2
작성	draft (a document)	5	집	house, home	1
잠깐	for a moment	6	집들이	housewarming party	6
장소	place	1	짜다	be salty	9
재료	ingredients	9	짜장면	noodles with black bean paste sauce	3
재미있다	be funny, interesting	1	짬뽕	noodles with spicy seafood soup	3
저녁	evening	1	찍다	take (a photo)	2
전공	major	2	찜질방	sauna	7
전통 음악	traditional music	10	차다	wear (watch, bracelet)	4
전화번호	phone number	3	착하다	be good, nice (person)	6
전화하다	call (by phone)	2	참가비	participation fee	1
절대	absolutely, never (+negative verb)	3	참기름	sesame oil	9
접시	dish	9	참석하다	participate (in an event, meeting)	5
젓가락	chopsticks	9			

Korean	English	Unit
창문	window	3
찾다	find, search, look for	1
책	book	5
천천히	slowly	4
첫차 시간	time of the first train/subway	7
청소하다	clean (verb)	2
체육관	gymnasium	8
체크카드	debit card	10
초대하다	invite	2
초등학교	primary school	2
초록색	green	4
추다	dance	6
추천하다	suggest	1
축구	soccer	6
출근하다	go to work	1
출발하다	leave (verb)	7
출석하다	present (at an event, verb)	2
출입국관리사무소	immigration office	10
출장	business trip	5
춥다	be cold	1
치과	dentist clinic	8
치다	play (a chord instrument)	4
치마	skirt	4
치즈	cheese	9
치킨	fried chicken	4
친구	friend	1
친절하다	be kind	5
침대	bed	3
침실	bedroom	3
커피	coffee	2
케이크	cake	1
코	nose	8
콘서트	concert	1
콧물	running nose	8
퀴즈	quiz	2
크다	be big	1
타자	typing	9
태권도	taekwondo	1
택배	express delivery	10
택시	taxi	7
텔레비전	TV	1
토요일	Saturday	1

Korean	English	Unit
통장	bank passbook	10
퇴근하다	go home from work	5
튀기다	fry	9
틀다	turn on	7
티셔츠	t-shirt	4
티켓	ticket	2
파란색	blue	4
파일	file	2
팔	arm	8
팔다	sell	4
편의점	convenience store	7
편지	letter	10
편하다	be comfortable	1
풀다	solve (a quiz, a problem)	8
프라이팬	frypan	9
피곤하다	be tired	1
피시방	internet/game café	8
피아노	piano	2
피우다	smoke (verb)	3
필요하다	be necessary	1
하늘	sky	1
하루종일	all day	2
하숙집	boarding house	2
학교	school	1
학생	student	1
학생증	student ID card	10
학원	academy	2
한국	Korea	1
한국어	Korean language	1
한국학	Korean Studies	2
한복	traditional Korean dress	4
한옥	traditional Korean house	3
한의원	traditional medicine clinic	8
한자	Chinese character	9
할머니	grandmother	6
할아버지	grandfather	6
할인	discount	4
합격하다	pass (an exam, verb)	2
핫도그	battered fried sausage	6
핸드폰	mobile phone	2
허리	low back	8
현금	cash	10

Korean	English	Unit
형	older brother (of a male person)	6
형제	siblings	6
호주	Australia	1
혹시	perhaps	4
혼자	alone	5
홍삼	red ginseng	8
화장실	toilet (room)	3
회사	company	1
회색	grey	4
회원	member	1
회의	meeting	5
회장	president (of an association)	1
휴가	leave (worker vacation)	5
휴지	toilet paper, paper tissue	3
흐리다	be cloudy	1
흰색	white	4
힘들다	be hard, difficult, fatiguing	1

Korean–English vocabulary list (by unit)

Korean	English	Unit
1과		
가다	go	1
가방	bag	1
가수	singer	1
가을	autumn	1
간식	snack	1
같다	be the same	1
걸리다	take (time)	1
겨울	winter	1
경치	view, panorama	1
계절	season	1
공부하다	study (verb)	1
괜찮다	be fine, be ok	1
근처	near, nearby	1
기분	mood	1
기쁘다	be happy, glad	1
기온	temperature	1
기차	train	1
김치	kimchi	1
날씨	weather	1
낮	day (as opposed to night)	1
내리다	come down, fall (rain, snow)	1
높다	be high	1
눈	snow	1
대학교	university	1
덥다	be hot	1
도서관	library	1
돌아가다	go back	1
드라마	drama	1
듣다	listen	1
등산하다	go hiking	1
따뜻하다	be warm	1
마시다	drink	1
만들다	make	1
많다	be many	1
맑다	be clean (sky)	1
맛있다	be delicious	1
맥주	beer	1
모자	cap	1
무겁다	be heavy	1
무섭다	be scary	1
뭐	what	1
바람	wind	1
바쁘다	be busy	1
받다	receive	1
방학	vacation	1
백화점	department store	1
보내다	send/spend	1
보다	see/watch/look	1
봄	spring	1
불다	blow (verb)	1
비	rain	1
비싸다	be expensive	1
빠르다	be quick, be fast	1
사다	buy	1
산	mountain	1
선물	present	1
선생님	teacher	1
수업	class	1
수영하다	swim (verb)	1
스케이트	skate	1
스키	ski	1
시계	watch, clock	1
시원하다	be cool	1
시작하다	start (verb)	1
시험	exam	1
식사	meal	1
신나다	be excited	1
신발	shoes	1
심심하다	be bored	1
쌀쌀하다	be chilly	1
아름답다	be beautiful, pretty	1
아마도	perhaps, maybe	1
아침	morning	1
안내	guide	1
약속	appointment, promise	1
어렵다	be difficult	1
어머니	mother	1
어제	yesterday	1
언어	language	1
에어컨	air conditioning	1
여름	summer	1
여행	travel	1

Korean	English	Unit
영화	film	1
오늘	today	1
오다	come	1
오랜만	after a long time	1
옷	clothes	1
요리	cuisine	1
요즘	recently	1
우리	we, our	1
유명하다	be famous	1
음악	music	1
일	work	1
일기예보	weather forecast	1
장소	place	1
재미있다	be funny, interesting	1
저녁	evening	1
정말	really	1
좋다	be good	1
준비물	things, material to prepare	1
준비하다	prepare	1
지금	now	1
지난주	last week	1
지하철	subway	1
집	house, home	1
참가비	participation fee	1
찾다	find, search, look for	1
추천하다	suggest	1
출근하다	go to work	1
춥다	be cold	1
친구	friend	1
케이크	cake	1
콘서트	concert	1
크다	be big	1
태권도	taekwondo	1
텔레비전	TV	1
토요일	Saturday	1
편하다	be comfortable	1
피곤하다	be tired	1
필요하다	be necessary	1
하늘	sky	1
학교	school	1
학생	student	1
한국	Korea	1

Korean	English	Unit
한국어	Korean language	1
호주	Australia	1
회사	company	1
회원	member	1
회장	president (of an association)	1
흐리다	be cloudy	1
힘들다	be hard, difficult, fatiguing	1

2과

Korean	English	Unit
A/S 센터	service center	2
가깝다	be near	2
결석하다	absent (verb)	2
계시다	be (somewhere, honorific)	2
고등학교	high school	2
고장 나다	be broken	2
교과서	textbook	2
교실	classroom	2
교환 학생	exchange student	2
김밥	gimpap	2
꼭	surely, certainly	2
내일	tomorrow	2
노래	song	2
놀다	hang out	2
늦다	be late	2
다니다	go, attend	2
단어	word, vocab	2
대학원	graduate school	2
돕다	help (verb)	2
떡볶이	rice cake with spicy sauce	2
떨어지다	fail (an exam)/fall down	2
말하기 시험	speaking exam	2
말하다	speak, say	2
매일	every day	2
맵다	be spicy	2
머리	head	2
멀다	be far	2
무슨	which	2
미디어학	Media studies	2
미안하다	be sorry	2
발표	presentation	2
병	bottle	2

Korean-English vocabulary list (by unit)

Korean	English	Unit
병원	hospital	2
복습하다	review (verb)	2
부르다	sing (a song)	2
비자	visa	2
비행기	airplane	2
빌리다	borrow	2
사진	photo	2
숙제	homework	2
심리학	Psychology	2
아시아학	Asian Studies	2
아프다	be sick, be unwell	2
언어학	Linguistics	2
예습하다	prepare (view in advance)	2
외우다	memorize	2
운동하다	exercise (sport, verb)	2
음식	food	2
의학	medicine (specialization)	2
일어나다	wake up, stand up	2
읽다	read	2
자다	sleep (verb)	2
작다	be small	2
전공	major	2
전화하다	call (by phone)	2
정치학	Political Sciences	2
졸업하다	graduate (verb)	2
죄송하다	be sorry	2
중간시험	mid-term exam	2
중국	China	2
중학교	middle school	2
지각하다	be late	2
질문	question	2
찍다	take (a photo)	2
청소하다	clean (verb)	2
초대하다	invite	2
초등학교	primary school	2
출석하다	present (at an event, verb)	2
커피	coffee	2
퀴즈	quiz	2
티켓	ticket	2
파일	file	2
피아노	piano	2
하루종일	all day	2

Korean	English	Unit
하숙집	boarding house	2
학원	academy	2
한국학	Korean Studies	2
합격하다	pass (an exam, verb)	2
핸드폰	mobile phone	2

3과

가구	furniture	3
가전	electric appliances	3
거리	distance	3
거실	living room	3
구경하다	browse	3
구하다	find, look for, search for	3
구하다(집을)	find (a house, a place to stay)	3
규칙	rule, regulation	3
기다리다	wait	3
기숙사	dormitory	3
김치찌개	kimchi stew	3
깨끗하다	be clean	3
나가다	exit, go out	3
내다	pay	3
냉장고	fridge	3
넓다	be wide, be spacious	3
담배	cigarette	3
더럽다	be dirty	3
돌리다(세탁기를)	run the laundry	3
들어가다	enter, go in, get in	3
라면	ramyon	3
마스크	mask	3
마음에 들다	like, catch one's fancy	3
만나다	meet	3
모르다	not know	3
모임	gathering	3
문의하다	enquire	3
미술관	art gallery	3
바로	now, straight away	3
밝다	be bright	3
방학	vacation (school vacation)	3
버리다	throw away	3
버스	bus	3
배고프다	be hungry	3

Korean	English	Unit
변기	toilet	3
부동산	real estate	3
부엌	kitchen (house kitchen)	3
빙수	shaved ice	3
살다	live	3
새	new	3
생일	birthday	3
세탁기	laundry machine	3
소주	soju (spirit)	3
소파	sofa	3
쉬다	rest (verb)	3
시끄럽다	be noisy	3
식탁	dining table	3
쓰레기	trash	3
쓰레기통	trash bin	3
아파트	apartment	3
앉다	sit (verb)	3
알다	know	3
어둡다	be dark	3
열쇠	key	3
옷장	wardrobe	3
우산	umbrella	3
월세	rent (monthly)	3
이사하다	move (verb, moving house)	3
이어폰	earphone	3
잊다	forget	3
전화번호	phone number	3
절대	absolutely, never (+negative verb)	3
조심하다	be careful	3
조용하다	be quite	3
좁다	be narrow	3
짜장면	noodles with black bean paste sauce	3
짬뽕	noodles with spicy seafood soup	3
창문	window	3
침대	bed	3
침실	bedroom	3
피우다	smoke (verb)	3
한옥	traditional Korean house	3
화장실	toilet (room)	3
휴지	toilet paper, paper tissue	3

Korean	English	Unit
4과		
가게	shop (noun, place)	4
가격	price	4
가끔	sometimes	4
걷다	walk (verb)	4
검은색	black	4
계산하다	calculate/prepare the bill	4
고르다	choice (verb), pick up, select	4
고치다	fix, repair	4
공짜	free of charge	4
구두	shoes (formal)	4
노란색	yellow	4
동영상	video	4
디자인	design	4
막걸리	alcoholic beverage made with fermented rice	4
먼저	firstly, first of all	4
멋있다	be cool, nice	4
무료	free of charge	4
묻다	ask	4
바지	pants	4
벗다	take off (clothes)	4
보라색	purple	4
빈대떡	mung-bean pancake	4
빨간색	red	4
빵	bread	4
사이즈	size	4
새롭다	be new	4
색깔	color	4
선글라스	sunglasses	4
설명하다	explain	4
셔츠	shirt	4
시장	market	4
신다	wear (shoes or socks)	4
쓰다	wear (hat, cap)	4
양말	socks	4
어울리다	match, fit nice/get along well	4
운동화	training shoes	4
원피스	dress	4
유행	trend, vogue, popular	4
인기(가 있다)	be popular	4
입다	wear	4

Korean	English	Unit
자리	seat	4
정장	suit	4
차다	wear (watch, bracelet)	4
천천히	slowly	4
초록색	green	4
치다	play (a chord instrument)	4
치마	skirt	4
치킨	fried chicken	4
티셔츠	t-shirt	4
파란색	blue	4
팔다	sell	4
한복	traditional Korean dress	4
할인	discount	4
혹시	perhaps	4
회색	grey	4
흰색	white	4

5과

Korean	English	Unit
건강	health	5
광고	advertisement	5
구하다(직원을)	recruit (people)	5
구하다(직장을)	find (a job), get an employment	5
국수	noodles	5
그만두다	quit (verb)	5
대리(님)	deputy head of section (usually a young worker)	5
댁	house (honorific)	5
동료	colleague	5
드리다	give (honorific)	5
말씀하다	speak (honorific)	5
무역	commerce	5
문서	document	5
바꾸다	change	5
바닷가	seaside	5
번역	translation	5
보고서	report	5
부장(님)	head of section (on the workplace)	5
사무실	office	5
사이트	website	5
사장(님)	boss	5

Korean	English	Unit
생각	thought	5
생각하다	think	5
생강차	ginger tea	5
샤워하다	have a shower	5
수고가 많다	thank you for your efforts (idiomatic)	5
신문	newspaper	5
씻다	wash	5
야근하다	work until late	5
오후	afternoon	5
온라인	online	5
올리다	upload/rise	5
웹툰	webtoon	5
이력서	CV	5
이야기	story	5
일찍	early	5
작성	draft (a document)	5
직원	employee	5
직장	workplace	5
참석하다	participate (in an event, meeting)	5
책	book	5
출장	business trip	5
친절하다	be kind	5
퇴근하다	go home from work	5
혼자	alone	5
회의	meeting	5
휴가	leave	5

6과

Korean	English	Unit
갈비	rib (pork or beef, Korean dish)	6
결혼하다	marry (verb)	6
과목	subject (university course)	6
관심	interest	6
기억하다	remember	6
남편	husband	6
농구	basketball	6
누나	older sister (of a male person)	6
닭갈비	spicy stir-fried chicken	6
닮다	be similar, look like (person)	6
동생	younger brother/sister	6
두껍다	be thick	6

Korean	English	Unit
딸	daughter	6
똑똑하다	be smart	6
방문하다	visit (verb)	6
부모님	parents	6
부부	married couple	6
부인	wife (somebody else's)	6
부지런하다	be diligent, hard working	6
붕어빵	pancake filled in with sweet bean paste	6
삼겹살	pork belly	6
선물	present	6
손님	guest	6
아내	wife (one's own)	6
아들	son	6
아버지	father	6
아이	child	6
어머니	mother	6
언니	older sister (of a female person)	6
연세	age (honorific)	6
열심히	diligently, hard	6
오빠	older brother (of a female person)	6
와인	wine	6
잠깐	for a moment	6
집들이	housewarming party	6
착하다	be good, nice (person)	6
추다	dance	6
축구	soccer	6
할머니	grandmother	6
할아버지	grandfather	6
핫도그	battered fried sausage	6
형	older brother (of a male person)	6
형제	siblings	6

7과

Korean	English	Unit
가져가다	bring	7
갈아타다	transfer (verb)	7
걱정하다	be worried	7
계획	plan	7
교통	traffic	7
교통 카드	traffic card	7
그냥	just, simply, as it is	7
끝나다	finish (intransitive verb)	7
내리다	get off	7
다이어트	diet	7
닫다	close	7
도착하다	arrive	7
막차 시간	time of the last train/subway	7
막히다	be jammed	7
문자	text message	7
바이올린	violin	7
방향	direction	7
복잡하다	be complicated/be jammed (traffic)	7
불꽃놀이	fireworks	7
세우다	stop (verb, a mean of transportation)	7
신호등	traffic light	7
연락하다	contact (verb)	7
열다	open	7
운전하다	drive	7
정류장	bus stop	7
주문하다	order (verb)	7
찜질방	sauna	7
첫차 시간	time of the first train/subway	7
출발하다	leave (verb)	7
택시	taxi	7
틀다	turn on	7
편의점	convenience store	7

8과

Korean	English	Unit
감기	cold, flu	8
걸리다	catch (a cold, flu)	8
귀	ear	8
금방	soon	8
낫다	be better	8
내과	internal medicine clinic	8
눈	eye	8
눈물	tear	8
다리	leg	8
다치다	get hurt	8
딱딱하다	be hard	8
맞다(주사를)	get a jab	8

Korean-English vocabulary list (by unit)

Korean	English	Unit
목	neck/throat	8
몸	body	8
문제	problem	8
발	foot	8
배	stomach, belly, abdomen	8
배	pear	8
배터리	battery	8
사탕	candy	8
소화제	digestive medicine	8
손	hand	8
스트레칭	stretching	8
안과	ophtalmology clinic	8
알	pill, capsule	8
야식	night snack	8
약	medicine	8
어깨	shoulders	8
열	fever	8
응급실	ER	8
의사	doctor	8
이틀	two days	8
입	mouth	8
입원하다	get admitted to hospital	8
정형외과	orthopedic clinic	8
주사	jab	8
죽	congee	8
체육관	gymnasium	8
치과	dentist clinic	8
코	nose	8
콧물	running nose	8
팔	arm	8
풀다	solve (a quiz, a problem)	8
피시방	internet/game café	8
한의원	traditional medicine clinic	8
허리	low back	8
홍삼	red ginseng	8

9과

Korean	English	Unit
간장	soy sauce	9
계란	egg	9
고기	meat	9
고추	chilli pepper	9

Korean	English	Unit
고추장	chilli paste	9
고춧가루	chilli powder	9
과일	fruit	9
굽다	roast	9
그릇	bowl	9
깎다	peel (verb)	9
끓다	boil (ramyon, soup etc.)	9
냄비	pot	9
넣다	put, put in	9
달다	be sweet	9
당근	carrot	9
돼지고기	pork	9
된장	fermented bean paste	9
된장찌개	soup made with fermented bean paste	9
마늘	garlic	9
맛	taste	9
맵다	be spicy	9
밥	rice (cooked)	9
볶다	stir-fry	9
부탁(이 있다)	favour	9
사과	apple	9
삶다	boil (egg, spaghetti etc.)	9
섞다	mix (verb)	9
설탕	sugar	9
소고기	beef	9
소금	salt	9
숟가락	spoon	9
시다	be sour	9
쌀	rice (uncooked)	9
썰다	slice (verb)	9
쓰다	be bitter	9
알람시계	alarm clock	9
야채	vegetable	9
양파	onion	9
예매하다	book (a ticket), make a reservation (verb)	9
자몽	grapefruit	9
재료	ingredients	9
접시	dish	9
젓가락	chopsticks	9
짜다	be salty	9

Korean	English	Unit
참기름	sesame oil	9
치즈	cheese	9
타자	typing	9
튀기다	fry	9
프라이팬	frypan	9
한자	Chinese character	9

Korean	English	Unit
학생증	student ID card	10
현금	cash	10

10과

Korean	English	Unit
관광	tourism	10
기대하다	expect	10
누르다	press	10
문	door	10
문화	culture	10
배달하다	deliver (verb)	10
봉사활동	volunteering activity	10
부치다	send	10
불	light/fire	10
붙이다	attach	10
비밀번호	PIN number	10
사용하다	use (verb)	10
사인하다	sign (verb)	10
소개하다	introduce, present (verb)	10
소포	parcel	10
신용카드	credit card	10
쓰다	use (verb)	10
어린이	children, kid	10
여권	passport	10
예약하다	book, make a reservation (verb)	10
외국인등록증	alien registration card	10
우체국	post office	10
우표	stamp	10
유럽	Europe	10
은행	bank	10
전통 음악	traditional music	10
정보	information	10
지원	support	10
체크카드	debit card	10
출입국관리사무소	immigration office	10
택배	express delivery	10
통장	bank passbook	10
편지	letter	10

English–Korean vocabulary list

English	Korean	Unit
absent (verb)	결석하다	2
absolutely, never (+negative verb)	절대	3
academy	학원	2
advertisement	광고	5
after a long time	오랜만	1
afternoon	오후	5
age (honorific)	연세	6
air conditioning	에어컨	1
airplane	비행기	2
alcoholic beverage made with fermented rice	막걸리	4
alien registration card	외국인등록증	10
all day	하루종일	2
alarm clock	알람시계	9
alone	혼자	5
apartment	아파트	3
apple	사과	9
appointment, promise	약속	1
arm	팔	8
arrive	도착하다	7
art gallery	미술관	3
Asian Studies	아시아학	2
ask	묻다	4
attach	붙이다	10
Australia	호주	1
autumn	가을	1
bag	가방	1
bank	은행	10
bank passbook	통장	10
basketball	농구	6
battered fried sausage	핫도그	6
battery	배터리	8
be (somewhere, honorific)	계시다	2
be beautiful, pretty	아름답다	1
be better	낫다	8
be big	크다	1
be bitter	쓰다	9
be bored	심심하다	1
be bright	밝다	3
be broken	고장 나다	2
be busy	바쁘다	1
be careful	조심하다	3

English	Korean	Unit
be chilly	쌀쌀하다	1
be clean	깨끗하다	3
be clean (sky)	맑다	1
be cloudy	흐리다	1
be cold	춥다	1
be comfortable	편하다	1
be complicated/be jammed (traffic)	복잡하다	7
be cool	시원하다	1
be cool, nice	멋있다	4
be dark	어둡다	3
be delicious	맛있다	1
be difficult	어렵다	1
be diligent, hard working	부지런하다	6
be dirty	더럽다	3
be excited	신나다	1
be expensive	비싸다	1
be famous	유명하다	1
be far	멀다	2
be fine, be ok	괜찮다	1
be funny, interesting	재미있다	1
be good	좋다	1
be good, nice (person)	착하다	6
be happy, glad	기쁘다	1
be hard	딱딱하다	8
be hard, difficult, fatiguing	힘들다	1
be heavy	무겁다	1
be high	높다	1
be hot	덥다	1
be hungry	배고프다	3
be jammed	막히다	7
be kind	친절하다	5
be late	지각하다	2
be late	늦다	2
be many	많다	1
be narrow	좁다	3
be near	가깝다	2
be necessary	필요하다	1
be new	새롭다	4
be noisy	시끄럽다	3
be popular	인기(가 있다)	4
be quick, be fast	빠르다	1

English	Korean	Unit
be quite	조용하다	3
be salty	짜다	9
be scary	무섭다	1
be sick, be unwell	아프다	2
be similar, look like (person)	닮다	6
be small	작다	2
be smart	똑똑하다	6
be sorry	미안하다	2
be sorry	죄송하다	2
be sour	시다	9
be spicy	맵다	2, 9
be sweet	달다	9
be the same	같다	1
be thick	두껍다	6
be tired	피곤하다	1
be warm	따뜻하다	1
be wide, be spacious	넓다	3
be worried	걱정하다	7
bed	침대	3
bedroom	침실	3
beef	소고기	9
beer	맥주	1
birthday	생일	3
black	검은색	4
blow (verb)	불다	1
blue	파란색	4
boarding house	하숙집	2
body	몸	8
boil (egg, spaghetti etc.)	삶다	9
boil (ramyon, soup etc.)	끓다	9
book	책	5
book (a ticket), make a reservation (verb)	예매하다	9
book, make a reservation (verb)	예약하다	10
borrow	빌리다	2
boss	사장(님)	5
bottle	병	2
bowl	그릇	9
bread	빵	4
bring	가져가다	7
browse	구경하다	3

English	Korean	Unit
bus	버스	3
bus stop	정류장	7
business trip	출장	5
buy	사다	1
cake	케이크	1
calculate/prepare the bill	계산하다	4
call (by phone)	전화하다	2
candy	사탕	8
cap	모자	1
carrot	당근	9
cash	현금	10
catch (a cold, flu)	걸리다	8
change	바꾸다	5
cheese	치즈	9
child	아이	6
children, kid	어린이	10
chilli paste	고추장	9
chilli pepper	고추	9
chilli powder	고춧가루	9
China	중국	2
Chinese character	한자	9
choice (verb), pick up, select	고르다	4
chopsticks	젓가락	9
cigarette	담배	3
class	수업	1
classroom	교실	2
clean (verb)	청소하다	2
close	닫다	7
clothes	옷	1
coffee	커피	2
cold, flu	감기	8
colleague	동료	5
color	색깔	4
come	오다	1
come down, fall (rain, snow)	내리다	1
commerce	무역	5
company	회사	1
concert	콘서트	1
congee	죽	8
contact (verb)	연락하다	7
convenience store	편의점	7
credit card	신용카드	10

English–Korean vocabulary list 245

English	Korean	Unit	English	Korean	Unit
cuisine	요리	1	exam	시험	1
culture	문화	10	exchange student	교환 학생	2
CV	이력서	5	exercise (sport, verb)	운동하다	2
dance	추다	6	exit, go out	나가다	3
daughter	딸	6	expect	기대하다	10
day (as opposed to night)	낮	1	explain	설명하다	4
debit card	체크카드	10	express delivery	택배	10
deliver (verb)	배달하다	10	eye	눈	8
dentist clinic	치과	8	fail (an exam)/fall down	떨어지다	2
department store	백화점	1	father	아버지	6
deputy head of section (usually a young worker)	대리(님)	5	favour	부탁(이 있다)	9
design	디자인	4	fermented bean paste	된장	9
diet	다이어트	7	fever	열	8
digestive medicine	소화제	8	file	파일	2
diligently, hard	열심히	6	film	영화	1
dining table	식탁	3	find (a house, a place to stay)	구하다(집을)	3
direction	방향	7	find (a job), get an employment	구하다(직장을)	5
discount	할인	4	find, look for, search for	구하다	3
dish	접시	9	find, search, look for	찾다	1
distance	거리	3	finish (intransitive verb)	끝나다	7
doctor	의사	8	fireworks	불꽃놀이	7
document	문서	5	firstly, first of all	먼저	4
door	문	10	fix, repair	고치다	4
dormitory	기숙사	3	food	음식	2
draft (a document)	작성	5	foot	발	8
drama	드라마	1	for a moment	잠깐	6
dress	원피스	4	forget	잊다	3
drink	마시다	1	free of charge	무료	4
drive	운전하다	7	free of charge	공짜	4
ear	귀	8	fridge	냉장고	3
early	일찍	5	fried chicken	치킨	4
earphone	이어폰	3	friend	친구	1
egg	계란	9	fruit	과일	9
electric appliances	가전	3	fry	튀기다	9
employee	직원	5	frypan	프라이팬	9
enquire	문의하다	3	furniture	가구	3
enter, go in, get in	들어가다	3	garlic	마늘	9
ER	응급실	8	gathering	모임	3
Europe	유럽	10	get a jab	맞다(주사를)	8
evening	저녁	1	get admitted to hospital	입원하다	8
every day	매일	2	get hurt	다치다	8

English	Korean	Unit	English	Korean	Unit
get off	내리다	7	invite	초대하다	2
gimpap	김밥	2	jab	주사	8
ginger tea	생강차	5	just, simply, as it is	그냥	7
give (honorific)	드리다	5	key	열쇠	3
go	가다	1	kimchi	김치	1
go back	돌아가다	1	kimchi stew	김치찌개	3
go hiking	등산하다	1	kitchen (house kitchen)	부엌	3
go home from work	퇴근하다	5	know	알다	3
go to work	출근하다	1	Korea	한국	1
go, attend	다니다	2	Korean language	한국어	1
graduate (verb)	졸업하다	2	Korean Studies	한국학	2
graduate school	대학원	2	language	언어	1
grandfather	할아버지	6	last week	지난주	1
grandmother	할머니	6	laundry machine	세탁기	3
grapefruit	자몽	9	leave	휴가	5
green	초록색	4	leave (verb)	출발하다	7
grey	회색	4	leg	다리	8
guest	손님	6	letter	편지	10
guide	안내	1	library	도서관	1
gymnasium	체육관	8	light/fire	불	10
hand	손	8	like, catch one's fancy	마음에 들다	3
hang out	놀다	2	Linguistics	언어학	2
have a shower	샤워하다	5	listen	듣다	1
head	머리	2	live	살다	3
head of section (on the workplace)	부장(님)	5	living room	거실	3
health	건강	5	low back	허리	8
help (verb)	돕다	2	major	전공	2
high school	고등학교	2	make	만들다	1
homework	숙제	2	market	시장	4
hospital	병원	2	married couple	부부	6
house (honorific)	댁	5	marry (verb)	결혼하다	6
house, home	집	1	mask	마스크	3
housewarming party	집들이	6	match, fit nice/get along well	어울리다	4
husband	남편	6	meal	식사	1
immigration office	출입국관리사무소	10	meat	고기	9
information	정보	10	Media studies	미디어학	2
ingredients	재료	9	medicine	약	8
interest	관심	6	medicine (specialization)	의학	2
internal medicine clinic	내과	8	meet	만나다	3
internet/game café	피시방	8	meeting	회의	5
introduce, present (verb)	소개하다	10	member	회원	1
			memorize	외우다	2

English–Korean vocabulary list

English	Korean	Unit
middle school	중학교	2
mid-term exam	중간시험	2
mix (verb)	섞다	9
mobile phone	핸드폰	2
mood	기분	1
morning	아침	1
mother	어머니	1, 6
mountain	산	1
mouth	입	8
move (verb, moving house)	이사하다	3
mung-bean pancake	빈대떡	4
music	음악	1
near, nearby	근처	1
neck/throat	목	8
new	새	3
newspaper	신문	5
night snack	야식	8
noodles	국수	5
noodles with black bean paste sauce	짜장면	3
noodles with spicy seafood soup	짬뽕	3
nose	코	8
not know	모르다	3
now	지금	1
office	사무실	5
ophtalmology clinic	안과	8
older brother (of a female person)	오빠	6
older brother (of a male person)	형	6
older sister (of a female person)	언니	6
older sister (of a male person)	누나	6
onion	양파	9
online	온라인	5
open	열다	7
order (verb)	주문하다	7
orthopedic clinic	정형외과	8
pancake filled in with sweet bean paste	붕어빵	6
pants	바지	4
parcel	소포	10
parents	부모님	6

English	Korean	Unit
participate (in an event, meeting)	참석하다	5
participation fee	참가비	1
pass (an exam, verb)	합격하다	2
passport	여권	10
pay	내다	3
peel (verb)	깎다	9
pear	배	8
perhaps	혹시	4
perhaps, maybe	아마도	1
phone number	전화번호	3
photo	사진	2
piano	피아노	2
pill, capsule	알	8
PIN number	비밀번호	10
place	장소	1
plan	계획	7
play (a chord instrument)	치다	4
Political Sciences	정치학	2
pork	돼지고기	9
pork belly	삼겹살	6
post office	우체국	10
pot	냄비	9
prepare	준비하다	1
prepare (view in advance)	예습하다	2
prepare (things, material to)	준비물 (noun)	1
present	선물	1, 6
present (at an event, verb)	출석하다	2
presentation	발표	2
president (of an association)	회장	1
press	누르다	10
price	가격	4
primary school	초등학교	2
problem	문제	8
Psychology	심리학	2
purple	보라색	4
put, put in	넣다	9
question	질문	2
quit (verb)	그만두다	5
quiz	퀴즈	2
rain	비	1
ramyon	라면	3

English	Korean	Unit	English	Korean	Unit
read	읽다	2	sing (a song)	부르다	2
real estate	부동산	3	singer	가수	1
really	정말	1	sit (verb)	앉다	3
receive	받다	1	size	사이즈	4
recently	요즘	1	skate	스케이트	1
recruit (people)	구하다(직원을)	5	ski	스키	1
red	빨간색	4	skirt	치마	4
red ginseng	홍삼	8	sky	하늘	1
remember	기억하다	6	sleep (verb)	자다	2
rent (monthly)	월세	3	slice (verb)	썰다	9
report	보고서	5	slowly	천천히	4
rest (verb)	쉬다	3	smoke (verb)	피우다	3
review (verb)	복습하다	2	snack	간식	1
rib (pork or beef, Korean dish)	갈비	6	snow	눈	1
rice (cooked)	밥	9	soccer	축구	6
rice (uncooked)	쌀	9	socks	양말	4
rice cake with spicy sauce	떡볶이	2	sofa	소파	3
roast	굽다	9	soju (spirit)	소주	3
rule, regulation	규칙	3	solve (a quiz, a problem)	풀다	8
run the laundry	돌리다(세탁기를)	3	sometimes	가끔	4
running nose	콧물	8	son	아들	6
salt	소금	9	song	노래	2
Saturday	토요일	1	soon	금방	8
sauna	찜질방	7	soup made with fermented bean paste	된장찌개	9
school	학교	1	soy sauce	간장	9
seaside	바닷가	5	speak (honorific)	말씀하다	5
season	계절	1	speak, say	말하다	2
seat	자리	4	speaking exam	말하기 시험	2
see/watch/look	보다	1	spicy stir-fried chicken	닭갈비	6
sell	팔다	4	spoon	숟가락	9
send	부치다	10	spring	봄	1
send/spend	보내다	1	stamp	우표	10
service center	A/S 센터	2	start (verb)	시작하다	1
sesame oil	참기름	9	stir-fry	볶다	9
shaved ice	빙수	3	stomach, belly, abdomen	배	8
shirt	셔츠	4	stop (verb, a mean of transportation)	세우다	7
shoes	신발	1	story	이야기	5
shoes (formal)	구두	4	now, straight away	바로	3
shop (noun, place)	가게	4	stretching	스트레칭	8
shoulders	어깨	8	student	학생	1
siblings	형제	6			
sign (verb)	사인하다	10			

English–Korean vocabulary list

English	Korean	Unit
student ID card	학생증	10
study (verb)	공부하다	1
subject (university course)	과목	6
subway	지하철	1
sugar	설탕	9
suggest	추천하다	1
suit	정장	4
summer	여름	1
sunglasses	선글라스	4
support	지원	10
surely, certainly	꼭	2
swim (verb)	수영하다	1
taekwondo	태권도	1
take (a photo)	찍다	2
take (time)	걸리다	1
take off (clothes)	벗다	4
taste	맛	9
taxi	택시	7
teacher	선생님	1
tear	눈물	8
temperature	기온	1
text message	문자	7
textbook	교과서	2
thank you for your efforts (idiomatic)	수고가 많다	5
think	생각하다	5
thought	생각	5
throw away	버리다	3
ticket	티켓	2
time of the first train/subway	첫차 시간	7
time of the last train/subway	막차 시간	7
today	오늘	1
toilet	변기	3
toilet (room)	화장실	3
toilet paper, paper tissue	휴지	3
tomorrow	내일	2
tourism	관광	10
traditional Korean dress	한복	4
traditional Korean house	한옥	3
traditional medicine clinic	한의원	8
traditional music	전통 음악	10
traffic	교통	7

English	Korean	Unit
traffic card	교통 카드	7
traffic light	신호등	7
train	기차	1
training shoes	운동화	4
transfer (verb)	갈아타다	7
translation	번역	5
trash	쓰레기	3
trash bin	쓰레기통	3
travel	여행	1
trend, vogue, popular	유행	4
t-shirt	티셔츠	4
turn on	틀다	7
TV	텔레비전	1
two days	이틀	8
typing	타자	9
umbrella	우산	3
university	대학교	1
upload/rise	올리다	5
use (verb)	쓰다	10
use (verb)	사용하다	10
vacation	방학	1, 3
vegetable	야채	9
video	동영상	4
view, panorama	경치	1
violin	바이올린	7
visa	비자	2
visit (verb)	방문하다	6, 10
volunteering activity	봉사활동	10
wait	기다리다	3
wake up	일어나다	2
walk (verb)	걷다	4
wardrobe	옷장	3
wash	씻다	5
watch, clock	시계	1
we, our	우리	1
wear	입다	4
wear (hat, cap)	쓰다	4
wear (shoes or socks)	신다	4
wear (watch, bracelet)	차다	4
weather	날씨	1
weather forecast	일기예보	1
website	사이트	5

English	Korean	Unit
webtoon	웹툰	5
what	뭐	1
which	무슨	2
white	흰색	4
wife (one's own)	아내	6
wife (somebody else's)	부인	6
wind	바람	1
window	창문	3
wine	와인	6
winter	겨울	1
word	단어	2
work (noun)	일	1
work until late	야근하다	5
workplace	직장	5
yellow	노란색	4
yesterday	어제	1
younger brother/sister	동생	6

Listening transcripts

1과

🎧 1.3

안녕하세요? 김현미입니다.
올해 겨울은 아주 춥습니다. 오늘 기온은 서울 영하 2도로 어제와 기온이 같습니다. 부산은 4도, 광주와 제주도는 8도입니다.
다음은 내일 전국 일기예보입니다.
서울은 낮부터 바람이 불겠습니다. 오후부터는 눈이 내리겠습니다. 그렇지만 많이 내리지는 않겠습니다.
부산은 하늘이 맑겠습니다. 날씨가 쌀쌀하겠습니다.
광주도 하늘이 맑겠습니다.
제주도는 오전에는 비가 내리겠습니다. 오후부터는 바람이 불겠습니다.
지금까지 날씨였습니다.

🎧 1.4

1. 오늘 서울 기온은 어제와 같습니다.
2. 오늘 제주도 기온은 8도입니다.
3. 내일 서울에는 비가 내리겠습니다.
4. 내일 광주와 부산은 비가 내리겠습니다.
5. 내일 제주도는 하늘이 맑겠습니다.

2과

🎧 2.3

1. 이 책으로 학생들이 한국어를 공부해요.
2. 이것을 몰라요. 그래서 사전을 찾아요.
3. 이것은 말하기 시험이에요.
4. 수업 후에 집에서 다시 공부해요.
5. 다니엘 씨는 오늘 한국어 수업에 갔어요.

🎧 2.4

여러분 안녕하세요? 저는 김현미입니다. 만나서 반갑습니다. 이번 학기에 저와 함께 한국어를 공부할 겁니다.
먼저 이것은 우리 교과서입니다. 수업에 교과서가 꼭 있어야 합니다.
그리고 선생님이 매주 출석을 부를 거예요. 그래서 여러분이 꼭 수업에 와야 합니다.
시험은 중간시험과 기말시험이 있습니다. 그리고 기말 인터뷰 시험도 있습니다.
이번 학기에 새로운 단어가 많습니다. 그래서 공부가 조금 어려울 수 있습니다. 그런데 여러분은 잘 할 수 있을 겁니다.
혹시 질문이 있으세요?
...
네 시메이 씨, 질문이 뭐예요?

🎧 2.5

1. 수업에 교과서는 필요하지 않습니다.
2. 선생님이 매주 출석을 부를 겁니다.
3. 기말시험이 있지만 기말 인터뷰 시험은 없습니다.
4. 이번 학기에 새로운 단어가 많지 않습니다.
5. 이번 학기 공부가 어렵지 않을 겁니다.

3과

🎧 3.3

1. 학교에서 멀어요.
2. 넓은 집이에요.
3. 냉장고와 세탁기가 있어요.
4. 에어컨이 없어요.
5. 침대가 있어요.
6. 집을 보고 싶어요? 그러면 부동산에 전화하세요.

🎧 3.4

아저씨: 어서 오세요.
토마스: 저...방을 찾고 있어요. 혹시 방이 있어요?
아저씨: 기차역 근처에 방 하나가 있어요.
토마스: 음...기차역은 학교에서 너무 멀어요.
보라: 맞아요, 토마스 씨. 거기로 이사하지 마세요.
   아저씨, 학교 근처에는 방이 없어요?
아저씨: 학교 근처에도 방 하나가 있어요. 8층이에요. 아주 밝아요. 그리고 방이 깨끗해요.

Mission Accomplished: Korean 2

보라: 월세는 얼마예요?
아저씨: 60만원이에요.
토마스: 저는 깨끗한 방이 마음에 들어요. 그 집에는 냉장고하고 세탁기도 있어요?
아저씨: 네, 냉장고와 세탁기가 있어요. 그런데 침대는 없어요.
토마스: 네, 알겠습니다. 학교 근처 방으로 이사할래요. 혹시 지금 방을 볼 수 있어요?
아저씨: 네, 그럼요. 바로 볼 수 있어요.

4과

4.3

1. 한번 구경할 수 있어요?
2. 다른 색을 보여 주세요.
3. 이 치마는 인기가 많아요. 한번 입어 보세요.
4. 이 바지는 4만 원이에요.
5. 죄송합니다. 미디엄 사이즈는 없어요.
6. 조금 비싸요. 할인해 줄 수 있어요?
7. 카드로 계산해 주세요.

4.4

점원: 어서 오세요!
수진: 옷 좀 구경할 수 있어요?
점원: 네, 천천히 보세요.
수진: 음...이 흰 치마가 너무 예뻐요.
점원: 이 치마는 요즘 인기가 많아요. 한번 입어 보세요.
수진: 네. 그럼 미디엄 사이즈로 주세요.
점원: 죄송합니다 고객님. 미디엄 사이즈는 없어요. 지금 라지 사이즈밖에 없어요.
수진: 그래요? 저는 라지 사이즈는 안 맞아요.
점원: 검은색은 미디엄 사이즈가 있어요.
수진: 괜찮습니다. 고맙습니다.
...
점원: 어서 오세요!
수진: 혹시 편한 구두 있어요?
점원: 네, 이 구두는 어때요? 요즘 이 디자인이 유행이에요.
수진: 신어 볼 수 있어요?
점원: 네, 신어 보세요.
수진: 정말 편하네요. 색깔도 마음에 들어요. 얼마예요?
점원: 20만원이에요.
수진: 좀 비싸네요. 혹시 할인 해 줄 수 있어요?
점원: 죄송합니다, 고객님. 새로운 디자인이에요. 그래서 할인 해 드릴 수 없어요.
수진: 네, 알겠습니다. 그럼 계산해 주세요.

4.5

1. 수진 씨는 옷 가게와 신발 가게에 갔어요.
2. 수진 씨는 치마가 마음에 들었어요.
3. 수진 씨 치마 사이즈가 없어요.
4. 수진 씨는 치마를 샀어요.
5. 수진 씨는 구두 색깔이 마음에 들지 않았어요.
6. 구두 가격이 2만 원이에요.
7. 수진 씨는 구두를 샀어요.

5과

5.3

1. 제가 작년부터 이 회사에서 번역 일을 시작했어요.
2. 직원들이 다 같이 회의를 했어요.
3. 요즘 사람들은 온라인으로 신문을 읽거나 뉴스를 많이 봐요.
4. 좋은 아이디어예요. 여러분은 어떻게 생각하세요?
5. 버스나 지하철에서 핸드폰을 사용하지 마세요.
6. 회사들이 온라인으로 광고를 많이 해요.

5.4

사라: 팀장님, 사람들이 모두 도착했습니다.
예린: 네. 알겠습니다. 그럼 지금부터 회의를 시작하겠습니다. 우리 회사 제품을 광고해야 해요. 어떻게 할까요? 김 대리님부터 말씀해

주세요.
김 대리: 아, 네. 요즘 사람들이 신문을 많이 읽지
　　　　　 않습니다. 그래서 SNS를 사용해야 합니다.
예린: 네, 좋습니다. 사라 씨는 어떻게 생각하세요?
사라: 저도 그렇게 생각합니다. 호주에서 많은
　　　회사들이 SNS에 광고를 합니다.
예린: 네, 알겠습니다. 김 대리와 사라 씨의 생각이
　　　마음에 듭니다. 다른 분들은 또 다른 생각
　　　있으십니까?
다른 직원: 없습니다.
예린: 그럼 김 대리와 사라 씨는 다음 주까지
　　　보고서를 저에게 보내 주세요. 다음 주
　　　회의에서 뵙겠습니다. 고맙습니다.

🎧 **5.5**

1. 요즘 회사들은 신문에 광고를 많이 합니다.
2. 김 대리님과 사라 씨는 생각이 다릅니다.
3. 예린 팀장님이 사라 씨의 생각을 좋아합니다.
4. 다음 주까지 사라 씨는 보고서를 써야 합니다.
5. 다음 주에는 회의가 없을 겁니다.

6과

🎧 **6.3**

1. 수진 씨 오빠는 뭐 하세요?
2. 보라 씨는 형제가 있어요?
3. 보라 씨, 어머니는 어떤 분이세요?
4. 집들이에 무슨 선물을 가져가야 해요?
5. 사라 씨 아버지께서는 무슨 일을 하세요?

🎧 **6.4**

보라: 토마스 씨, 우리 오빠가 지난달에 결혼했어요.
　　　그래서 주말에 집들이를 할 거예요. 우리 오빠
　　　집들이에 같이 갈래요?
토마스: 네, 좋아요! 보라 씨 오빠는 어떤 분이세요?
보라: 우리 오빠는 착하고 부지런해요. 지금 큰
　　　회사에서 열심히 일을 하고 있어요.
토마스: 오빠 부인은요?

보라: 새언니는 아주 예뻐요. 새언니는 대학교에서
　　　외국인 학생들한테 한국어를 가르치고 있어요.
토마스: 그런데 보라 씨, 집들이에 선물도 가져가야
　　　해요?
보라: 네, 보통 사람들이 휴지를 많이 선물해요. 비싼
　　　선물보다 집주인한테 필요한 선물을 해요.
토마스: 휴지요? 좋은 아이디어예요. 휴지는 꼭
　　　필요해요. 보라 씨, 혹시 오빠는 술을
　　　좋아하세요?
보라: 네, 우리 오빠는 술을 잘 마셔요. 왜요?
토마스: 선물로 휴지하고 와인을 가져가고 싶어요.
　　　보통 호주에서는 손님이 선물로 와인을
　　　가져가요.

🎧 **6.5**

1. 보라 씨는 지난달에 결혼했어요.
2. 보라 씨 오빠는 집들이를 할 거예요.
3. 보라 씨 오빠 부인은 한국어 선생님이에요.
4. 토마스 씨는 선물로 휴지만 가져갈 거예요.
5. 보라 씨 오빠는 술을 잘 안 마셔요.

7과

🎧 **7.3**

서울 여름 밤 날씨가 더워요. 그래서 여름에
한강공원은 인기가 많아요. 사람들이 여기에서 많이
만나요. 친구와 함께 이야기하고 놀아요. 그리고
술도 마시고 맛있는 음식을 먹어요. 공원에서
치킨도 주문할 수 있어요.
　여름에 한강공원에서는 불꽃놀이를 해요. 이때
많은 사람들이 불꽃놀이를 보려고 해요. 그래서
한강공원 근처 교통이 좀 복잡해요. 한강공원에
한번 가고 싶으세요? 그럼 고려대학교에서 지하철
6호선을 타고 5호선으로 갈아타세요. 그럼
여의도역에 갈 수 있어요.

🎧 7.4

수진: 토마스 씨, 토요일에 한강공원에서 보라 씨하고 불꽃놀이를 보려고 해요. 같이 갈래요?
토마스: 불꽃놀이요? 좋아요. 그런데 한강공원에 어떻게 가요? 저는 잘 몰라요.
보라: 고려대학교에서 6호선을 타세요. 그리고 공덕역에서 5호선으로 갈아타세요. 그다음에 여의도역에서 내리세요. 50분쯤 걸려요.
토마스: 와, 오래 걸려요. 버스는 없어요?
수진: 버스는 지하철보다 더 오래 걸려요. 그리고 버스는 좀 더 복잡해요.
토마스: 알겠어요. 지하철을 탈게요. 그리고 제가 카메라를 가져갈게요. 멋있는 사진을 찍어줄게요.
보라: 그럼 저는 맥주를 살게요.
수진: 저는 도착한 다음에 치킨을 주문할게요. 한강공원에서 치킨을 배달시킬 수 있어요.
토마스: 좋아요. 그러면 토요일에 한강공원에서 만나요.

🎧 7.5

1. 토마스 씨는 보라 씨와 수진 씨하고 불꽃놀이를 보려고 해요.
2. 고려대학교에서 한강공원에 갈 거예요. 그러면 지하철로 40분 걸려요.
3. 한강공원에 빨리 가고 싶어요. 그러면 버스를 타야 해요.
4. 토마스 씨는 불꽃놀이 사진을 찍으려고 해요.
5. 보라 씨는 한강공원에서 소주를 사려고 해요.
6. 수진 씨는 치킨을 학교 앞에서 주문하려고 해요.

8과

🎧 8.3

1. 지호 씨는 다리를 다쳤어요. 어느 병원에 가야 해요?
2. 요즘 날씨가 추워서 수진 씨는 머리도 목도 아파요. 어느 병원에 가야 해요?
3. 시메이 씨는 컴퓨터를 많이 해서 눈이 아파요. 어느 병원에 가야 해요?
4. 토마스 씨는 어제 딱딱한 음식을 먹어서 이가 아파요. 어느 병원에 가야 해요?

🎧 8.4

보라: 수진 씨, 얼굴이 정말 안 좋아요. 어디 아파요?
수진: 며칠 전부터 머리가 조금 아파요. 그리고 목도 아프고 콧물이 나요.
보라: 혹시 감기에 걸렸어요? 병원에 한번 가 보세요.
수진: 네, 내과에 한번 가 볼게요.
...
의사: 들어오세요. 어디가 아프세요?
수진: 머리가 아파요. 그리고 목도 아파요.
의사: 열도 나요?
수진: 아니요, 열은 나지 않아요.
의사: 요즘 많이 피곤하세요?
수진: 네, 아르바이트도 많이 하고 학교 시험도 많아서 좀 피곤했어요.
의사: 감기예요. 요즘 날씨가 추워서 감기에 잘 걸려요.
수진: 아, 네.
의사: 약은 병원 1층 약국에 찾으러 가세요. 약을 드시고 이틀 동안 푹 쉬세요.
수진: 네, 알겠어요. 그런데 선생님, 다음 주에 인턴십을 하러 호주 대사관에 가야 해요. 괜찮을까요?
의사: 감기는 금방 나아요. 걱정하지 마세요.
수진: 네, 감사합니다.

🎧 8.5

1. 수진 씨는 배가 아파서 내과에 갔어요.
2. 수진 씨는 감기에 걸렸지만 열이 나지 않아요.
3. 날씨가 추워서 요즘 사람들이 감기에 잘 걸려요.
4. 수진 씨는 3일 쉬어야 해요.
5. 수진 씨는 이번 주에 시험이 있어서 걱정하고 있어요.

🎧 8.6

수진: 감기약을 주세요.
약사: 여기 있어요.
수진: 어떻게 먹어요?
약사: 하루에 세 번, 한 번에 한 알, 식사 후에 드세요.
수진: 알겠습니다. 고맙습니다.

9과

🎧 9.3

보라: 토마스 씨, 오늘 김치전하고 닭갈비를 만들 거예요. 필요한 재료는 김치, 밀가루, 기름, 닭고기, 양파, 감자, 마늘, 고추, 고춧가루, 설탕, 참기름이에요.

🎧 9.4

토마스: 오늘 저녁에 학교 축제에서 우리가 무슨 요리를 할 거예요?
보라: 음...오늘 김치전하고 닭갈비를 만들려고 해요. 토마스 씨는 김치전을 만들 줄 알아요?
토마스: 네, 만들 줄 알아요. 김치하고 밀가루로 만들어요.
보라: 네, 맞아요. 오늘은 우리 어머니 김치를 쓸 거예요. 우리 어머니 김치가 최고예요.
토마스: 맛있겠어요! 그런데 보라 씨, 닭갈비는 어떻게 해요? 닭갈비 재료가 뭐예요?
보라: 닭갈비는 재료가 좀 많이 필요해요. 닭고기, 양파, 감자, 고추가 있어야 해요. 그리고 간장, 고추장, 설탕, 고춧가루, 마늘과 참기름을 섞어서 소스를 만들어야 해요.
토마스: 알겠어요. 닭갈비 레시피가 어려워요?
보라: 조금 어렵지만 걱정하지 마세요. 저녁에 가르쳐 줄게요.
토마스: 우리 술도 팔아요?
보라: 네. 학교 축제에서 술을 팔 수 있어요.
토마스: 재미있겠어요!.

🎧 9.5

1. 오늘 보라 씨하고 토마스 씨는 김치전과 닭갈비를 만들려고 해요.
2. 보라 씨는 김치전을 만들려고 김치를 사러 갔어요.
3. 닭갈비 재료보다 김치전 재료가 많이 필요해요.
4. 토마스 씨는 닭갈비를 잘 만들 줄 알아요.
5. 축제에서 학생들이 술을 팔 수 없어요.

10과

🎧 10.3

1. 통장을 만들고 싶어요.
2. 체크카드도 만들어 드릴까요?
3. 비밀번호를 눌러 주세요.
4. 외국인등록증을 주세요.
5. 여권을 갖고 오셨어요?
6. ATM에 현금을 찾으러 갈 거예요.

🎧 10.4

직원: 어서 오세요. 어떻게 오셨어요?
토마스: 통장을 만들고 싶어요.
직원: 외국인등록증을 주세요. 그리고 여기에 사인해 주세요.
토마스: 외국인등록증은 아직 없어요. 여권을 드려도 돼요?
직원: 네, 여권도 괜찮습니다.
토마스: 여권이 여기 있습니다.
직원: 고맙습니다. 잠깐 기다려 주세요.
...
직원: 고객님, 체크카드도 만들어 드릴까요?
토마스: ATM에서 체크카드로 현금을 찾을 수 있어요?
직원: 네, 맞습니다. 그리고 저희 은행 체크카드를 교통카드로 사용하셔도 돼요.
토마스: 정말 편하네요. 네, 그러면 체크카드도 만들어 주세요.

직원: 네, 체크카드를 만들어 드리겠습니다. 여기에 다시 한 번 사인해 주세요. 그리고 여기에 카드 비밀번호를 두 번 눌러 주세요.

…

직원: 네, 다 됐습니다. 여기 있습니다. 고객님의 통장과 카드입니다. 안녕히 가세요.

🎧 10.5

1. 토마스 씨는 외국인등록증이 있어요.
2. 토마스 씨는 여권으로 통장을 만들었어요.
3. 토마스 씨는 통장과 체크카드를 만들었어요.
4. 체크카드로 ATM에서 돈을 찾을 수 있어요.
5. 체크카드는 교통카드로 사용할 수 없어요.

🎧 10.6

1. 학생증을 주시겠어요?
2. 여권을 가지고 오셨어요?
3. 이것을 다음 달까지 빌려도 돼요?
4. 외국인등록증이 집에 있어요. 여권을 드려도 돼요?
5. 다시 한 번 비밀번호를 눌러 주세요.
6. 오늘 이용 시간이 끝났습니다. 가방을 놓고 가지 마세요.

Translation of dialogues, main listening and main reading texts

1과

대화 1

Ms Kim: Shimei, long time no see you. How did you spend your holidays?
Shimei: Yes, I had a fun holiday.
Ms Kim: Really? What did you do?
Shimei: I travelled to Korea during the holiday.

대화 2

Bora: Thomas, what will you do on the weekend?
Thomas: Recently the weather is warm. So I'll go hiking on the weekend.
Bora: Thomas, have you watched the weather forecast? It will rain on the weekend.
Thomas: Oh, really?
Bora: Yes. You must be upset.

듣기 2

Hello. This is Hyunmi Kim.
This year the winter is very cold. The temperature in Seoul today is 2 degrees below zero, the same temperature as yesterday. Busan is four degrees, Gwangju and Jeju Island are eight degrees. Tomorrow's forecast for all South Korea is as follows: Seoul will be windy from the morning. In the afternoon it will snow. However, it will not snow much. In Busan, the sky will be clear, and the weather will be chilly. In Gwanju too the sky will be clear. In Jeju island it will rain in the morning, and it will be windy from the afternoon.
This is all for the weather forecast.

읽기 2

Hiking Club
Information about October's hiking excursion.
Mountain: Mt. Bukhan.
Meeting place: Bulgwang Station, subway line n. 6.
Meeting time: 8 am.
Start: 8:30 am.
Course: Bulgwang Station → Mt. Bukhan → restaurant (12 pm) → Bulgwang Station (2 pm).
Participation fee: 20,000 won (lunch + water)
Things to prepare: warm clothes + cap + comfortable shoes.
Participant application: 010-6570-0394

2과

대화 1

Shimei: You speak Korean really well!
Senior student: No, I am not very good yet.
Shimei: Me too I want to speak Korean well. How should I do it?
Senior student: Mmm...you have to remember many words.
Shimei: Really? And then, what else should I do?
Senior student: Then you have to review every day.

대화 2

Teacher: There is the mid-term test next week Monday.
Daniel: I have another class on Monday.
Teacher: Then can you sit the test on Tuesday?
Daniel: Yes, I can sit it on Tuesday.

듣기 2

Hello everybody. I am Hyunmi Kim. Nice to meet you. We will study Korean together this semester. First of all, this is our textbook. You must have the textbook in class. Then, I will call attendance every week, so you have to come to class. For the tests, there will be a mid-term test and a final test. There will also be a final interview test.
There will be a lot of new vocabulary to learn this semester. So study can be a bit hard, but you can do

well. Do you have any questions?
...
Yes, Shimei, what's your question?

읽기 2

Dear Ms. Kim,
Hello.
I am Shimei, a first year student. I would like to ask you a few questions.
I am taking many classes this semester and I also have a lot of homework. So I am very busy. I have to submit my Korean homework by next week Monday, but I do not have time. Is it ok if I submit the homework by Tuesday? I am very sorry. Next time I will not be late.
Then, I have another question. There is a final exam in the last week of classes, but in that time I have to sit the test of my major class. Would it be possible to take the Korean exam at another time?
I would like to go on exchange to Korea next semester, but I cannot speak Korean well yet. How can I prepare well to go on exchange? Also, which university can I go to on exchange?
My last question is about a Korean study group. I want to join a study group but I have not made any friends yet in my Korean class. What should I do?
Thank you.
Best regards
Shimei

3과

대화 1

Landlady: Sujin! Are you late again?
Sujin: I am sorry!
Landlady: Why are you late?
Sujin: I had a student gathering which finished late.
Landlady: Don't you know the rules of the boarding house? Don't be late the next time.
Sujin: Yes...sorry...

대화 2

Thomas: I want to move.
Bora: Why? Don't you like the dormitory?
Thomas: No, the room is too small. So I want to look for a new room. How should I do that?
Bora: Mmm...ask the real estate agency.
Thomas: The real estate agency? I don't speak Korean well...would you help me?

듣기 2

Man: Please come in.
Thomas: I am looking for a house. Are there any?
Man: There is a house near the train station.
Thomas: Mmm...the train station is too far from the university.
Bora: That's right, Thomas. Don't move there. Is there a house near the university?
Man: There is also a house near the university. It's on the 8th floor. It is very bright. And it's clean.
Bora: How much is the rent?
Man: It's 600,000 won.
Thomas: I like a clean house. Is there also a fridge and a washing machine?
Man: Yes, there is a fridge and a washing machine, but there is not a bed.
Thomas: I see. I want to move into the house near the university. Is it possible to have a look at the house now?
Man: Yes, of course. You can have a look now.

읽기 2

Regulations of the dormitory of Korea University. Welcome! In our dormitory there are the following regulations. Please, absolutely follow these regulations so that we can all live together. The regulations are as follows.

1) Clean your room at least once a week.
2) Do not smoke in your room.
3) Do not drink alcohol in the dormitory.
4) Do not invite friends to your room.
5) Do not cook food in your room.
6) Do not forget food in the fridge.
7) Put the trash in the trash bin.
8) Do not throw paper in the toilet.
9) Do not talk with a loud voice in your room.
10) Listen to music with earphones after 10 pm.
11) Do not enter the dormitory later than 11 pm.
12) Do not give the key of your room to friends.
13) You can work out in the dormitory gym only from 7 am to 11 am, and from 4 pm to 7 pm.
14) Do not use the laundry machine at night.
If you have any questions, email or call the dormitory manager.

4과

대화 1

Daniel: Shimei, show me the photos of your trip to Korea, please.
Shimei: Yes, here they are.
Daniel: So cool! This is Gyeongbok palace, right?
Shime: Yes, have you been there before?
Daniel: Yes, I went there. What did you do at Gyeongbok palace?
Shimei: I toured Gyeonbok palace, then I tried on a hanbok.

대화 2

Bora: Erm...how much is this dress?
Clerk: It's 120,000 won. Try it on.
...
Bora: What it is like? Does it look good?
Clerk: Yes, it looks really good.
Bora: I want this. But it's a bit expensive. Can you please give me a discount?

듣기 2

Clerk: Hello.
Sujin: Can I have a look at the dresses?
Clerk: Yes, please take your time.
Sujin: Mmm... this white skirt is really beautiful.
Clerk: This is popular now. Try it on.
Sujin: Ok, please give me a medium size.
Clerk: I am sorry. We don't have (more) of the medium size. We just have large sizes.
Sujin: Really? The large size doesn't fit me.
Clerk: We have the medium size of the black skirt.
Sujin: That's ok, thank you.
...
Clerk: Hello.
Sujin: Do you have comfortable shoes?
Clerk: Yes. What about these shoes? This design is in fashion now.
Sujin: Can I try them on?
Clerk: Yes, try them.
Sujin: They are really comfortable. I like the color too. How much are they?
Clerk: They are 200,000 won.
Sujin: That's a bit expensive. Is there any discount?
Clerk: I am sorry. It's a new design. So there is no discount.
Sujin: I see. I'll buy these.

읽기 2

Hi everybody! This is Sara's fashion blog.
Where do you shop for clothes? This time I bought them through an online department store, and I enjoyed it.
In Australia now comfortable clothes are popular. I also wanted to buy comfortable clothes, so I bought these pants. They are really comfortable! And they are warm. Autumn weather in Australia is not cold, but sometimes is chilly, isn't it? So these pants will

be really good. I bought it in a medium size, in yellow.

My boy-friend works in a company. So he needs a suit. I bought him a suit for his birthday. How is it? It's cool, isn't it? I also got a 40% discount. Blue suits are popular now. It's blue, but it is also available in green and black. I wanted to buy him a white shirt too, but I did not have enough money. So he bought the white shirt himself.

Try an online department store yourself, then please write your review down here.

5과

대화 1

Yerin: Sara, have you drafted the report?
Sara: No, I haven't drafted it yet.
Yerin: So draft the report, then go home.
Sara: Yes.

대화 2

Sara: Is the boss in the office?
Yerin: No, today the boss is on a business trip.
Sara: Ah, really? When is he back?
Yerin: He will be here tomorrow.

듣기 2

Sara: Everybody has arrived.
Yerin: Ok, now we start the meeting. How should we advertise the products of our company? Mr Kim, can you start?
Mr. Kim: Ah yes. Lately people don't read many newspapers, so we have to use social media.
Yerin: Ok, good. What do you think, Sara?
Sara: I am of the same opinion. In Australia many companies do their advertising through social media.
Yerin: Ok. I like your idea, Mr. Kim and Sara. Does anybody else have any other idea?
Other people: No, we don't.
Yerin: Mr. Kim and Sara, please send me a report by next week. See you all at the meeting next week. Thank you.

읽기 2

The magazine 'Commerce Today' has interviewed three famous company presidents. Below is the story of Ms. Kim, Ms. Park, and Mr. Choi.

Ms. Kim is the president of "Busan Commercial". Ms. Kim at university did an internship in a big commerce company, and after graduation she got a job in the same company. At the time Ms. Kim used to go to work early and finish late. Five years ago she left that company and created "Busan Commercial". Now "Busan Commercial" has offices in Korea, Singapore, Australia, and New Zealand.

Ms. Park is the president of "The Country of Translation". Ms. Park majored in English at university, and she worked part-time as a translator. Ms. Park created "The Country of Translation" after graduating from university. At the beginning she worked alone, then she hired staff. Now Ms. Park's company translates popular Korean webtoons, dramas, and films into English.

Mr. Choi is the president of "Green Korea". Mr. Choi Studied at Australia University, and he found a job in Australia after graduation. He went back to Korea after working for ten years in Australia. Then, seven years ago, he created the company "Green Korea". This company buys energy from Australia, and sells it back to Korea.

6과

대화 1

Bora: Thomas, do you have brothers or sisters?

Translation of dialogues, main listening and main reading texts

Thomas: I have an older brother.
Bora: Really? What kind of person is he?
Thomas: My brother is kind. And he is better at sport than me. Here is a photo of my brother.
Bora: He really looks like you!

대화 2

Jiho: Hello? Sara, do you have time to talk?
Sara: I am sorry. I am busy now. I am working.
Jiho: Oh sorry.
Sara: No, it's alright. I'll call you back later.
Jiho: Ok, got it. Thank you.

듣기 2

Bora: Thomas, my brother got married last month. So he will prepare a housewarming party on the weekend. Would you like to go together with me?
Thomas: Yes! But Bora, what kind of person is your brother?
Bora: My brother is kind and he works hard. Now he is working in a big company.
Thomas: And his wife?
Bora: She is beautiful. She teaches Korean to foreigners at the university.
Thomas: But Bora, do we have to bring a present to the housewarming party?
Bora: Yes, usually people bring toilet paper as a present to a housewarming party. They bring to the owner a useful present rather than an expensive one.
Thomas: Toilet paper? It's a good idea. Toilet paper is useful. Bora, does your brother like alcohol?
Bora: Yes, my brother is a good drinker. Why?
Thomas: I want to bring him toilet paper and wine as a present. In Australia we usually bring wine as a present.

읽기 2

This month's drama
My unfamiliar family
(review by Sujin)
Hello! I could not write many drama reviews recently, but I am going to write one now. So I start with the review.
Last month I watched the drama "My unfamiliar family". It is the story of one familiy. In this family there are a father, a mother, a big sister, a little sister, and a little brother. The big sister is already married and lives with her husband. The little brother lives with the parents, and the little sister lives alone. Usually, family members know each other well. But in this drama, people do not really talk much to the other family members, although they do love each other. So they do not know each other very well. The children do not really know their parents, the wife does not know her husband, and the siblings do not know each other very well either. So it's hard for everybody.
The family in the drama begin to talk to each other little by little, and at the end they get to know each other. This is the drama I liked the most among last month's dramas, because for me, family is the most important thing. Also, by watching this drama I learned something. That you need to talk with your family.
That's all for my review. Next month I'll write about another drama. See you later!

7과

대화 1

Thomas: Excuse me. I want to go to The Kyobo bookstore. How do I get there?
Lady: Take the subway n. 6 at Anam station. Then transfer to the line n. 5 at Cheongu station.

Thomas: Where do I get off?
Lady: Get off at Gwanghwamun.
Thomas: Thank you

대화 2

Thomas: Sujin, how do I get to the gathering of the film club?
Sujin: You need to take the bus first.
Thomas: Which bus do I need to take?
Sujin: I'll text you.
Thomas: Thanks.

듣기 2

Sujin: Thomas, Bora and I will go together to watch the fireworks on Saturday at the Han river park. do you want to go together?
Thomas: Fireworks?
Sujin: Yes.
Thomas: Ok. But how do I get there? I don't know the Han river park well.
Bora: Take the line n. 6 at Korea Univ. station. Then transfer to the line n.5 at Gondeok station. Then get off at Yeouido station. It takes about 50 minutes.
Thomas: It takes a lot of time. Is there a bus?
Sujin: The bus takes longer than the subway. And also the bus is more complicated.
Thomas: Ok. I'll take the subway. I'll bring my camera. I'll take beautiful photos for you.
Bora: Then I'll buy the beer.
Sujin: I'll order the fried chicken after I get there. You can get chicken delivered at the Han river park.
Thomas: Ok. See you Saturday at the Han river park.

읽기 2

Thomas, Sujin and Bora went together to the Han river park.
Thomas took the subway number 6 at Korea University, then he transferred to line n.5 at Geondeok station. Thomas took the wrong train at Geondeok station and went in the opposite direction. After taking the train for Yeouido, he got off at Yeouido station. Yeouido station is a bit far from the Han river park, so he walked for about twenty minutes. He was fifteen minutes late.
His friends were already waiting for him at the Han river park. They toured Building 63 and after they went for a stroll. Then they bought alcohol at a convenience store and ordered fried chicken. There were a lot of people but they sat in a good spot. They watched the fireworks from 8 pm.
After watching the fireworks they drank alcohol. They chatted together and had a good time. So the time passed quickly. At 12 pm they wanted to take the subway to go home but the time of the last train had already passed. The first train in the morning leaves at 5:46. Thomas wanted to take a taxi, but the Han river park is far from Korea University. The taxi fare is 18,000 won.
Thomas found a sauna near the Han river park. The sauna is 8,000 won. Since the sauna is more [blank] than the taxi, that day Thomas [blank].

8과

대화 1

Daniel: I couldn't make it to class last week. I am sorry.
Ms. Kim: That's ok. what happened?
Daniel: I had fever, so I couldn't come to school.
Ms. Kim: Are you ok now?
Daniel: Yes, now I am better, thank you.

대화 2

Shimei: Where are you going, Jiho?
Jiho: I am going to the pharmacy to buy some medicine.
Shimei: Why?

Jiho: Because I don't feel ok today.

듣기 2

Bora: Sujin, you don't look very well. Are you sick?
Sujin: I have had a headache for a few days. Also, my throat is sore, and I have a runny nose.
Bora: Did you catch a cold? Go to see a doctor!
Sujin: Yes, I'll go to a clinic.
...
Doctor: Come in. Where does it hurt?
Sujin: I have a headache and a sore throat.
Doctor: Do you also have a fever?
Sujin: No, I don't have a fever.
Doctor: Are you feeling very tired recently?
Sujin: Yes, I am tired because I work part-time a lot and I also have many exams at school.
Doctor: It's a cold. Recently many people are catching a cold, because the weather is cold.
Sujin: Oh, I see.
Doctor: You can get medicine at the pharmacy on the ground floor of the clinic. Take the medicine, then get a good rest at home for a couple of days.
Sujin: Ok. But I need to go to the Australian embassy for an internship next week. Will I be ok?
Doctor: You will get better quickly. Don't worry.
Sujin: Thank you.

읽기 2

Healthy foods and drinks

Recently, people have an interest in foods and drinks good for their health. Healthy foods and drinks popular among Koreans are red ginseng, congee, and juices.

Koreans often enjoy red ginseng. Red ginseng is good for your health. Students study a lot and they get tired. When this happens, students have red ginseng and get stronger. Then, if you have red ginseng you do not easily catch a cold. You can eat or drink red ginseng, because it's available as a candy or also as a tea. Since red ginseng is popular among Koreans, good red ginseng is a bit pricey. When winter is cold, do you easily catch a cold? Sometimes you eat but you do not have any strength? When this happens, eat congee. Congee is made with rice, and it's good for your health. Congee is delicious when it is warm, and it's good for people who are unwell. You can make congee at home, but you can also order it from a restaurant. Juices are also popular among Koreans. There are several kinds of juice. Some teachers have pear juice after their class, because pear juice is good for the throat. Try grape juice after a heavy sport activity. It's sweet and it will make you feel stronger. Juice is not usually expensive, and you can buy it from a pharmacy or a supermarket.

9과

대화 1

Thomas: Bora, can you do me a favor?
Bora: Yes, Thomas. What it is?
Thomas: Do you know how to cook Korean food?
Bora: Yes, I know how.
Thomas: I want to try to make tteokpokki. Can you teach me?
Bora: Ok, I'll teach you.

대화 2

Jiho: Shimei, what video are you watching?
Shimei: I am watching a video of the Korean class.
Jiho: Shimei, why do you study Korean?
Shimei: I study Korean to get a job in a Korean company in the future.

듣기 2

Thomas: Which food are we going to prepare at the

university student festival tonight?
Bora: Mmm...today we will prepare kimchi pancakes and spicy stir-fried chicken. Do you know how to make kimchi pancakes?
Thomas: Yes, I know. You need kimchi and flour.
Bora: Yes, right. We will use my mom's kimchi. My mom's kimchi is the best.
Thomas: That sounds tasty! But Bora, I don't know how to make spicy stir-fried chicken, what are the ingredients?
Bora: You need a lot of ingredients. You need... chicken, onions, potatoes, and chilli. Then you prepare a sauce with soy sauce, chilli paste, sugar, powdered chilli, garlic and sesame oil.
Thomas: Ok. Is the recipe for the spicy fried chicken difficult?
Bora: It is a bit difficult, but don't worry. I'll teach you tonight.
Thomas: Will we sell alcohol too?
Bora: Yes, we can sell alcohol at the school festival.
Thomas: That will be fun.

읽기 2

Ms. Kim's ttoppokki.
I like ttoppokki and when I was a high school student I always came out of school quickly after class to go with my friends to eat ttoppokki at a restaurant in front of the school. It was so good I cannot forget that taste even now. Then I found the recipe below on the internet, and I went shopping for groceries to make ttoppokki. This recipe tastes exactly like the food in the restaurant in front of my school, so I want to share it with you. This recipe is easy and you can make ttoppokki quickly.
Ingredients
Rice cake for ttoppokki: 2 cups
Water: 2 cups
Spring onion: half a cup
Sauce

Sugar: 3 spoons
Chilli paste: 1 spoon
Chilli powder: 1 spoon
Soy sauce: 2 spoons
So now I am going to tell you the recipe. First, put the rice cakes in water and wait for 30 minutes. Then put those rice cakes with two cups of fresh water and sugar in a pot, and boil. When the water boils, add the chilli paste and mix well. After you have mixed the chilli paste well add the soy sauce. Then add the chilli powder and mix again. Chop the spring onions and prepare them. At the end, add the spring onions and mix one more time. Done! Easy, isn't it? You can try to make ttoppokki like the restaurant at home. You can also add other ingredients. I always add a boiled egg. Is ttoppokki too spicy for you? Then try adding cheese. Are you very hungry? Then you can add ramyon and make rappokki!

10과

대화 1

Library staff: How can I help you?
Thomas: Can I use the library computer?
Library staff: Yes, you can. But before using the computer please tag your student card here.
Thomas: Ah ok. Thank you.

대화 2

Jiho: Sara, are you going to Korea next month?
Sara: Yes, I am so excited.
Jiho: Have you bought your plane ticket?
Sara: No, before buying the plane ticket I need to get my passport.
Jiho: Good idea. Have a good trip.
Sara: Thanks!

듣기 2

Staff: Hello. How can I help you?

Thomas: I want to open an account.

Staff: Please give me your alien registration card and sign here.

Thomas: I don't have an alien registration card yet. Can I give you my passport?

Staff: Yes, the passport is fine too.

Thomas: Here is my passport.

Staff: Thank you. Please wait a moment.

...

Staff: Would you like also to make a check-card?

Thomas: Can I withdraw money from an ATM with the check-card?

Staff: Yes, that's correct. You can also use the check-card of our bank as a transport card.

Thomas: It's really easy. Yes please, make me a check-card too.

Staff: Yes, I'll make you a check-card. Please sign here one more time. Then please enter your card pin number here.

...

Staff: It's done. Here is your bank passbook and your card. Thank you.

읽기 2

Seoul Foreigner Support Center

Welcome to the Seoul Foreigner Support Center. Is your life hard since you have come to Korea? If so, visit our center! At our center, we provide foreigners with the information they need for their life in Korea. At our center you can receive information in both Korean and English. We have support programs, educational programs, cultural programs and volunteering activities.

Support programs:

Do you need a mobile phone?
Don't you have a bank account yet?
Are you unwell and need to visit a hospital?
Do you need to obtain your alien registration card at the immigration office?
Do you find it hard to get around with the bus and subway?
Do you not speak Korean well yet?
Are you looking for a place to stay?
Do you have problems with the phone, bank, or hospital? At our center we can help you.

Educational programs:

Is Korean hard for you? At our center, foreigners can learn Korean and about the Korean culture for free.

Korean classes
Period: 10 weeks
Levels: beginner, intermediate
Location: Seoul Foreigner Support Center classrooms.
Information: info@seouljiwon.go.kr

Cultural programs:
Seoul visit (Gyeonbokgung, DDP, Mt. Bukhan)
Korean cooking classes (every second and fourth Saturday of the month, 10 am)
Library (700 English volumes, magazines, newspapers; Korean language textbooks)

Volunteering activities:

Do you want to do volunteering? We are always looking for Koreans and foreigners to do volunteering.

Volunteering for Koreans: Korean language teacher, guide for cultural programs, English/Korean translation and interpretation.

Volunteering for foreigners: Center information, English/Korean translation and interpretation.

Information: volunteering@seouljiwon.go.kr

Answer keys

1과

연습 1
1. 초대합니다.
2. 만납니다.
3. 먹습니다.
4. 읽습니다.
5. 입니다.
6. 들었습니다.
7. 배웠습니다.

연습 2
1. 준비해요.
2. 찾았습니다.
3. 올 겁니다.
4. 탔어요.
5. 마십니다.
6. 괜찮습니다.
7. 많았어요.
8. 들을 겁니다.

연습 3
1. 맑은 하늘
2. 빠른 기차
3. 좋은 선생님
4. 맛있는 요리
5. 시원한 맥주
6. 어려운 시험
7. 높은 산
8. 추운 날씨

연습 4
1. 기쁘겠어요.
2. 비가 오겠어요.
3. 무겁겠어요.
4. 춥겠어요.
5. 무섭겠어요.

연습 5
1. 맛있겠어요.
2. 좋겠어요.
3. 피곤하겠어요.
4. 힘들겠어요.
5. 늦겠어요.
6. 시원하겠어요.
7. 배고프겠어요.

연습 6
1. 겨울
2. 내립니다
3. 따뜻합니다
4. 맑습니다
5. 덥습니다
6. 비
7. 바람

듣기 1
1. 부산은 비가 옵니다.
2. 광주는 하늘이 맑습니다.
3. 제주도는 바람이 붑니다.

듣기 2
서울 → 2번과 4번   부산 → 1번
광주 → 1번   제주도 → 2번과 3번

듣기 3
1. O   2. O   3. X
4. X   5. X

읽기 1
1. 춥습니다.
2. 하늘이 맑습니다. 시원합니다.
3. 하늘이 흐립니다. 쌀쌀합니다.
4. 따뜻합니다.
5. 덥습니다.
6. 시원합니다.
7. 하늘이 맑습니다. 따뜻합니다.
8. 하늘이 맑습니다. 덥습니다.

읽기 2
1. 10월 16일에 북한산에서 등산 할 겁니다.
2. 오전 8시 반부터 등산 할 겁니다.
3. 따뜻한 옷, 모자, 편한 신발이 필요합니다.
4. 토마스 씨는 전화로 참가 신청을 해야 합니다. 그리고 참가비 20,000원을 내야 합니다.
5. 8시 30분: 출발; 12시: 식사; 2시: 불광역으로 돌아갑니다.

2과

연습 1
1. 말할 수 있어요.
2. 잘 수 없었어요.
3. 먹을 수 있어요.
4. 할 수 있어요.

5. 일어날 수 없었어요.   6. 갈 수 없었어요.
7. 만날 수 없어요.   8. 만들 수 있어요.

연습 3

1. 청소해야 해요.   2. 연습해야 해요.
3. 받아야 해요.   4. 일해야 해요.
5. 전화해야 해요.   6. 사야 해요.
7. 가야 해요.   8. 씻어야 해요.

연습 5

1. 하숙집은 학교에서 멀지만 싸요.
2. 지하철은 사람이 많지만 빨라요.
3. 김치는 맵지만 맛있어요.
4. 운동은 힘들지만 신나요.
5. 학교 식당은 맛없지만 싸요.

연습 6

1. 한국 요리를 먹고 싶지만 근처에 한국 식당이 없어요.
2. 다니엘 씨한테 전화했지만 전화를 받지 않아요.
3. 공부를 많이 했지만 시험을 못 봤어요.
4. 늦게 일어났지만 지각하지 않았어요.
5. 여행 가방이 크지만 무겁지 않아요.

연습 7

1. 전공해요.   2. 외워요.
3. 졸업해요.   4. 결석해요.
5. 복습해요.   6. 지각했어요.

듣기 1

1. 교과서   2. 단어   3. 인터뷰
4. 복습해요   5. 출석

듣기 2

1. X   2. O   3. X
4. X   5. X

읽기 1

2, 4, 1, 3

읽기 2

1. X   2. O   3. X
4. X

3과

연습 1

1. 타세요/타지 마세요
2. 쓰세요/쓰지 마세요
3. 쉬세요/쉬지 마세요
4. 앉으세요/앉지 마세요
5. 닫으세요/닫지 마세요
6. 들으세요/듣지 마세요
7. 만드세요/만들지 마세요
8. 드세요/드시지 마세요
9. 말씀하세요/말씀하지 마세요

연습 2

1. 연습하세요.   2. 가세요.
3. 바꾸세요.   4. 앉으세요.
5. 하세요.

연습 3

1. 지각하지 마세요./늦지 마세요.
2. 담배를 피우지 마세요.
3. 요리하지 마세요.

연습 5

1. 놀래요.   2. 마실래요.
3. 볼래요.   4. 부를래요.
5. 탈래요.   6. 쉴래요.

연습 6

1. 버스를 탈래요? 지하철을 탈래요?
2. 짬뽕을 먹을래요? 짜장면을 먹을래요?
3. 소주를 마실래요? 맥주를 마실래요?
4. 빙수를 먹을래요? 아이스크림을 먹을래요?
5. 베트남 여행을 갈래요? 태국 여행을 갈래요?

연습 7

1. 깨끗해요.
2. 이사할 거예요.
3. 부엌
4. 거실
5. 세탁기
6. 한옥

듣기 1

1. – B
2. – A
3. – A/B
4. – B
5. – B
6. – A/B

듣기 2

1. 토마스 씨는 집을 구하고 싶어요.
2. 기차역은 학교에서 멀어요.
3. 학교 근처 집은 밝아요. 그리고 깨끗해요.
4. 60만 원이에요.
5. 냉장고하고 세탁기가 있어요.

읽기 1

1. 쓰레기를 버리지 마세요.
2. 음악을 듣지 마세요.
3. 음식을 먹지 마세요.
4. 큰 소리로 말하지 마세요.
5. 술을 드시지 마세요.

읽기 2

1. X
2. X
3. O
4. X
5. O
6. X

4과

연습 1

1. 가 보세요/가 봤어요
2. 만들어 보세요/만들어 봤어요
3. 보내 보세요/보내 봤어요
4. 해 보세요/해 봤어요
5. 찾아 보세요/찾아 봤어요
6. 불러 보세요/불러 봤어요
7. 들어 보세요/들어 봤어요
8. 걸어 보세요/걸어 봤어요

연습 2

1. 프랑스에 가 봤어요?
2. 김치를 먹어 봤어요?
3. 등산해 봤어요?
4. 소주를 마셔 봤어요?
5. 태권도를 배워 봤어요?
6. 사진을 찍어 봤어요?
7. 한복을 입어 봤어요?

연습 3

1. 가 보세요.
2. 먹어 보세요.
3. 입어 보세요.
4. 신어 보세요.
5. 읽어 보세요.
6. 마셔 보세요.
7. 들어 보세요.

연습 4

1. 닫아 주세요.
2. 빌려 주세요.
3. 찍어 주세요.
4. 가르쳐 주세요.
5. 말씀해 주세요.
6. 불러 주세요.

연습 5

1. 도와주세요.
2. 가 주세요.
3. 전화해 주세요.
4. 만들어 주세요.
5. 쳐 주세요.

연습 6

1. 할인
2. 벗어요.
3. 신었어요.
4. 찼어요/썼어요.
5. 가격

듣기 1

1. 고객님
2. 고객님
3. 점원
4. 점원
5. 점원
6. 고객님
7. 고객님

듣기 2

1. O
2. O
3. O
4. X
5. X
6. X

7. O

읽기 1

1. 다
2. 나
3. 라
4. 마
5. 가

읽기 2

바지: D   정장과 셔츠: E

1. 노란 바지와 파란색 정장을 샀어요.
2. 온라인 백화점에서 쇼핑했어요.
3. 편한 옷을 사고 싶었어요.
4. 사라 씨 남자 친구가 회사에 다녀요. 그래서 정장이 필요해요.
5. 남자 친구가 흰 셔츠를 샀어요.

읽기 3

C

5과

연습 1

1. 가세요/가셨어요/가실 거예요
2. 출근하세요/출근하셨어요/출근하실 거예요
3. 사세요/사셨어요/사실 거예요
4. 들으세요/들으셨어요/들으실 거예요
5. 예쁘세요/예쁘셨어요/예쁘실 거예요
6. 쓰세요/쓰셨어요/쓰실 거예요
7. 말씀하세요/말씀하셨어요/말씀하실 거예요
8. 아프세요/아프셨어요/아프실 거예요
9. 주무세요/주무셨어요/주무실 거예요
10. 드세요/드셨어요/드실 거예요

연습 2

1. 가셨어요.
2. 드세요.
3. 계세요.
4. 오셨어요.
5. 가르치세요.
6. 가셨어요.
7. 주무셨어요.
8. 이세요.

연습 3

1. 아버지께서는 어디에서 일하세요?
2. 오늘 차를 타고 오셨어요?
3. 무엇을 사고 싶으세요?
4. 무엇을 찾으세요?
5. 내일 몇 시에 출근하실 거예요?
6. 보통 주말에 뭐 하세요?
7. 어디가 아프세요?

연습 4

1. 아프고
2. 맑고
3. 공부하고
4. 하고
5. 끼고, 쓰고
6. 좋고
7. 듣고
8. 재미있고

연습 5

1. 시메이 씨는 테니스를 치고 학교에서 수업을 들어요.
2. 수진 씨는 식사하고 공부를 해요.
3. 다니엘 씨는 아르바이트를 하고 드라마를 봐요.

연습 6

1. 먹거나
2. 읽거나
3. 하거나
4. 없거나
5. 흐리거나
6. 치거나

연습 7

1. 주말에 러닝을 하거나 자전거를 타요.
2. 햄버거를 먹거나 피자를 먹어요.
3. 음악을 듣거나 책을 읽어요.
4. 등산하거나 영화를 봐요.
5. 쉬거나 친구를 만나요.

연습 8

1. 참석하셨어요.
2. 동료
3. 이력서
4. 출근해요, 퇴근해요.
5. 보고서
6. 구할 거예요.

듣기 1

1. 시작했어요.
2. 회의
3. 신문
4. 생각하세요?
5. 사용하지 마세요.
6. 광고

듣기 2

1. X
2. X
3. O
4. O
5. X

읽기 1

1. – C
2. – D
3. – E
4. – A
5. – B

읽기 2

1. 무역 회사에 취직하셨습니다.
2. 한국, 싱가포르, 호주, 뉴질랜드에 있습니다.
3. 영어를 공부하셨습니다.
4. 웹툰, 드라마, 영화를 번역합니다.
5. 한국에서 일하십니다.
6. 호주에서 에너지를 사고 그 에너지를 한국에 팝니다.

쓰기 1

1. 고려대학교에서 미디어를 공부하셨어요.
2. 졸업 후에 '한국 신문' 기자로 일하셨어요.
3. '오늘 뉴스' 회사를 만들었어요.

6과

연습 1

1. 여동생은 나보다 키가 작아요.
2. 로마가 시드니보다 멀어요.
3. 김밥이 샌드위치보다 맛있어요.
4. 삼겹살이 치킨보다 싸요.
5. 호텔이 기숙사보다 비싸요.
6. 테니스는 수영보다 재미있어요.

연습 2

1. 한라산과 에베레스트산 중에서 뭐가 더 높아요?
2. 핫도그와 붕어빵 중에서 뭐가 더 맛있어요?
3. 버스와 지하철 중에서 뭐가 더 빨라요?
4. 농구와 축구 중에서 뭐가 더 재미있어요?
5. 닭갈비와 불고기 중에서 무엇을 더 좋아해요?

연습 4

1. 읽고 있어요.
2. 보고 있어요.
3. 공부하고 있어요.
4. 찾고 있어요.
5. 운동하고 있어요.
6. 하고 있어요.
7. 입고 있어요.

연습 5

1. 토마스 씨는 청소하고 있어요.
2. 예린 씨는 일하고 있어요.
3. 선생님이 한국어를 가르치고 있어요.
4. 시메이 씨는 자고 있어요.
5. 다니엘 씨는 손을 씻고 있어요.
6. 수진 씨는 음악을 듣고 있어요.
7. 지호 씨는 책을 읽고 있어요.

연습 6

1. 오빠
2. 형, 부인
3. 형제
4. 부모님
5. 할머니.

듣기 1

1. – C
2. – D
3. – E
4. – B
5. – A

듣기 2

1. X
2. O
3. O
4. X
5. X

읽기 2

1. O
2. X
3. X
4. O
5. O

읽기 3

1. 이 드라마는 가족 이야기예요.
2. 서로 이야기를 잘 하지 않아요.
3. 수진 씨한테 가족이 중요해서요.
4. 다

7과

연습 1

1. 입으려고 해요.
2. 빌리려고 해요.
3. 보내려고 해요.
4. 가려고 해요.
5. 하려고 해요.
6. 사려고 해요.
7. 배우려고 해요.

연습 3

1. 탈게요
2. 전화할게요
3. 줄게요
4. 말할게요
5. 갈게요
6. 살게요
7. 닫을게요
8. 돌아올게요
9. 내릴게요
10. 앉을게요
11. 있을게요
12. 열게요

연습 4

1. 살게요.
2. 공부할게요.
3. 일어날게요.
4. 할게요.
5. 나올게요.
6. 기다릴게요.

연습 5

1. 세수를 한 다음에 잠을 자요.
2. 한국어 시험을 본 다음에 쉬어요.
3. 점심을 먹은 다음에 친구를 만나요.
4. 버스에서 내린 다음에 지하철로 갈아타요.
5. 도서관에 간 다음에 친구하고 같이 공부해요.
6. 택시를 부른 다음에 집에 가요

연습 6

1. 타세요, 갈아타세요.
2. 정거장
3. 막혀요
4. 걸려요.
5. 이용 방법
6. 세워 주세요.

듣기 1

1. 인기가 많아요.
2. 술도 마시고
3. 주문할 수 있어요.
4/5. 불꽃놀이
6. 교통이 좀 복잡해요.

듣기 2

1. O
2. X
3. X
4. O
5. X
6. X.

읽기 1

1. 달라요.
2. 5시 46분
3. 휴일에 막차 시간이 제일 빨라요.
4. 토요일에 막차 시간이 제일 늦어요.

읽기 2

2. 싸요.
3. 찜질방에서 자려고 해요.

읽기 3

1. 63빌딩을 구경하고 술을 사고 치킨을 먹고 불꽃놀이를 구경했어요.
2. 지하철 반대 방향을 타서 늦었어요.
3. 막차 시간이 지났어요.
4. 택시비가 더 비싸요.

쓰기 1

1. 타세요, 내리세요
2. 을, 에서, 으로, 에서

8과

연습 1

1. 잊어서
2. 다쳐서
3. 좁아서
4. 없어서
5. 시작해서
6. 매워서

7. 아파서   8. 걸어서   9. 추워서

연습 3

1. 보라 씨는 친구를 만나러 커피숍에 가요.
2. 토마스 씨는 쇼핑하러 백화점에 가요.
3. 수진 씨는 태권도를 배우러 체육관에 가요.
4. 저는 한국어 수업을 들으러 학교에 가요.
5. 예린 씨는 버스를 타러 고속 터미널에 가요.
6. 지호 씨는 손을 씻으러 화장실에 가요.
7. 토마스 씨는 게임을 하러 피시방에 가요.
8. 저는 가야금을 배우러 학원에 다녀요.

연습 4

1. 은행에 뭐 하러 가요? 돈을 찾으러 가요.
2. 회사에 뭐 하러 가요? 일하러 가요.
3. 헬스장에 뭐 하러 가요? 운동하러 가요.
4. 수영장에 뭐 하러 가요? 수영하러 가요.
5. 노래방에 뭐 하러 가요? 노래를 부르러 가요.
6. 학교에 뭐 하러 가요? 수업을 들으러 가요.
7. 공항에 뭐 하러 가요? 비행기를 타러 가요.
8. 야구장에 뭐 하러 가요? 야구를 보러 가요.

연습 5

1. 걸렸어요.   2. 아프고   3. 나서
4. 좋아서   5. 내과   6. 맞고
7. 나아서

듣기 1

안과 – 3   치과 – 4   정형외과 – 1
내과 – 2

듣기 2

1. X   2. O   3. O
4. X   5. X

듣기 3

나

읽기 2

1. X   2. O   3. X
4. X   5. O

9과

연습 1

1. 부를 줄 알아요.   2. 운전할 줄 알아요.
3. 만들 줄 알아요.   4. 탈 줄 알아요.
5. 칠 줄 알아요.   6. 할 줄 알아요.
7. 읽을 줄 알아요.

연습 2

1. 기타를 칠 줄 알아요?
2. 수영할 줄 알아요?
3. 케이크를 만들 줄 알아요?
4. 떡볶이를 먹을 줄 알아요?
5. 소주를 마실 줄 알아요?
6. 테니스를 칠 줄 알아요?
7. 사진을 찍을 줄 알아요?

연습 3

1. 한국 여행을 가려고 아르바이트를 해요.
2. 헬스장에서 음악을 들으려고 이어폰을 샀어요.
3. 저녁에 친구를 만나려고 숙제를 빨리 끝냈어요.
4. 감기에 안 걸리려고 따뜻한 옷을 입어요.
5. 해외 여행을 가려고 여권을 만들었어요.
6. 일찍 일어나려고 일찍 자요.
7. 불고기를 만들려고 불고기 재료를 샀어요.
8. 김치찌개를 끓이려고 레시피를 찾아요.

연습 5

1. 넣으세요   2. 냄비   3. 삶으세요
4. 볶으세요   5. 매운

듣기 1

1. 김치   2. 닭고기   3. 마늘

4. 설탕, 참기름

듣기 2

1. O 2. X 3. X
4. X 5. X

듣기 3

김치전: 김치, 밀가루
닭갈비: 닭고기, 양파, 감자, 고추, 간장, 고추장,
        설탕, 고춧가루, 마늘, 참기름

읽기 1

1. 떡 2. 고추장 3. 물
4. 고춧가루 5. 간장 6. 설탕
7. 파

읽기 2

1. X 2. X 3. X
4. X 5. O

읽기 3

A → F → C → E → G → B → H → D

10과

연습 1

1. 구경해도 돼요. 2. 앉아도 돼요.
3. 찍어도 돼요. 4. 가도 돼요.
5. 퇴근해도 돼요. 6. 주차해도 돼요.

연습 2

1. 이야기해도 돼요. 2. 마셔도 돼요.
3. 쉬어도 돼요. 4. 앉아도 돼요.
5. 가도 돼요. 6. 써도 돼요.
7. 신어 봐도 돼요. 8. 먹어 봐도/먹어도 돼요.

연습 3

1. 은행에 가기 전에 신분증과 통장을 가방에 넣어요.
2. 점심을 먹기 전에 손을 씻어요.
3. 편지를 부치기 전에 우표를 사요.
4. 퇴근하기 전에 사무실 불을 꺼요.
5. 출근하기 전에 커피숍에서 커피를 마셔요.
6. 취직하기 전에 한번 인턴십을 하고 싶어요.

연습 5

1. 통장, 외국인등록증 2. 택배
3. 부치러 4. 현금

듣기 1

A – 4 B – 6 C – 1
D – 2 E – 3 F – 5

듣기 2

1. X 2. O 3. O
4. O 5. X

듣기 3

은행: 2, 4, 5
대학교 도서관: 1, 3, 6

읽기 2

1. 외국인에게 한국 생활에 필요한 정보를 알려 줍니다.
2. 영어와 한국어로 지원 프로그램 안내를 받을 수 있고 한국어 수업을 들을 수 있어요.
3. 초급과 중급 한국어 수업이 있어요.
4. 서울 구경, 요리 수업, 도서관이 있어요.
5. 한국어 선생님, 문화 프로그램 가이드, 통역/번역, 지원 센터 안내, 봉사 활동을 할 수 있어요.